INCLUSION OF CENTRAL EUROPEAN COUNTRIES IN THE EUROPEAN MONETARY UNION

INCLUSION OF CENTRAL EUROPEAN COUNTRIES IN THE EUROPEAN MONETARY UNION

Edited by

Paul De Grauwe
University of Leuven

Vladimir Lavrač
Institute for Economic Research, Ljubljana

KLUWER ACADEMIC PUBLISHERS
BOSTON / DORDRECHT / LONDON

A C.I.P. Catalogue record for this book is available from the Library of Congress.

ISBN 0-7923-8385-0

Published by Kluwer Academic Publishers,
P.O. Box 17, 3300 AA Dordrecht, The Netherlands.

Sold and distributed in North, Central and South America
by Kluwer Academic Publishers,
101 Philip Drive, Norwell, MA 02061, U.S.A.

In all other countries, sold and distributed
by Kluwer Academic Publishers,
P.O. Box 322, 3300 AH Dordrecht, The Netherlands.

Printed on acid-free paper

Printed in the Netherlands

Contents

Contributing Authors

Yunus Aksoy
University of Leuven

Peter Backé
Österreichische Nationalbank, Vienna

Oldrich Dedek
Czech National Bank, Prague

Paul De Grauwe
University of Leuven

Daniel Gros
Center for Economic Policy Studies, Brussels

Vladimir Lavrač
Institute for Economic Research, Ljubljana

Ivan Ribnikar
University of Ljubljana

Giuseppe Tullio
University of Brescia

Guy Vandille
University of Leuven

Abbreviations

BIS............................Bank for International Settlements
BLEU........................Belgium-Luxembourg Economic Union
BoS..........................Bank of Slovenia
CAP..........................Common Agricultural Policy
CE countries............Central European countries
CEE countries..........Central and Eastern European countries
CEFTA ....Central European Free Trade Agreement
CMEA.....................Council of Mutual Economic Aid
CNB.........................Czech National Bank
EBRD......................European Bank for Reconstruction and Development
ECB.........................European Central Bank
ECU.........................European Currency Unit
EFTA.......................European Free Trade Area
EMS.........................European Monetary System
EMU ....European Economic and Monetary Union
ERM ....Exchange Rate Mechanism
ERM II.....................Exchange Rate Mechanism 2
ESCB.......................European System of Central Banks
EU............................European Union
GDP.........................Gross Domestic Product
IMF..........................International Monetary Fund
IFS...........................International Financial Statistics
ILO..........................International Labour Organisation
NAFTA....................North Atlantic Free Trade Area
NATO......................North Atlantic Treaty Organisation
NCBs.......................National Central Banks
OCA........................Optimum Currency Area
OECD......................Organisation for Economic Co-operation and Development
PPP..........................Purchasing Power Parity
SITC ....Standard International Trade Classification
TEU.........................Treaty on European Union
VAT.........................Value-Added Tax

Preface

The creation of the European Economic and Monetary Union (EMU) and the introduction of the euro is a historical event for the EU countries. The debates on the desirability of the EMU provoked a vast economic literature dealing with the theory of the optimum currency area, costs and benefits of the EMU, symmetric vs. asymmetric shocks, alternative mechanisms of adjustment in a monetary union and so forth. Until recently, for the Central European candidate countries for a full membership in the EU, these issues seemed to be too far away, as they concentrated on devising their own monetary and exchange rate systems suitable for their transition period. The challenges of the EMU for the Central European countries were practically not dealt with in both Western and Eastern economic literature. The present book aims to fill this gap, by focusing on the most direct issue of relevance for the Central European countries with respect to the EMU - why, how and when these countries are expected to join the EMU. The papers included in this volume study the relationship between the EU accession process of the Central European candidate countries and their involvement in the process of European monetary integration. The book focuses on two main issues: First, are these countries (now or possibly later) a part of the European optimum currency area, so that they should belong to the euro area in the near future? Second, if so, how and when should they undertake necessary adjustments in their monetary and exchange rate policies and join the ERM 2 and the EMU?

This book contains the collection of working papers resulting from the research project "Inclusion of Central European Countries in the European Monetary Integration Process", which were presented at two workshops in Leuven in February 1997 and in Ljubljana in September 1997. This research project was financed by the European Commission through its ACE-Phare research programme. We would like to thank the European Commission for its financial support, which gave us a valuable opportunity to establish research links and exchange expertise between Western and Central European economists involved in the research on monetary integration in Europe. Finally, we would like to express our thanks to all those who in various ways contributed to this volume in its final form.

Paul de Grauwe and Vladimir Lavrač

Chapter 1

Introduction
Challenges of European Monetary Union for Central European Countries

PAUL DE GRAUWE AND VLADIMIR LAVRAČ

The creation of the European economic and monetary union (EMU) and the introduction of the European single currency, the euro, is a historic event, which will lead to fundamental changes in the EU economies. These changes will undoubtedly have a significant impact on the economies of the Central European countries, candidates for a full membership in the EU, similarly as the preparations of the EU countries for the EMU and their efforts to meet the Maastricht convergence criteria have already affected the Central European economies. Decision-makers at various levels (governments, enterprises, banks) will have to adapt to the changing environment, first by adjusting to the irrevocably fixed exchange rates among the EU currencies participating in the EMU and then by adjusting to the introduction of the euro and to the elimination of national currencies in the euro zone. The present volume, however, does not concentrate on these otherwise important issues of the impact of the EMU on the Central European countries. It focuses primarily on the most direct questions related to the EMU for these countries - why, how and when the Central European EU candidate countries will join the EMU.

The group of Central European countries under consideration includes the Czech Republic, Hungary, Poland and Slovenia. They (together with Estonia and Cyprus) belong to the group of countries which started official negotiations for a full membership in the EU in March 1998. In some cases, Slovakia is also included in the analysis, as it geographically belongs to the same group and as it is a member of the CEFTA (Central European Free Trade Agreement). It should be mentioned at the outset that this group of countries is rather homogenous as regards the fulfilment of the Maastricht convergence criteria. In general, they fulfil both fiscal criteria (fiscal deficit, public debt), but fail to meet the three monetary convergence criteria (inflation rate, long-term interest rate, stability of the exchange rate). The Czech Republic and Slovenia, where the inflation rate has stabilised in the high single-digit figures, perform better than Hungary and Poland in terms of both fiscal and monetary Maastricht criteria. While the analysis in this book covers the entire group of the Central European countries, special attention is given to the Czech Republic and Slovenia, as these two countries are the most advanced within the group in terms of their per capita GDP and their readiness to join the European monetary integration process. The book includes the case studies of these two countries on their way towards joining the EMU.

In the period of transition individual Central European countries have chosen very different and completely uncoordinated monetary and exchange rate systems and policies. The exchange rate regimes of these countries cover the whole spectrum of possible solutions: Slovenia decided for a (managed) floating exchange rate system, the Czech Republic used a fixed exchange rate system until recently, when it switched to a floating regime. Poland and Hungary opted for some interim solutions. Poland first decided for a fixed, but adjustable peg system, while now it practices a crawling peg regime, which is also in use in Hungary. Membership of these countries in the CEFTA has remained an unused opportunity to harmonise their monetary and exchange rate policies. Their association agreements with the EU do not restrain their monetary and exchange rate autonomy either. However, it can be expected that in their EU accession period and in the negotiations for a full membership in the EU, the Central European countries will be subject to some pressures and obligations for the co-ordination and harmonisation of their monetary and exchange rate systems and policies, with the aim of better preparing them for their future inclusion in the ERM 2 (Exchange Rate Mechanism 2) and in the EMU.

For the moment the Central European countries are not included in any form of the European monetary integration. They enjoy their full monetary sovereignty, with their own currency, their central bank and autonomous monetary and exchange rate policies.

Obligations and opportunities related to the European monetary integration derive from the prospective membership of the Central European countries in the EU. In principle, member countries of the EU are included in the European monetary institutions, such as the EMS (European Monetary System) and the EMU. However, at least until now it could be observed that the inclusion in the European monetary integration process did not occur at the same pace. Greece became member of the ERM only in March 1998, and some of the other EU member countries did not join the ERM until they were monetarily mature enough. It should be mentioned that they joined the ERM at their own will and they were able to leave the ERM when they found its requirements too constraining (Great Britain, Italy). In the case of the EMU, the opt-out countries (Great Britain, Denmark) decided not to participate in the third stage of EMU in 1999.

Until the Central European countries join the EU, they can not formally and institutionally enter its mechanisms of monetary integration. Membership in the EMS, in the ERM 2 and in the EMU is open only to EU members. The Central European countries can therefore for the moment only unilaterally, informally and functionally adjust to the mechanisms of the European monetary integration. In the transitional period they can shadow the euro, with the aim of better preparing themselves for the future inclusion in the ERM 2 and in the EMU. If we take the case of Slovenia, which uses a floating exchange rate system, it could (after bringing its inflation rate down to the level near to the EU inflation rate) make a switch to a system of fixed but adjustable exchange rate in line with the requirements of ERM 2.

The Central European countries could go even further in their unilateral adaptations to the prerequisites of the European monetary integration by irrevocably fixing the exchange rate. They could peg their currencies to the euro, when this opportunity opens in 1999. In this case they commit themselves to a de facto monetary union with the monetary area of the euro. This would lead to the loss of their monetary sovereignty, as their monetary policy would be directed towards sustaining the fixed exchange rate. The problem of unilateral de facto monetary unions is that the country involved bears all the costs (loss of the monetary sovereignty), while it participates in only some of the benefits of the monetary union. Additionally, such a unilateral commitment to the irrevocable fixing of the exchange rate would lack credibility compared to a formalised monetary union.

In this book, the focus is primarily on the other alternative - the formal and institutional inclusion of the Central European countries in the European monetary integration process. This process is closely related to the accession of the Central European countries in the EU. This link between membership in the EU and in EMU is not always correctly appreciated in the candidate countries. This could be due to the fact that some EU countries were in a position to decide whether or not to join EMU. It is unlikely that this option will exist for the Central European countries. Criteria for the EU accession, which were formulated at the Copenhagen Summit in 1993, include, among others, the capacity of a candidate country to take up all obligations from the EU membership (acquis communautaire), including the adherence to the aims of political, economic and monetary union. In practice this means that a candidate country has to agree to join the EMU as soon as it is ready, i.e., as soon as it meets the Maastricht convergence criteria on a sustainable basis. In other words, obligation to participate in the EMU arises from the membership in the EU. The Central European countries will therefore not be in a position to opt-out of the EMU. If they have some problems with surrendering their monetary sovereignty, they would be advised not to join the EU in the first place and would probably be excluded from the negotiations for the EU membership.

Any considerations about the expected costs and benefits of the EMU for the Central European countries may be analytically interesting, but are not relevant any more for decision-making on whether or not to join the EMU. These issues were relevant at the time before these countries decided they wanted to join the EU. Today it would look odd if the candidate countries invested a lot of efforts in the EU accession, but would then not be willing to participate in its crowning project, the EMU, because they felt that the implied loss of their monetary sovereignty was too high a sacrifice. The fact that an EU member country like Great Britain could afford to do so does not mean that Central European countries would be allowed to do the same. Another theoretical possibility is that a candidate country, when joining the EU, would deliberately delay the fulfilment of the Maastricht convergence criteria. Sweden followed this strategy. It is doubtful, however, whether the Central European countries would get away with this.

To what extent the loss of the exchange rate instrument is really a cost of the inclusion in the EMU, depends mostly on two factors - exposure to the asymmetric shocks and functioning of the alternative mechanisms of adjustment to these shocks, which substitute for the exchange rate when this instrument is given up as a result of the inclusion in the EMU.

So far we have concentrated on general assessment of costs and benefits of the monetary union, which at least in principle holds true for all present and potential member countries of EMU. The theory of the optimum currency areas also emphasises certain structural characteristics of the economy which determine whether for an individual country it is better to join a broader monetary union. According to this theory, the main structural characteristics which determine whether a country should join a monetary union, are the following: size, openness, diversification of production and exports, and geographical concentration of trade.

The research reported in this book allows us to shed some light on these issues of whether the Central European countries form an optimum currency area with the euro zone.

More particularly, this research indicates that individual Central European countries are not expected to be exposed to serious specific asymmetric shocks which would hit their economies but not other parts of the EMU or EU as a whole. This results from the findings that, first, the Central European countries (Slovenia and the Czech Republic in the first place) have a product structure of their exports to the EU which is very similar to that of the intra-EU trade, and second, from the evidence that more symmetric than asymmetric shocks can be expected in the Central European countries (in Slovenia in particular) and that their economies are rather synchronised with the cycles in the EU economies. If this is the case, Slovenia and other Central European countries should not meet specifically difficult problems when joining the EMU, since they will not have to rely heavily on the exchange rate as an instrument of adjustment to these asymmetric shocks. In these circumstances, giving up the exchange rate as an instrument of adjustment when joining the EMU is not a severe sacrifice. This improves the expected ratio of benefits/costs of the EMU for the Central European candidate countries. To deal with symmetric shocks which hit the entire EMU, traditional instruments of adjustment - monetary and exchange rate policy - can be used.

Adjustments which the Central European countries will still need to face when joining the EMU will have to be borne (just like in the EU member countries in the EMU) by greater flexibility of the labour market. Possible alternative mechanisms of adjustment, such as mobility of labour within the EMU or fiscal transfers within the EMU area, are for well known reasons not expected to play a role worth mentioning. It can, therefore, be concluded that for the Central European countries the inclusion in the EMU will make sense only when they prepare themselves to be able to sustain the competitive pressures on the EU internal market. Not surprisingly, this is the main point and the main requirement in the process of negotiations of these countries for their full membership in the EU. In the opposite case, the loss of the exchange rate as an instrument of adjustment might really become a very large sacrifice of the participation in EMU. If the exchange rate policy is no longer available while alternative mechanisms of adjustment do not function, a candidate country which faces problems with its international competitiveness in the EU markets could experience negative effects on its economic growth. It would become a depressed region in the EMU, which would be the final high costs of an unsuccessful inclusion in the EMU.

Having dealt with the question of why joining EMU, we now come to the question of how and when the Central European countries should join. This question involves a set of related sub-questions. The first one refers to the time they are expected to join the EMU. This question has also to do with the issue of whether the Central European countries should join EMU after or at the time of their EU accession. The second one addresses the issue of whether these countries will join the EMU directly, or whether they will first join the ERM 2.

According to the most probable scenario which is implicit in the documents of the European Commission, the Central European countries are first expected to join the ERM 2, probably at the time of their accession to the EU, and then somewhat later, perhaps after a few years, to join the EMU. In Agenda 2000 the possibility of their simultaneous entrance in the EU and in the EMU is not excluded, but it is considered undesirable. This attitude derives from the belief that these countries will not be able to reach the required macroeconomic stability as defined in the Maastricht convergence criteria on a sustainable basis in the relatively short time before their accession in the EU. Any postponement of the Eastern enlargement process of the EU would of course increase the possibilities of the simultaneous inclusion of these countries in both the EU and the EMU. It would give them more time to meet the required standards of macroeconomic stability. However, such a delay would not be in the interest of the candidate countries and would bring out some new problems.

It is clear that the Central European countries will not be able to join the EMU before the time of their accession in the EU. Membership in the EMU is open only to the members of the EU. The present rules which restrict the membership in the EMU only to EU members will certainly not change.

Will the Central European countries be in a position to join the EMU at the time of their accession in the EU? In principle this is possible, but two problems, a formal one and a substantial one, would have to be overcome. The formal problem lies in the definition of the Maastricht convergence criterion relating to the exchange rate stability. It requires, among other things, that for at least two years, the currency of an EMU candidate country has to be participating in the ERM (or ERM 2, which is going to be the relevant reference at the time), before it can join the EMU. On the other hand, according to the present rules, a country cannot join the EMS and its ERM (or ERM 2) until it becomes a member of the EU. It follows that the Central European candidate countries will first have to join the EU and the ERM 2 at the same time, and then wait for at least two years, merely to formally fulfil this convergence criterion, even if all other Maastricht criteria were already met. The way out of this formal obstacle to a simultaneous entry into the EU and the EMU could be found in one of the following solutions:

a) The Maastricht convergence criterion relating to the exchange rate stability could be modified or at least flexibly interpreted in view of changed circumstances at that time (newly established ERM 2, emergence of new candidate countries, already functioning euro etc.). It seems that some flexibility of this criterion was already applied when it was decided that Italy and Finland fulfil this Maastricht criterion, even though their currencies were not participating in the ERM for two years beforehand.

b) The rules which define that membership in the ERM (or ERM 2) is open only to EU members and not to the candidate countries, could be modified or at least flexibly interpreted. In academic circles the idea of an early inclusion of the Central European candidate countries in the ERM 2, even before their accession to the EU, emerged some years ago. One possible timing for the inclusion of the Central European countries in the ERM 2 could be after they conclude the negotiations for a full membership in the EU, but before the ratification of their EU membership agreement. At that time they would already be assessed as ready for joining the EU.

The arguments in favour of an early inclusion of the Central European countries in the ERM 2 are the following:

a) It would enable these countries to overcome the above mentioned rigidity of the Maastricht criterion relating to the exchange rate stability. At the moment this prevents the simultaneous entrance of the Central European candidate countries in the EU and in the EMU, even if they are economically ready for it and fulfil all other Maastricht convergence criteria.
b) It would give the ERM 2 some meaning, substance and needed critical mass. If these countries were not allowed to join the ERM before their EU membership, the ERM 2 may be a rather "lonely" place in the period 1999-2002 or even further, as it would include only a couple of voluntarily participating pre-in EU countries. Wider membership would give the ERM 2 more meaning and importance. It should be remembered that at the time the ERM 2 was designed, there was a general belief there would be more, say some five or six countries participating in the ERM 2.
c) An early inclusion of the Central European candidate countries in the ERM 2 would give them the opportunity to get used to the European concepts of monetary and exchange rate discipline and co-operation. They could learn to see their exchange rates as a matter of common concern and collective decision-making, thereby preparing themselves for an easier inclusion in the EMU after the required two-year period in the ERM 2.

Another obstacle to the simultaneous entry of the Central European countries into EU and EMU has to do with the Maastricht convergence criteria. Today in 1998, the Central European countries fulfil both fiscal criteria, but fail to meet the three monetary criteria. In particular, the inflation rate is, even in the best performing Central European countries, still much too high for the standards of the European monetary integration. Lowering the inflation rate is the main task of the policy-makers in these countries in the next few years before their EU accession. This is a prerequisite for their further steps on the way to the European monetary integration and finally for joining the EMU.

If we take the example of Slovenia, its Strategy of the EU accession (adopted in 1997) defines the expected timing of both accession in the EU and in the EMU. According to the Strategy, Slovenia should become EU member in 2002 and join the EMU in 2005, three years later. The main reason for this two-stage approach to joining the EMU lies in the assessment of realistic timing of reaching the required macroeconomic stability on a sustainable basis. The Strategy starts from the assumption that structural reforms and sectoral adjustments should be undertaken first, while concentration on macroeconomic stability should follow next. If these reforms were not undertaken or were delayed, and macroeconomic policies were overburdened with chasing the Maastricht convergence criteria, the result could be unnecessary losses in terms of economic growth and employment. On the other hand, if the Maastricht criteria were reached earlier, at any price by aggressive monetary and fiscal policies, the structural problems would simply be swept under the carpet. Such macroeconomic stability could hardly be sustained and structural problems would soon break open. In fact, the European Commission warns against such an overambitious approach and suggests that the Central European candidate countries should first concentrate on the EU accession requirements and then focus on meeting the Maastricht convergence criteria.

This volume is the collection of the papers prepared in the framework of the ACE-Phare research project "Inclusion of the Central European Countries in the European Monetary Integration Process". Additionally, the paper by D. Gros and G. Vandille, which was prepared for the preceding ACE-Phare research project "Monetary Integration and Disintegration in Europe - the Case of Slovenia" was also included. All of these research papers focus on the issue of the European monetary integration for the Central European countries candidates for the EU accession, but they approach the issue from different viewpoints. The following two chapters use empirical analysis to investigate the questions of costs and benefits of the EMU and of symmetric vs. asymmetric shocks in a monetary union. The next four chapters discuss issues of transition of the inclusion of the Central European countries in the EMU. The analysis includes, beside economic, some political and institutional aspects. The last two chapters are the case studies of the Czech Republic and Slovenia. They place the monetary integration in the context of their transition process and of their aspiration for the EU membership.

The chapter **"Are Central European Countries Part of the European Optimum Currency Area?"**, by Paul De Grauwe and Yunus Aksoy, starts from the theory of optimal currency area which has identified the conditions countries must satisfy to benefit from joining a currency union. In this chapter the authors concentrate on one such condition, the size of asymmetric shocks, and analyse it empirically for Central European countries. They find that the degree of asymmetry in the movement of output and employment of Central European countries is surprisingly small and even smaller than in the Scandinavian countries. Two main conclusion can be drawn from the analysis for Central European countries as a group and for some of them, like Slovenia in particular. First, these countries can be expected to be more exposed to symmetric than to asymmetric shocks, which makes them potentially suitable for joining the monetary integration, and second, their economic cycles are rather synchronised with those in the EU economies which again is an argument in favour of their inclusion in the EMU.

The chapter **"Central European and EU Trade Structures"**, by Daniel Gros and Guy Vandille, is an empirical analysis of the similarities of trade structures between the Central European countries and the EU countries. It compares the structure of intra-EU trade to the trade between individual Central European countries and the EU. Information about the extent to which the nature of CE-EU trade differs from that of intra-EU trade is useful to assess whether Central European countries should seek stronger economic and/or monetary integration with the EU. The underlying hypothesis is that countries with similar trade structure are natural candidates for integration leading eventually to EMU, because differences in economic structure indicate the likelihood of country-specific shocks for which the exchange rate would be a useful adjustment mechanisms (which is lost once a country joins the EMU). Finally, the paper presents some rough estimates of the relative size of the benefits and costs of EMU for Central European and EU countries.

The chapter **"Fiscal Consolidation in the Central European Countries and European Monetary Union"**, by Paul de Grauwe and Vladimir Lavrač, addresses the fiscal dimension of Central European countries' inclusion in the EMU. The paper first analyses fiscal convergence of Central European countries in terms of their past and present performance on budgetary deficits and public debt. Next, the paper relates fiscal convergence to monetary convergence and, when discussing the sustainability of the fiscal convergence of the Central European countries, to the so-called real convergence, i.e. to the growth rates and current account balances of these countries. The paper concludes that the prospects for sustaining fiscal convergence in the Central European countries in the next few years before their accession in the EU seem rather good.

The chapter **"Exchange Rate Policy of Central European Countries in the Transition to EMU"** by Giuseppe Tullio deals with the risks and costs that Central European economies in transition may incur if they join the EMU too soon. It argues that the catching-up process will be very long and is likely to be the source of asymmetric shocks hitting these countries individually and as a group. This will require a freer hand in determining real exchange rates and competitiveness than the joining of EMU would allow. Some inherent defects of EMU (lack of flexibility of national fiscal policies, lack of a sizeable enough "federal budget" and a possible deflationary bias) are additional arguments for adopting a wait-and-see attitude. The paper also criticises the exchange rate policy followed so far by all Central European countries and argues that they could have struck a better balance between the anchor role that the exchange rate can provide and the need to avoid losses in competitiveness. Central European countries should adopt an exchange rate "corridor" announced in advance for each year, with sufficient margins, a positive slope and a small appreciation of the real exchange rate incorporated into the pre-announced nominal devaluation. This system, beside striking a better balance between the two conflicting objectives mentioned above, also has the advantage of guaranteeing a smooth transition into an ERM-type arrangement with the euro.

The chapter **"Inclusion of Central European Countries in the European Monetary Integration Process"** by Vladimir Lavrač aims at analysing the possibilities for the inclusion of Central European countries in the European monetary integration process. First, it discusses the relationship between the EU membership and the inclusion in the European monetary integration process. Next, it analyses the exchange rate regimes and policies of individual Central European countries and compares them to the requirements of the present EMS. As the requirements of the future EMU are defined in the Maastricht convergence criteria, the paper addresses the question of how the Central European economies comply with these standards, and how the Maastricht convergence criteria should be interpreted and applied in these countries. The paper analyses present and expected readiness of the Central European countries for joining the EMS and EMU in the future, and indicates the adjustments in their exchange rate policies which they should undertake while preparing themselves for the inclusion in the European monetary integration process.

The chapter **"Integrating Central Europe into the European Union: The Monetary Dimension"** by Peter Backé places the preparations of the Central European countries, candidates for a full EU membership, for their inclusion in the ERM 2 and in the EMU in the context of their process of transition and their EU approximation process. Since 1997 accession preparations for a widening of the EU to the East have reached a considerable momentum. Against this backdrop, the perspectives of Central European countries for monetary integration have increasingly been discussed. The purpose of this chapter is to look into the main points of this unfolding debate. The analysis sets out by putting the issue of monetary integration into the wider context of the Central European countries' quest for EU membership. This is followed by an examination of the prospects of the Central European countries for an eventual joining of the Stage Three of the EMU. The chapter concludes by shedding some light on the potential economic consequences an accession to the euro area would entail for the front-runner transition countries.

The chapter **"Echoing the European Monetary Integration in the Czech Republic"** by Oldrich Dedek is a case study of the Czech policy making related to the perspective membership in the EMU. The underlying idea is that although in the current stage of transition the issue of the single currency is still far from being on the top of the agenda, the very progress of economic transition with a substantial flexibility both on the current and capital account of the balance-of-payments urges to pay much more attention to preserving a healthy macroeconomic environment, much in line with that indicated in the Maastricht convergence criteria. This observation is even more accentuated if a small and open economy acknowledges benefits from a stable exchange rate. By not respecting this causality, a country may get into trouble as was the case of currency turbulence that affected the Czech economy in May 1997. From this perspective, the paper evaluates the progress achieved in individual areas such as disinflation, fiscal consolidation and exchange rate policies. Finally, the paper identifies potential risks that may cause delays in the catching-up with the EU.

The chapter **"Monetary Arrangements and Exchange Rate Regime in a Small Transitional Economy (Slovenia)"** by Ivan Ribnikar is the case study of Slovenian preparations for a move from monetary sovereignty with a floating exchange rate system towards joining the EMU some time in the future. In the Central European economies, the monetary policy regime so far has been largely determined by previous economic systems and the chosen method of transition - in the case of Slovenia in the first place by the method of abolishment of the social ownership of business enterprises. Therefore, in analysing monetary arrangements and exchange rate regimes, these determinants are taken into account. How monetary arrangements and exchange rate regimes have been changing and how the country is approaching EU and perhaps finally the European single currency area follows in the second part of the text.

Chapter 2

Are Central European Countries Part of the European Optimum Currency Area?

PAUL DE GRAUWE AND YUNUS AKSOY

1. COSTS AND BENEFITS OF MONETARY UNION FOR A CENTRAL EUROPEAN COUNTRY: THE THEORY

The theory of optimum currency areas (OCA) has analysed the conditions that countries should satisfy if they want to profit from joining a monetary union. The main insights of the theory can be summarised as follows. When countries are different in economic structures, they are likely to face 'asymmetric shocks'. In the absence of the exchange rate instrument, they will need a lot of flexibility in their labour markets (e.g. wage flexibility, labour mobility) so as to adjust to these asymmetric shocks and to prevent these shocks from leading to permanent unemployment. The OCA-theory also stresses that the cost of relinquishing the exchange rate instrument declines with the openness of the country. For very open countries the exchange rate instrument loses much of its effectiveness to affect output and employment, and therefore to correct for asymmetric shocks. Thus, very open (and typically small) countries bear fewer costs by joining a monetary union than large and relatively closed economies. Conversely, the benefits of a single currency increase with the degree of openness of a country, because more contracts involve exchange rate transactions in small open economies than in large and relatively closed ones.

We can represent the main insights of the OCA-theory graphically as follows. In Figure 1, on the vertical axis we set out the degree of divergent movements of output and employment between a representative Central European country (CE-country) and the European Union. We call this the degree of economic divergence[1]. On the horizontal axis, we set out a measure of the degree of trade integration between these countries. This measure could be the trade of the CE-country with the EU-countries as a share of the CE-country's GDP. The downward sloping line (TT) says that as trade integration between the CE-country and the EU increases the degree of economic divergence between the countries involved declines, i.e. countries become more alike and face less asymmetric shocks. The presumption here is that economic integration between the CE-country and the EU will take the form of intra-industry specialisation. As a result, when a shock occurs in one industry, it will affect all countries in a similar way. (This is only one view, however. There is another view, however, that will be discussed shortly).

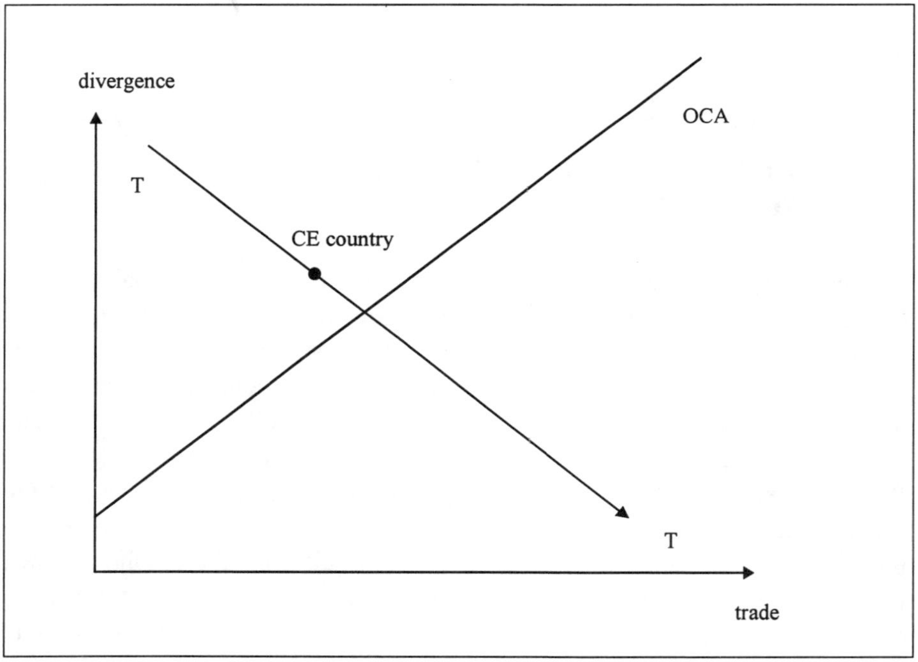

Figure 1. Costs and benefits of monetary integration for the CE country

The upward sloping line (called OCA) represents the combinations of divergence and trade integration that makes monetary union a break-even operation (costs = benefits). It is derived as follows. The OCA-theory tells us that as trade integration increases the benefits for the CE-country rise and the costs decline. Put differently, the net gains of a monetary union increase with the degree of trade integration. At the same time, when economic divergence increases, the costs of a monetary union increase. The two phenomena together allow us to interpret the upward sloping OCA-schedule as follows: an increase in economic divergence makes a monetary union more costly; this increase in the cost of a monetary union, however, is offset by increasing economic integration. All points on the OCA-line are then combinations of divergence and integration for which the monetary union has a zero net gain. Note that all the points to the right of the OCA-line are points for which the benefits of monetary union exceed the costs. We call it the OCA-zone.

The effect of changes in labour market flexibility can be presented by shifts in the OCA-line. When labour market flexibility increases, the cost of a monetary union declines. Thus, a country can afford to experience larger asymmetric shocks and still find monetary union gainful. The OCA-line shifts upwards when labour market flexibility increases. This also increases the size of the OCA-zone relative to the non-OCA-zone.

The crucial question now is where we should put the CE-country? In Figure 1, we have put the CE-country on the downward sloping TT-line to the left of the OCA-line. That is, we assume that today the CE-country is not yet part of the European optimum currency area, basically because the degree of economic divergence is still too high and/or the degree of trade integration too low. This is however a purely empirical matter. We will return to this issue in section where we analyse some of the important factors to check whether our hypothesis is the right one.

The model of Figure 1 allows us to say something about the long-term perspectives of monetary union for the CE-country. As trade integration between the CE-country and the EU proceeds, the CE-country will be moving downwards along the TT-line. This will inevitably bring the country into the OCA-zone. Thus, in this view, monetary unification of the CE-country with the EU will increasingly become more profitable. In this sense, monetary union of the CE-country with the EU is inevitable.

The analysis of Figure 1 also makes clear that steps towards increasing the degree of labour market flexibility in the CE-country speed up the moment in which a monetary union yields a net gain for the CE-country. Graphically policies introducing more flexibility in the labour market shift the OCA-curve upwards and bring the CE-country closer to the OCA-zone (they could even bring the CE-country immediately into the OCA-zone).

The view presented in Figure 1 can be called the conventional view of the dynamics of monetary integration. It has been defended most forcefully by the European Commission in its well-known report 'One Market, One Money'. There is an alternative view, however, that can be derived from

Krugman's analysis of the effects of economic integration on the occurrence of asymmetric shocks. This view is based on the idea that by increasing the size of the markets, economic integration leads to a better exploitation of (static and dynamic) economies of scale. As a result, economic integration leads to regional concentration and agglomeration effects. This leads to a more specialised industrial structure of countries, which in turn increases the probability of asymmetric shocks. Thus, in this view economic integration leads to more divergence in the growth rates of output and employment between countries. We represent this alternative view in Figure 2. Instead of a downward sloping TT-line, we have a positively sloped TT-line. Thus, when economic integration between the CE-country and the EU increases, the CE-country becomes more specialised so that it will be subject to more rather than less asymmetric shocks[2].

We now have to consider two possibilities for the long-term prospects of monetary union. One is represented by the TT-line, the slope of which is flatter than the slope of the OCA-line. In this case, although today the CE-country may not be an optimum currency area, it will move into the OCA-zone over time. In this case more integration leads to more specialisation and thus to more asymmetric shocks. However, the benefits of a monetary union also increase steeply with the degree of integration. As a result, despite the increase in asymmetric shocks, more integration will lead the CE-country into the OCA-zone.

The second case is represented by the steep TT'-line. Here integration brings the CE-country increasingly farther away from the OCA-zone. This is so because the net gains of a monetary union do not increase fast enough with the degree of integration. As a result, the costs of divergence overwhelm all the other benefits a monetary union may have. In the long run the prospects for a monetary union of the CE-country with the EU-15 are poor.

From the discussion of the Krugman model, we conclude that even if integration leads to more asymmetric shocks, this may still lead to increasing net gains of a monetary union for the CE-country. We cannot exclude, however, that the process of integration will make monetary union for the CE-country more and more unattractive.

What is the right view of the world? A clear-cut answer will be difficult to formulate. Nevertheless, it is reasonable to claim that a presumption exists in favour of the European Commission view. The reason can be formulated as follows. The fact that economic integration can lead to concentration and agglomeration effects cannot be disputed. At the same time, however, it is also true that as market integration between countries proceeds, national borders become less and less important as factors that decide about the location of economic activities. As a result, it becomes more and more likely that concentration and agglomeration effects will be blind for the existence of borders. This creates the possibility that the clusters of economic activity will encompass borders. Put differently, it becomes more and more likely that the relevant regions in which some activity is centralised will transgress one or more borders. For example, it could very well be that the agglomeration effects lead to concentration of industries in Northern Italy and the CE-country. If this is the case, shocks in these industries will affect Italy and the CE-country, so that the lira/CE exchange rate cannot be used to absorb this shock.

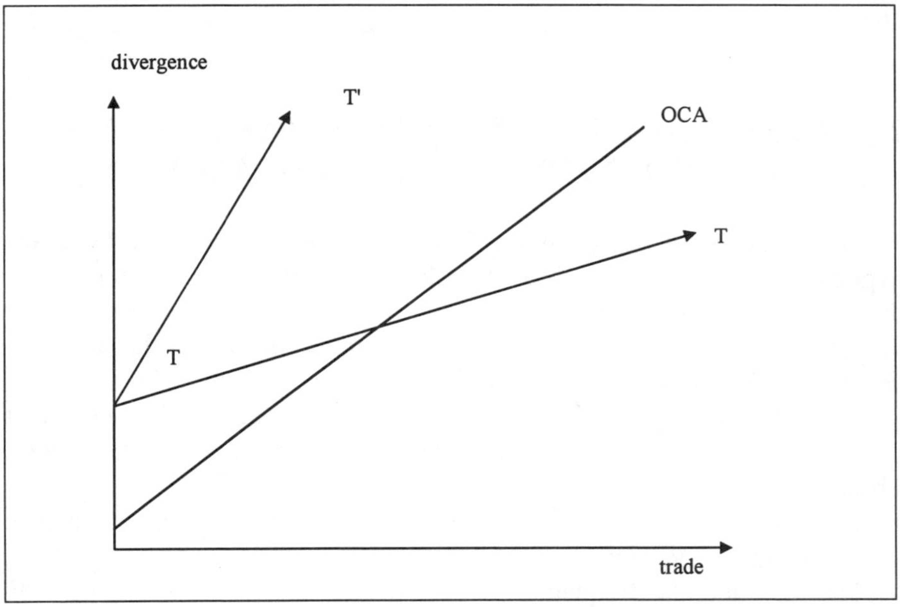

Figure 2. The Krugman view of monetary integration

Note that the argument we develop here is not that integration may not lead to concentration effects (it probably will), but rather that national borders will increasingly be less relevant in influencing the shape of these concentration effects. As a result, regions may still be very much affected by asymmetric shocks. The probability that these regions overlap existing borders, however, will increase as integration moves on. We conclude that the economic forces of integration are likely to rob the exchange rates between national currencies of their capacity to deal with these shocks.

From the preceding arguments it should not be concluded that economists know for sure what the relationship is between economic integration and the occurrence of asymmetric shocks. All we can say is that there is a theoretical presumption in favour of the hypothesis that integration will make asymmetric shocks between nations less likely. The issue remains essentially an empirical one. Recently Frankel and Rose (1996) have undertaken important empirical research relating to this issue. They analysed the degree to which economic activity between pairs of countries is correlated as a function of the intensity of their trade links. Their conclusion was that a closer trade linkage between two countries is strongly and consistently associated with more tightly correlated economic activity between the two countries. In terms of Figures 1 and 2 this means that the relationship between divergence and trade integration is negatively sloped.

Similar evidence is presented in Artis and Zhang (1995), who find that as the European countries have become more integrated during the 1980s and 1990s, the business cycles of these countries have become more correlated.

2. COSTS AND BENEFITS OF MONETARY UNION FOR THE CE-COUNTRY: SOME EMPIRICAL TESTS

In this section, we develop some empirical tests to find out whether our hypothesis about the location of the CE-country in Figure 1 is the correct one. The reader should be warned that these empirical tests are far from definitive. They can only give some approximate idea about the costs and benefits of a monetary union for the CE-country.

The OCA-theory has identified three sets of factors that matter in determining whether the CE-country would benefit from a monetary union. These are:

- The degree of trade integration of the CE-country with the EU and its likely future development.
- The size and the frequency of asymmetric shocks to which the CE-country is likely to be subject. In this context, the different economic and industrial structure of the CE-country versus the other EU-countries matters.
- The degree of flexibility of the labour markets in the CE-country.

In this section, we concentrate our attention on the nature of the asymmetric shocks in the CE-country. We use a panel data model that allows us to find out to what extent the growth rates of output and employment in the CE-country have been different from those observed in the European Union. Ideally one should separate the shocks that are induced by different monetary policies (and that will disappear in a future monetary union) from the shocks that are structural (and that will not disappear in a monetary union). A procedure to separate these shocks has been proposed by Blanchard and Quah (1989). This consists in using the neo-classical macroeconomic model to separate demand and supply shocks in the time series of output and employment. It is reasonable to assume that demand shocks are very much conditioned by the nature of the monetary regime, whereas supply shocks are not. Put differently, in a monetary union supply shocks will not disappear. As a result, an analysis of the degree of correlation of these supply shocks across countries can teach us whether these countries are likely to be hit by asymmetric shocks once they form a monetary union. In so doing, we gain insights into an important question, i.e. the size of the asymmetric shocks that potential members of a monetary union will face. (For applications of the Blanchard-Quah procedure see Bayoumi and Eichengreen (1992), Erkel-Rousse and Mélitz (1995).

Unfortunately, this procedure requires relatively long time series. These are as yet unavailable for CE-countries. As a result, we will rely on a procedure, which does not attempt to separate demand and supply shocks.

The model used in this paper aims at separating the common (international) and the country (asymmetric) sources of shocks in output and employment.[3] In order to do so, we proceed in two steps. We first specify a static panel data model. In a second step, we add some dynamics to the model.

2.1 The Static Model

The static model is specified as follows:

$$\Delta y_{i,t} = a + \sum_{t}^{T-1} b_t D_t + \sum_{i}^{N-1} c_i D_i + e_{i,t} \tag{1}$$

where $\Delta y_{i,t}$ is the percentage change in the dependent variable (GDP, employment, and industrial production, respectively) in year t and country i; a is the constant term; D_t is a set of time dummies, one for each year; D_i is a set of country dummies, one for each country; and $e_{i,t}$ is the disturbance term to country i at time t and assumed to be an i.i.d. random variable.

In this simple form the model explains yearly changes in, say, GDP of country i by two variables. The first one is the common shock D_t. This variable expresses the influence exerted each year by a component which is common to all countries in the sample. The second variable is the country specific (asymmetric) shock, D_i. The latter measures the extent to which the yearly changes in GDP of country i differ from the changes observed in the other countries in the sample. In both sets of variables, we have imposed two necessary normalisations to avoid perfect co-linearity. We will set a benchmark country, here Germany, taking the value zero and a benchmark year, the last year of the sample taking the value of zero. Accordingly, the estimated coefficients of the country dummies should be interpreted as differences with respect to Germany and those of the time dummies as differences with respect to the last year in the sample.

We estimated equation (1) using data of the EU-countries and the CE-countries during the 1990s. We had to use quarterly data and to restrict the analysis to the 1990s due to the limited availability of the data in CE-countries.[4] The results are summarised in Table 1. (The complete estimation results are presented in Table 4 in Statistical Appendix). The results allow us to formulate the following conclusions. First, the R^2s suggest that employment changes are better explained by the model than either changes in industrial production or GDP. Second, the contribution of aggregate shocks to the total variability is generally higher than the contribution of country specific shocks. Put differently, changes in output and employment tend to be dominated by common shocks. This is most pronounced for employment changes and much less so for industrial production where common and country specific shocks are equally important. Third, there is still a large part of the total variability that is not explained by the model.

Table 1 also shows the F-tests of the joint significance of the coefficients of the CE-countries. They test whether adding observations of these CE-countries to the model lead to structural changes in the model. We generally find that we must reject the hypothesis of no structural changes. This is especially so for the time coefficients that show significant structural changes when the CE-countries are added to the sample. It is much less the case for the coefficients of the country dummies. This suggests that the time pattern of the changes in output and employment differs significantly between the CE-countries and the EU-countries. This is much less the case with the average growth rates of output and employment (as measured by the country dummies). Thus, on average changes in output and employment do not seem to be significantly different in the CE-countries as compared with the EU. The difference may lie in a different time pattern. This conclusion should be handled with care, however, because our sample period is extremely short.

In a next step, we test whether the CE-countries as a whole pass this test. In order to do so we grouped the CE-countries' observations together. We also grouped the other countries, i.e. the core, Scandinavia, Southern Europe, the UK and Ireland. The results are presented in Table 2. The benchmark group of countries is the core. As a result, the coefficients of the country dummies have to be interpreted as deviations from the core. A simple t-test then measures whether the changes of employment and output have deviated significantly in CE-countries from the core. As can be seen, we do not observe significant differences. The same holds for Southern Europe. It does

Table 1. Time vs. Country Effects (Static Analysis)

$$\Delta y_{i,t} = \alpha_1 + \Sigma_t^{T-1} \beta_t D_t + \Sigma_i^{N-1} \gamma_i D_i + \varepsilon_{i,t}$$

	R^2			No. of	F-tests		
	Aggregate Shock (%)	Country Specific Shock (%)	Total (%)	obs.	General	Time	Country
Dependent Variables $\Delta y_{i,t}$							
Czech Republic							
Industrial Production (93.2-95.3)	7	9	17	142	0.98	1.11	0.87
GDP (93.2-95.4)	14	1	15	103	0.78	1.44	0.15
Employment (93.2-95.4)	30	12	43	141	3.61	5.69*	1.27
Slovak Republic							
Industrial Production (93.2-95.3)	9	7	15	142	0.78	2.30*	0.61
GDP (93.2-95.4)	13	2	15	103	0.76	1.38	0.17
Employment (93.2-95.4)	34	10	43	141	3.71*	6.80*	0.92
Slovenia							
Industrial Production (92.1-95.3)	18	15	33	222	3.23*	3.68*	2.80*
GDP (93.1-95.4)	22	1	23	112	1.34	2.36*	0.08
Employment (92.1-95.4)	38	5	42	215	4.63*	7.89*	0.88
Hungary							
Industrial Production (92.1-95.3)	12	7	19	222	1.50	2.01*	0.98
Employment (92.4-95.4)	40	7	46	170	4.54*	8.72*	0.82
Poland							
Industrial Production (91.2-93.3)	11	11	21	160	1.50	1.95*	1.13
Employment (92.1-95.4)	38	4	42	261	4.72*	8.23*	0.72

not hold for the Scandinavian countries, which have experienced significantly different employment changes. Thus, surprisingly, CE-countries come closer to forming part of an optimum currency area with the core countries than the Scandinavian countries.

Table 2. Static Analysis[a]
(Regression analysis for the static equation; time dummy coefficients should be interpreted with respect to the last year and country dummies should be interpreted with respect to the core.)

$\Delta y_{i,t}$	Industrial Production	GDP	Employment
		Time Dummies	
α	-0.017	-0.008	-0.011
	(-1.00)	(-0.51)	(-1.78)*
1993:2	0.014	0.035	0.006
	(0.70)	(1.70)*	(0.79)
1993:3	0.022	0.017	0.007
	(1.10)	(0.84)	(1.00)
1993:4	0.03	0.02	-0.009
	(1.57)	(0.98)	(-1.33)
1994:1	0.024	-0.009	-0.0016
	(1.17)	(-0.43)	(-0.23)
1994:2	0.025	0.04	0.015
	(1.26)	(2.15)*	(2.21)*
1994:3	0.03	-0.016	0.022
	(1.52)	(-0.77)	(3.11)*
1994:4	0.016	0.026	-0.005
	(0.76)	(1.29)	(-0.65)
1995:1	0.029	-0.005	-0.002
	(1.33)	(-0.24)	(-0.29)
1995:2	0.02	0.03	0.023
	(1.01)	(1.64)	(3.06)*
1995:3	-	0.015	0.014
		(0.74)	(1.91)*
		Country Dummies	
Central Europe	0.015	0.004	0.0003
	(1.32)	(0.38)	(0.01)
Scandinavia	0.017	-0.0013	0.012
	(1.17)	(-0.12)	(2.52)*
Southern Europe	0.001	-0.004	0.004
	(0.10)	(-0.28)	(1.17)
Ireland	0.04	-	0.017
	(1.86)*		(2.72)*
UK	0.004	0.002	0.006
	(0.21)	(-0.13)	(0.92)
		Descriptive Statistics	
R^2 (%)	5.28	22.79	30.83
No. of observations	172	125	184

[a] t-values are in parenthesis. An asterix indicates that the coeficient is significant at the 95 % interval.

2.2 The Dynamic Model

The static model only allows for a country specific shock, which is assumed to be the same each year. We cannot distinguish constant and non-constant country effects over time. In this section, we incorporate an interaction term to the model which allows us to detect the non-constant country effects over time. We re-estimate the model by including this interaction term between the time and the country dummies for each country separately and we test whether the coefficients of these interaction terms are jointly significant. If they are, we can conclude that these country effects are not constant over time and that there is a typical output-employment cycle for the country concerned. We repeat the same regression for all the other EU-countries[5]. The model now can be written as follows

$$\Delta y_{i,t} = a + \sum_{t}^{T-1} b_t D_t + \sum_{i}^{N-1} c_i D_i + \sum_{t}^{T-1} e_t D_t D_k + e_{i,t} \qquad (2)$$

for $k = 1, \ldots, N$

where $D_t D_k$ is the interaction term.

We present the results concerning the significance of the interaction terms in Table 3. (In appendix, we show the full results in Tables 5 to 9). Table 3 allows us to derive the following conclusions. For industrial production, we find significantly different cycles in all CE-countries except for Slovenia. For GDP and employment, we do not find any significant time varying effects. Thus, the results are mixed. One variable (industrial production) appears to follow a different cycle in most CE-countries, the other variables do not exhibit such differences.

Table 3. Joint F (Wald) Test for Time Specific Country Dummies

Joint F-Tests	Industrial Production	GDP	Employment
Czech Republic	18.45*	1.37	1.58
Hungary	23.59*	-	1.44
Poland	4.96*	-	1.16
Slovak Republic	63.31*	1.23	0.48
Slovenia	0.84	0.39	0.76

Returning to the theoretical analysis of section 1 (Figure 1) we can conclude that some CE-countries may now be located on the right hand side of the OCA-line. Slovenia, for example, comes closest to this possibility. This conclusion, however, should be considered as a provisional one. As we have indicated earlier, the data set we have used is rather short so that considerable uncertainty continues to exist about the issue of whether the CE-countries belong to the European OCA.

NOTES

1 We could take as measure of divergence one minus the correlation coefficient between the growth rates of output of these countries. Thus when the correlation is 1, our measure of divergence is 0. When the correlation is -1 our measure of divergence would be 2, its maximum value.
2 This view could also be associated with Peter Kenen who stressed that countries with a less diversified output structure are subject to more asymmetric shocks making them less suitable to form a monetary union. The presumption is that small countries that are highly integrated with the rest of the world are also highly specialised. This leads to the paradox that small and very open countries should keep their own currencies and not join a monetary union (see Frankel and Rose (1996) on this paradox and how it can be resolved).
3 The model is described more fully in De Grauwe and Aksoy (1997). In this paper we also discuss the problems of the model.
4 Quarterly data are from IFS and OECD, Main Economic Indicators. Data cover 1992:1 - 1995:3 period for industrial production, 1993:1 - 1995:4 period for GDP and 1992:1 - 1995:4 period for employment.
5 Note that together with the European Union countries we include only one Central European country in the panel data set. Thus, we estimate equation (2) for each Central European country separately.

REFERENCES

Artis, M., and Zhang, W., 1995, "International Business Cycles and the ERM: Is There a European Business Cycle?" *CEPR Discussion Paper,* No. 1191.

Bayoumi, T., and Eichengreen, B., 1992, "Shocking Aspects of Monetary Unification", in: F. Giavazzi and F. Torres, eds., The Transition to Economic and Monetary Union in Europe, Cambridge University Press, Cambridge.

Bayoumi, T., and Prasad, E., 1995, "Currency Unions, Economic Fluctuations and Adjustment: Some Empirical Evidence", *CEPR Discussion Paper,* No. 1172.

Blanchard, O., and Quah, D., (1989), "The Dynamic Effects of Aggregate Demand and Supply Disturbances", *American Economic Review*, 79 (4).

De Grauwe, P., and Aksoy, Y., 1997, "Is Europe an Optimum Currency Area? Evidence from Panel Data", University of Leuven, January 1997.

Erkel-Rousse, H., and Mélitz, J., 1995, "New Empirical Evidence on the Costs of Monetary Union", *CEPR Discussion Paper*, No. 1169.

Frankel, J., and Rose, A., 1996, "The Endogeneity of the Optimum Currency Area Criteria", *NBER Discussion paper*, No. 5700, August 1996.

Stockman, A., 1988, "Sectoral and National Aggregate Disturbances to Industrial Outputs in Seven European Countries", *Journal of Monetary Economics,* No. 21.

STATISTICAL APPENDIX

Table 4. Static Analysis
(Regression analysis for the static equation; time dummy coefficients should be interpreted with respect to the last year and country dummies should be interpreted with respect to Germany.)

$\Delta y_{i,t}$	Industrial Production	GDP	Employment
		Time Dummies	
α	-0.019	-0.016	-0.020
	(-0.83)	(-0.67)	(-2.19)*
1993:2	0.015	0.035	0.006
	(0.02)	(1.67)*	(0.80)
1993:3	0.023	0.017	0.007
	(1.08)	(0.82)	(0.98)
1993:4	0.032	0.020	-0.009
	(1.53)	(0.96)	(-1.32)
1994:1	0.024	-0.009	-0.0008
	(1.15)	(-0.41)	(-0.11)
1994:2	0.026	0.045	0.017
	(1.24)	(2.10)*	(2.33)*
1994:3	0.031	0.016	0.023
	(1.49)	(0.76)	(3.22)*
1994:4	0.015	0.027	-0.004
	(0.72)	(1.26)	(-0.54)
1995:1	0.029	-0.006	-0.002
	(1.30)	(-0.25)	(-0.25)
1995:2	0.022	0.034	0.022
	(0.99)	(1.57)	(3.08)*
1995:3	-	0.014	0.014
		(0.69)	(1.94)*
		Country Dummies	
Austria	0.007	0.013	0.015
	(0.29)	(0.59)	(1.65)*
Belgium	-0.0002	-	-
	(-0.009)		
Czech Republic	0.004	0.01	-0.004
	(0.13)	(0.43)	(-0.40)
Denmark	0.002	0.016	0.023
	(0.07)	(0.68)	(1.76)*
Finland	0.018	0.014	0.024
	(0.70)	(0.63)	(2.67)*
France	0.004	0.003	0.006
	(0.14)	(0.14)	(0.66)
Greece	0.0024	-	0.015
	(0.09)		(1.68)*
Hungary	0.016	-	0.005
	(0.64)		(0.53)

Table 4. Continuation

$\Delta y_{i,t}$	Industrial Production	GDP	Employment
		Country Dummies	
Ireland	0.038	-	0.025
	(1.68)*		(2.82)*
Italy	0.006	-	0.009
	(0.22)		(0.98)
Luxembourg	-0.003	-	0.007
	(-0.09)		(0.69)
Netherlands	0.005	0.005	0.006
	(0.21)	(0.22)	(0.66)
Poland	-	-	0.013
			(1.41)
Portugal	-0.007	-	0.013
	(-0.23)		(1.29)
Slovakia	0.043	0.014	0.017
	(1.69)*	(0.62)	(1.94)*
Slovenia	0.007	0.011	0.01
	(0.26)	(0.51)	(1.13)
Spain	0.012	0.004	0.015
	(0.44)	(0.16)	(1.70)*
Sweden	0.021	-0.002	0.017
	(0.81)	(-0.09)	(1.90)*
UK	0.007	0.006	0.014
	(0.25)	(0.26)	(1.56)
		Descriptive Statistics	
R^2 (%)	7.59	14.41	36.91
No. of observations	172	125	184

Czech Republic (Dynamic Analysis)

Table 5a. Correlation Coefficients (in percent)

Joint F-Tests	Industrial Production	GDP	Employment
Austria	18.02	25.60	44.69
Belgium	18.04	-	-
Czech Republic	67.21	28.54	50.17
Denmark	26.70	24.72	-
Finland	34.28	18.19	64.68
France	17.62	16.70	47.02
Germany	18.23	14.59	43.80
Greece	19.03	-	52.49
Ireland	21.14	-	44.12
Italy	16.47	-	43.45
Luxembourg	24.91	-	43.75
Netherlands	19.31	17.30	49.47
Portugal	14.93	-	43.13
Spain	14.86	17.07	44.03
Sweden	19.34	65.27	44.93
U. K.	17.53	16.78	44.84

Table 5b. Joint F (Wald) Test for Time Dummies[a]

Joint F-Tests	Industrial Production	GDP	Employment
Austria	1.04	0.69	5.03*
Belgium	1.01	-	-
Czech Republic	1.04	1.56	6.50*
Denmark	1.68	1.21	-
Finland	1.25	0.89	5.71*
France	1.00	1.32	6.71*
Germany	1.15	1.36	6.00*
Greece	1.22	-	4.84*
Ireland	1.23	-	5.88*
Italy	1.13	-	5.26*
Luxembourg	0.87	-	6.08*
Netherlands	1.09	1.38	6.62*
Portugal	1.39	-	5.45*
Spain	1.14	1.37	5.84*
Sweden	1.21	2.56*	4.99*
U. K.	1.14	1.34	6.29*

[a] F-statistics with asterisks denote that the coefficients are significantly different at 95th percentile.

Table 5c. Joint F (Wald) Test for Country Dummies[a]

Joint F-Tests	Industrial Production	GDP	Employment
Austria	0.89	0.16	1.73*
Belgium	0.87	-	-
Czech Republic	2.88*	0.34	1.24
Denmark	0.71	0.37	-
Finland	0.81	0.21	2.18*
France	0.87	0.15	2.03*
Germany	0.81	0.16	1.52
Greece	0.92	-	2.40*
Ireland	0.50	-	1.39
Italy	0.46	-	1.62
Luxembourg	0.64	-	1.71*
Netherlands	0.90	0.15	1.77*
Portugal	0.42	-	1.70*
Spain	0.46	0.15	1.67*
Sweden	0.79	1.97*	1.71*
U. K.	0.84	0.16	1.72*

[a] F-statistics with asterisks denote that the coefficients are significantly different at 95th percentile.

Table 5d. Joint F (Wald) Test for Time Specific Country Dummies[a]

Joint F-Tests	Industrial Production	GDP	Employment
Austria	0.18	1.07	0.37
Belgium	0.21	-	-
Czech Republic	18.45*	1.37	1.58
Denmark	2.48*	1.05	-
Finland	0.37	0.27	6.58*
France	0.12	0.14	0.96
Germany	0.21	0.14	0.34
Greece	0.33	-	2.43*
Ireland	0.66	-	0.26
Italy	0.41	-	0.13
Luxembourg	1.36	-	0.32
Netherlands	0.33	0.19	1.58
Portugal	0.25	-	0.11
Spain	0.14	0.16	0.24
Sweden	0.38	11.87*	0.42
U. K.	0.11	0.14	0.45

[a] F-statistics with asterisks denote that the coefficients are significantly different at 95th percentile.

Hungary: (Dynamic Analysis)

Table 6a. Correlation Coefficients (in percent)

Joint F-Tests	Industrial Production	Employment
Austria	19.86	46.89
Belgium	19.76	-
Denmark	25.62	-
Finland	20.14	65.60
France	19.43	48.84
Germany	19.77	46.36
Greece	22.46	54.58
Hungary	72.26	44.95
Ireland	21.37	46.51
Italy	20.26	47.11
Luxembourg	23.61	46.27
Netherlands	19.86	51.30
Portugal	20.10	45.64
Spain	19.67	40.62
Sweden	20.56	42.42
U. K.	19.49	47.77

Table 6b. Joint F (Wald) Test for Time Dummies[a]

Joint F-Tests	Industrial Production	Employment
Austria	1.82*	7.05*
Belgium	1.80*	-
Denmark	2.27*	-
Finland	1.89*	7.92*
France	1.84*	8.75*
Germany	1.87*	8.09*
Greece	2.08*	6.86*
Hungary	4.49*	8.85*
Ireland	1.85*	7.41*
Italy	1.94*	7.81*
Luxembourg	2.02*	8.12*
Netherlands	1.80*	8.96*
Portugal	1.92*	7.33*
Spain	1.74*	8.21*
Sweden	1.67	7.37*
U. K.	1.99*	8.59*

[a] F-statistics with asterisks denote that the coefficients are significantly different at 95th percentile.

Table 6c. Joint F (Wald) Test for Country Dummies[a]

Joint F-Tests	Industrial Production	Employment
Austria	1.02	0.97
Belgium	0.94	-
Denmark	1.07	-
Finland	0.86	1.39
France	1.00	1.22
Germany	0.86	0.76
Greece	1.05	1.57
Hungary	3.74*	0.77
Ireland	0.53	0.61
Italy	1.00	0.92
Luxembourg	1.08	0.94
Netherlands	0.99	0.96
Portugal	0.96	0.93
Spain	1.00	0.86
Sweden	0.93	1.02
U. K.	0.97	0.89

[a] F-statistics with asterisks denote that the coefficients are significantly different at 95th percentile.

Table 6d. Joint F (Wald) Test for Time Specific Country Dummies[a]

Joint F-Tests	Industrial Production	Employment
Austria	0.21	0.33
Belgium	0.21	-
Denmark	1.57	-
Finland	0.26	6.46*
France	0.15	0.84
Germany	0.20	0.35
Greece	0.65	2.46*
Hungary	23.59*	1.44
Ireland	0.46	0.25
Italy	0.36	0.38
Luxembourg	1.21	0.32
Netherlands	0.21	1.48
Portugal	0.36	0.12
Spain	0.23	0.16
Sweden	0.35	0.62
U. K.	0.15	0.58

[a] F-statistics with asterisks denote that the coefficients are significantly different at 95th percentile.

Poland (Dynamic Analysis)

Table 7a. Correlation Coefficients (in percent)

Joint F-Tests	Industrial Production	Employment
Austria	22.62	42.75
Belgium	23.71	-
Denmark	34.43	-
Finland	24.46	62.02
France	21.78	43.21
Germany	22.63	41.48
Greece	31.57	49.96
Ireland	22.97	41.33
Italy	22.34	41.84
Luxembourg	29.77	41.65
Netherlands	22.53	45.59
Poland	45.75	45.30
Portugal	24.15	40.24
Spain	22.98	40.60
Sweden	26.98	42.70
U. K.	22.28	42.81

Table 7b. Joint F (Wald) Test for Time Dummies[a]

Joint F-Tests	Industrial Production	Employment
Austria	1.81*	6.53*
Belgium	1.80*	-
Denmark	2.44*	-
Finland	1.61	7.07*
France	1.88*	7.89*
Germany	1.76*	7.33*
Greece	1.79*	6.11*
Ireland	1.95*	7.00*
Italy	1.84*	7.10*
Luxembourg	2.44*	7.46*
Netherlands	1.59	8.02*
Poland	2.31*	8.10*
Portugal	1.68	6.53*
Spain	1.61	6.91*
Sweden	1.66	6.22*
U. K.	2.03*	7.89*

[a] F-statistics with asterisks denote that the coefficients are significantly different at 95th percentile.

Table 7c. Joint F (Wald) Test for Country Dummies[a]

Joint F-Tests	Industrial Production	Employment
Austria	1.14	0.83
Belgium	1.12	-
Denmark	2.27*	-
Finland	1.15	1.36
France	1.11	1.20
Germany	1.05	0.76
Greece	1.40	1.51
Ireland	0.77	0.52
Italy	1.13	0.85
Luxembourg	1.22	0.89
Netherlands	1.19	0.91
Poland	1.63	0.94
Portugal	1.12	0.84
Spain	1.11	0.85
Sweden	1.21	0.82
U. K.	1.13	0.88

[a] F-statistics with asterisks denote that the coefficients are significantly different at 95th percentile.

Table 7d. Joint F (Wald) Test for Time Specific Country Dummies[a]

Joint F-Tests	Industrial Production	Employment
Austria	0.29	0.59
Belgium	0.49	-
Denmark	2.86*	-
Finland	0.64	6.80*
France	0.13	0.73
Germany	0.29	0.41
Greece	2.29*	2.49*
Ireland	0.35	0.29
Italy	0.23	0.39
Luxembourg	1.74*	0.46
Netherlands	0.38	1.30
Poland	4.96*	1.16
Portugal	0.57	0.10
Spain	0.35	0.14
Sweden	1.12	0.57
U. K.	0.23	0.64

[a] F-statistics with asterisks denote that the coefficients are significantly different at 95th percentile.

Slovak Republic (Dynamic Analysis)

Table 8a. Correlation Coefficients (in percent)

Joint F-Tests	Industrial Production	GDP	Employment
Austria	14.79	25.76	45.52
Belgium	15.66	-	-
Denmark	17.72	25.48	-
Finland	14.58	18.08	65.99
France	14.74	16.31	47.77
Germany	14.03	15.92	44.84
Greece	15.52	-	54.62
Ireland	15.06	-	45.21
Italy	14.61	-	44.66
Luxembourg	17.44	-	44.72
Netherlands	15.77	16.91	50.36
Portugal	13.85	-	43.79
Slovak Republic	86.26	27.09	45.90
Spain	13.96	16.64	44.69
Sweden	14.76	64.62	45.60
U. K.	14.48	16.41	45.70

Table 8b. Joint F (Wald) Test or Time Dummies[a]

Joint F-Tests	Industrial Production	GDP	Employment
Austria	1.03	0.68	5.76*
Belgium	1.16	-	-
Denmark	1.08	1.26	-
Finland	1.01	0.85	6.41*
France	1.04	1.27	7.57*
Germany	0.95	1.31	6.92*
Greece	1.16	-	5.92*
Ireland	0.95	-	6.79*
Italy	1.01	-	6.15*
Luxembourg	1.14	-	6.99*
Netherlands	1.14	1.33	7.49*
Portugal	0.98	-	6.20*
Slovak Republic	1.04	1.57	6.50*
Spain	1.00	1.31	6.61*
Sweden	1.01	2.12*	5.67*
U. K.	1.06	1.28	7.16*

[a] F-statistics with asterisks denote that the coefficients are significantly different at 95th percentile.

Table 8c. Joint F (Wald) Test for Country Dummies[a]

Joint F-Tests	Industrial Production	GDP	Employment
Austria	0.77	0.19	1.31
Belgium	0.61	-	-
Denmark	0.64	0.44	-
Finland	0.58	0.24	1.65
France	0.60	0.16	1.55
Germany	0.56	0.18	1.04
Greece	0.60	-	2.01*
Ireland	0.48	-	1.06
Italy	0.62	-	1.18
Luxembourg	0.66	-	1.27
Netherlands	0.60	0.17	1.23
Portugal	0.58	-	1.27
Slovak Republic	2.10*	0.32	1.23
Spain	0.61	0.17	1.28
Sweden	0.58	1.87	1.25
U. K.	0.59	0.17	1.30

[a] F-statistics with asterisks denote that the coefficients are significantly different at 95th percentile.

Table 8d. Joint F (Wald) Test for Time Specific Country Dummies[a]

Joint F-Tests	Industrial Production	GDP	Employment
Austria	0.14	1.21	0.40
Belgium	0.30	-	-
Denmark	0.89	1.18	-
Finland	0.11	0.30	7.02*
France	0.13	0.13	0.98
Germany	0.03	0.17	0.45
Greece	0.25	-	2.92*
Ireland	0.18	-	0.34
Italy	0.18	-	0.23
Luxembourg	0.99	-	0.42
Netherlands	0.28	0.18	1.65
Portugal	0.02	-	0.11
Slovak Republic	63.31*	1.23	0.48
Spain	0.04	0.16	0.24
Sweden	0.14	11.58*	0.42
U. K.	0.10	0.14	0.49

[a] F-statistics with asterisks denote that the coefficients are significantly different at 95th percentile.

Slovenia (Dynamic Analysis)

Table 9a. Correlation Coefficients (in percent)

Joint F-Tests	Industrial Production	GDP	Employment
Austria	36	35	44
Belgium	36	-	-
Denmark	48	34	-
Finland	36	26	63
France	34	25	46
Germany	34	24	43
Greece	40	-	53
Ireland	39	-	44
Italy	35	-	44
Luxembourg	44	-	43
Netherlands	37	26	49
Portugal	35	-	42
Slovenia	37	26	45
Spain	35	25	43
Sweden	38	66	45
U. K.	34	26	45

Table 9b. Joint F (Wald) Test for Time Dummies[a]

Joint F-Tests	Industrial Production	GDP	Employment
Austria	3.31*	1.45	6.69*
Belgium	3.32*	-	-
Denmark	4.98*	2.17*	-
Finland	3.42*	1.53	7.10*
France	3.24*	2.30*	8.27*
Germany	3.17*	2.37*	7.62*
Greece	3.85*	-	6.45*
Ireland	3.59*	-	7.27*
Italy	3.34*	-	7.27*
Luxembourg	4.09*	-	7.64*
Netherlands	3.59*	2.40*	8.55*
Portugal	3.39*	-	6.85*
Slovenia	3.46*	2.21*	8.36*
Spain	2.96*	2.38*	7.19*
Sweden	3.18*	3.52*	6.43*
U. K.	3.64*	2.41*	8.26*

[a] F-statistics with asterisks denote that the coefficients are significantly different at 95th percentile.

Table 9c. Joint F (Wald) Test for Country Dummies[a]

Joint F-Tests	Industrial Production	GDP	Employment
Austria	2.83*	0.14	0.85
Belgium	2.65*	-	-
Denmark	3.40*	0.43	-
Finland	2.40*	0.15	1.23
France	2.72*	0.08	1.19
Germany	2.37*	0.11	0.64
Greece	3.05*	-	1.53
Ireland	1.52	-	0.56
Italy	2.73*	-	0.83
Luxembourg	3.27*	-	0.86
Netherlands	2.83*	0.08	0.89
Portugal	2.65*	-	0.83
Slovenia	2.91*	0.08	0.87
Spain	2.72*	0.08	0.84
Sweden	2.66*	1.60	0.87
U. K.	2.65*	0.07	0.85

[a] F-statistics with asterisks denote that the coefficients are significantly different at 95th percentile.

Table 9d. Joint F (Wald) Test for Time Specific Country Dummies[a]

Joint F-Tests	Industrial Production	GDP	Employment
Austria	0.53	1.63	0.46
Belgium	0.58	-	-
Denmark	4.77*	1.38	-
Finland	0.57	0.35	6.32*
France	0.26	0.19	0.81
Germany	0.27	0.26	0.35
Greece	1.52	-	2.79*
Ireland	1.35	-	0.32
Italy	0.62	-	0.45
Luxembourg	3.53*	-	0.32
Netherlands	0.79	0.27	1.55
Portugal	0.70	-	0.10
Slovenia	0.84	0.39	0.76
Spain	0.45	0.25	0.16
Sweden	1.06	10.27*	0.56
U. K.	0.27	0.27	0.67

[a] F-statistics with asterisks denote that the coefficients are significantly different at 95th percentile.

Chapter 3

Slovenian and European Trade Structures

DANIEL GROS AND GUY VANDILLE

1. EXPORTS TO THE EUROPEAN UNION

In this section we analyse the structure of trade between the EU and Central and Eastern Europe. We start by calculating the correlation coefficients[1] between the structure of intra-European Union imports and exports to the Union from the Central and Eastern European countries (CEE countries) considered here (Slovenia, former Czechoslovakia, Hungary, Poland, Romania, and Bulgaria) at the SITC 2-digit level. We also have a quick look at the issue of sensitive products. And finally we try to find some explanation for the differences or similarities in the trade structure of the individual countries.

1.1 Trade Structure Correlations

To establish a benchmark trade Table 1 shows the complete matrix of correlation coefficients between the EU and its member countries, as well as between the individual countries themselves. On the central diagonal, the standard deviations (STD) of the export shares are presented. They provide a summary statistic of the overall concentration of a member's intra-EU trade. A low standard deviation would indicate a low concentration of imports in specific categories. According to this criterion, Spain, Portugal and Greece have the highest concentration of exports to the EU.

The countries with a trade structure most like the European average are Germany, France, the BLEU (Belgium-Luxembourg Economic Union), the

UK, and Spain. All bilateral correlation coefficients in this group of countries are above 60 percent.[2]

Surprisingly the trade structure of the Netherlands and Denmark deviates from moderately to substantially from those of the other countries and the European average. This is a fortiori true for Ireland, Portugal and Greece. For the latter countries this could be expected, however, because they are much poorer. For the Netherlands the reason for the different trade structure is to be found in a rather high amount of agricultural exports and exports of energy[3], combined with a low amount of road vehicles (category 78), which is the product most heavily traded among EU members. For Denmark the reason for the low correlation is to be found in above average exports to the EU of agricultural products and furniture[4], combined with low exports of textiles and steel[5], and road vehicles.[6]

Table 1. EU Correlation Coefficients

STD	EUR12	BLEU	FRA	GER	ITA	SPA	UK	NETH	DEN	IRE	POR	GRE
EU12	1.9											
BLEU	91	2.4										
FRA	95	87	2.0									
GER	96	89	94	2.4								
ITA	82	67	71	76	2.0							
SPA	87	89	86	86	62	3.7						
UK	85	67	78	76	67	60	1.9					
NETH	66	55	50	47	45	47	73	1.7				
DEN	36	24	27	28	39	14	13	40	2.0			
IRE	34	15	25	20	26	6	53	57	40	2.6		
POR	44	36	34	34	68	31	31	20	17	7	3.2	
GRE	18	12	11	3	44	12	9	17	8	1	71	3.7

How does this intra-European trade structure compare to that of Central and Eastern Europe? Table 2 shows the correlation matrix of the CEE countries with the EU average, and among themselves, whereas Table 3 presents the correlation matrix of the CEE countries with individual EU-members. Again, the STD is presented on the diagonal. It is interesting to note that for all CEE countries except Romania, exports to the EU are less concentrated than those of Spain, Portugal and Greece, as the STD of their export structure is lower!

Table 2 shows that the Slovenian trade structure is not that different from the average intra-EU trade structure. Together with former Czechoslovakia, it is ranked at the top among the CEE countries concerning the resemblance of its trade structure to the intra-EU one. The Slovenian correlation coefficient is about as high as the one for the Netherlands. Slovenian trade shows an even higher affinity with that of the trade of the other CEE countries (also with the EU). The correlation hovers around 70 percent, and except for Bulgaria is always marginally higher than that with the EU.[7]

Table 2. Central and Eastern European Correlation Coefficients

	EUR12	SLO	CZE	HUN	POL	ROM	BUL
SLO	68	3.0					
CZE	64	71	2.0				
HUN	42	73	59	2.3			
POL	34	72	66	72	2.2		
ROM	19	70	57	74	76	4.4	
BUL	21	65	57	78	79	81	2.4

Table 1 and 2 together thus imply that Slovenia's trade with the EU has a structure that is "midway" between the Visegrad countries and of the most highly integrated countries of the Union.

However, as Table 3 shows, the Slovenian trade structure is even more strongly correlated with the trade structure of two of the Southern EU-members, namely neighbouring Italy and especially Portugal. The latter country's trade structure bears quite a close resemblance to that of almost all CEE countries.

The resemblance of Slovenia to the EU average is caused by the importance in Slovenia's exports towards the EU of SITC-categories belonging to the category of basic manufactures (e.g. paper, textile yarn and fabrics, iron and steel) and of motor vehicles. The resemblance to Portugal comes out clearly in the importance of exports of clothing and accessories. In this limited sense, there might be some direct competition between Slovenia and the Southern European EU-members. The latter apparently determined the position of the EU during recent negotiations with Slovenia.

Table 3. Central and Eastern Europe and the EU Members, Correlation Coefficients

	SLO	CZE	HUN	POL	ROM	BUL
BLEU	62	68	32	32	14	17
FRA	61	54	30	25	9	13
GER	65	59	30	25	8	9
ITA	78	75	64	52	50	51
SPA	60	50	23	27	4	9
UK	46	47	29	18	11	10
NETH	27	29	38	22	8	14
DEN	23	19	45	21	22	16
IRE	7	6	24	-1	4	6
POR	85	61	75	67	77	78
GRE	57	42	67	69	74	82

1.2 Exports of "Sensitive" Products

It has often been argued that the trade relations of Central and Eastern Europe with the EU are different because of the high proportion of "sensitive" exports. However, when we calculate the share of sensitive products[8] in EU imports it becomes clear that the share of these products in imports from the Eastern European countries is not higher than in imports from the Southern EU members, except for Romania. Table 4 presents these shares.

Table 4. Share of Sensitive Products in EU Imports

EUR12	38.08		
UK	25.23	LAT	7.03
IRE	27.83	LIT	10.99
NET	33.37	EST	26.98
GER	35.99	CZE	46.40
FRA	37.93	BUL	47.67
ITA	43.41	HUN	51.75
BLEU	45.26	SLO	53.85
DEN	46.51	POL	54.61
POR	54.44	ROM	72.16
SPA	55.21		
GRE	60.66		

1.3 Explaining Differences in Trade Structures

What determines similarities or differences in trade structures? Are they just an expression of the overall level of development? In order to investigate this question Figure 1 plots the correlation coefficients of trade structures with the EU against the income per capita (GDP/cap) of each country. The figure shows that countries with a higher GDP/cap are on average more closely correlated to the EU average. There is only one clear outliner: Denmark. In order to go beyond the visual impression we regressed the correlation coefficients (for trade with the EU) on GDP/cap in USD. We had to use dummy for Denmark in order to obtain a good estimate ($R^2 = 63$). The coefficient on GDP/cap turned out positive and highly significant (= 0.28, t-stat = 4.81, on the dummy -0.66, t-stat = 3.16). Adding a dummy for the transforming economies, we were able to increase the R^2 to 72. However, this dummy is only significant at the 90 percent confidence level (t-stat = 1.90). The coefficient is positive, which means that the countries in Eastern Europe have a trade structure more similar to the EU average than would be expected on the basis of their GDP/cap. This is certainly true for former Czechoslovakia, which seems to be an outliner among the economies in transition. The positive value of the dummy was to be expected, since it is widely assumed that their GDP is currently undervalued.

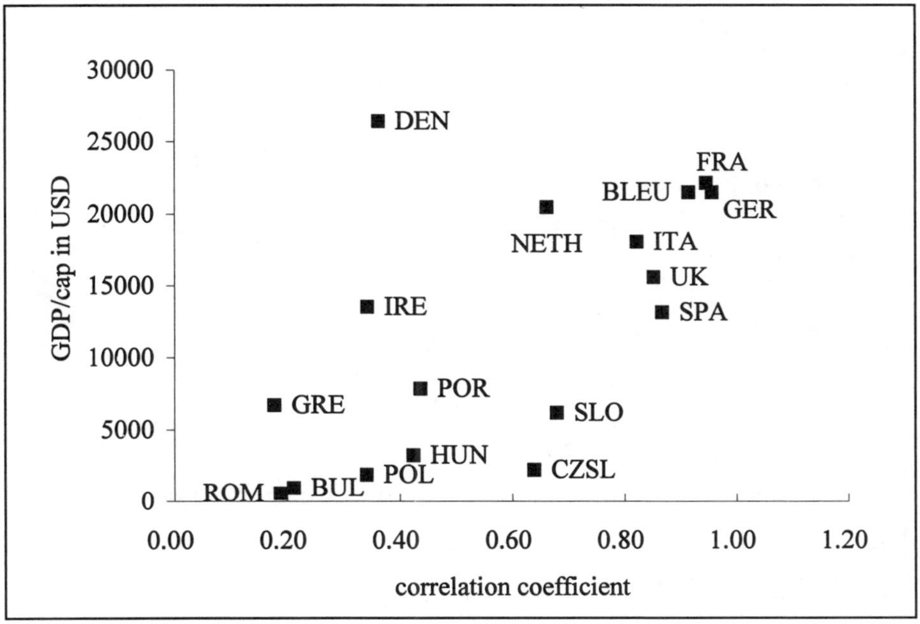

Figure 1. The correlation of the structure of trade with EUR12 and GDP/cap

A similar regression was performed using GDP/cap adjusted for Purchasing Power Parity (PPP). The conclusions were the same. Statistically we obtained even better results. The R^2 was 83, and the significance of the dummy for the transforming economies became clearer (t-stat = 2.21).[9]

In order to test the robustness of the relationship between income levels and trade structures Figure 2 shows the relation between the correlation coefficient and GDP/economically active person (as defined by the ILO).[10] The difference with the GDP/cap approach is that this kind of measure shows the value of production per person instead of how rich on average everybody is. The position of Denmark from this perspective is less out of line with the other countries. The position of former Czechoslovakia is not affected. The regression of the correlation coefficient on GDP/economically active person is nevertheless again significantly improved upon by the introduction of a dummy for Denmark. The goodness of fit parameter R^2 rose from 37 to 54, when the Denmark dummy was included. The coefficient on GDP was 0.11 (t-stat = 3.74), the coefficient on the Danish dummy -0.48 (t-stat = 2.24). This means that Denmark can still be considered as an outliner. Adding a dummy for the transforming economies again increased the R^2 (to 63). The coefficient was again positive, but with a t-statistic of 1.65 not even significant at the 90 percent confidence level.

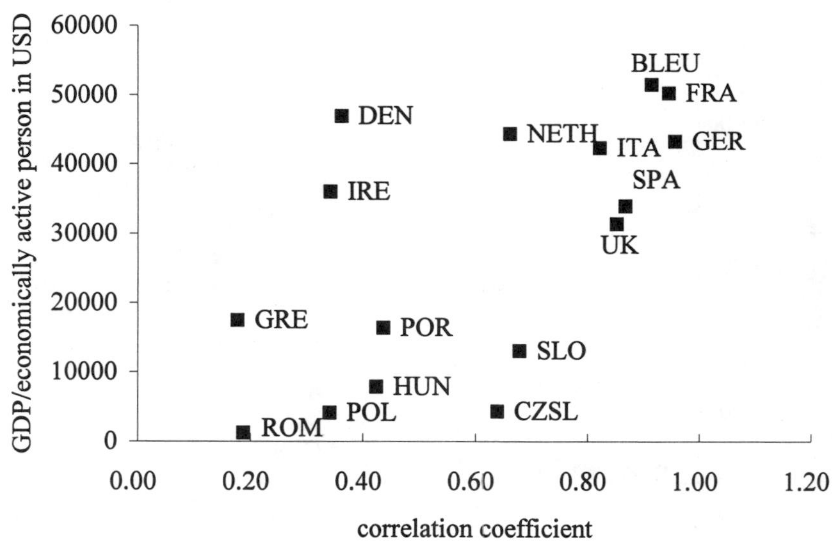

Figure 2. The correlation of the structure of trade with EUR12 and GDP/economically active person

Could the different behaviour of Denmark be explained by the importance of agricultural exports? Figure 3 shows the relation between the correlation coefficients and the share of agriculture in GDP. For the EU countries, the share of agriculture in gross value added was used. There is a clear negative relation between the resemblance of the trade structure to the EU average and the importance of agriculture in the economy. A regression of the correlation coefficient on the share in agriculture resulted in a coefficient of -0.04, with a t-statistic of 6.05. The R^2 was 71. Again the Danish dummy coefficient was -0.36 (t-stat = 2.66), when this dummy was included. A dummy for the economies in transition did not yield any significant results.

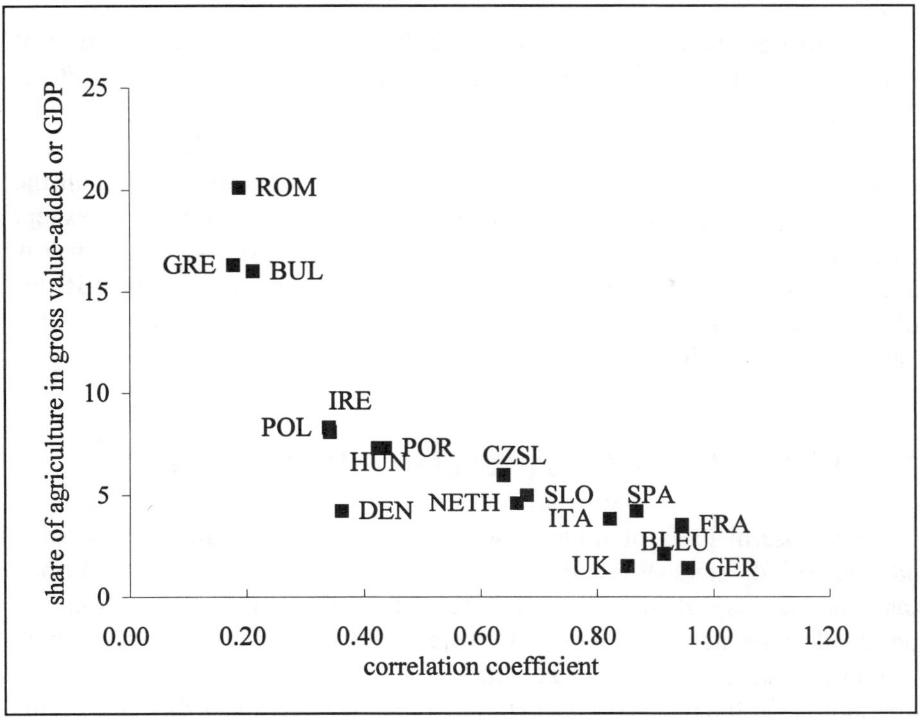

Figure 3. The correlation of the structure of trade with EUR12 and share of agriculture

The importance of agricultural exports turns out to be an important factor in the different behaviour of Denmark. The correlation coefficient between the trade structure of Denmark and the EU for manufactures only is indeed higher than when agriculture is included. It rises from 36 to 45. This is still on the low side nevertheless.[11]

When both income per capita and the share of agriculture were included in the regression we found these two variables to be strongly correlated, making it possible to distinguish between their influence. This implies that we cannot draw any clear conclusions about the specific influence of the factors explaining trade structure differences. Both income per capita and the share of agriculture in gross value added are nevertheless strongly correlated with the trade structure when allowing for Denmark as an outliner.

2. IMPORTS FROM THE EUROPEAN UNION

We also calculated the correlation coefficients between the structure of intra-EU exports from the Union to the individual countries at the SITC-2-digit level. Here the differences are much less marked than for the calculations using imports into the EU. This is to be expected. The EU exports a similar mix of products to all its partner countries. Among all the EU member countries the correlation coefficient is at least 90 percent, except for Denmark and Ireland (87 and 75 percent respectively).[12] Their below average car imports (because of heavy indirect taxes on automobiles) is one of the explanations for their lower correlation coefficients. Among the CEE partner countries, the correlation is at least 75 percent.

3. REVEALED COMPARATIVE ADVANTAGES

Other useful tools of trade structure analysis are revealed comparative advantage indicators. We calculated two indices: the net exports/total trade index and the export specialisation index. The definition of these indices can be found in the statistical annex. Both are used to reveal the sectors in which a country bears a comparative advantage.

Looking at the net exports/total trade index we noted that Slovenia seems to have a comparative advantage for the categories of live animals other than fish, cork and wood, gas, animal oils and fats, rubber manufactures, cork and wood manufactures, furniture, clothing, and footwear. As such Slovenia is indeed a competitor to Portugal for cork and wood (and manufactures), clothing, and footwear. The latter is confirmed by the export specialisation index, which shows that sectors are indeed among the best performers of all Slovenian exporting sectors. The sectors that are at least double as competitive as Slovenia is on average are cork and wood (and manufactures), pulp and waste paper, leather (and manufactures), rubber manufactures, prefabricated building equipment (sanitary, plumbing, heating, lighting equipment), furniture, clothing, and footwear. For cork and wood (and manufactures), rubber manufactures, furniture, clothing, and footwear both indices point to a comparative advantage for Slovenia. These are the Slovenian sectors, which are most competitive in the European context.

We also included the correlation coefficients for the index of net exports to the EU. All these coefficients turned out to be very low. This shows that trade is randomly distributed. There is no bias towards particular countries in the EU trade.

However, when comparing these correlation coefficients within the groups of EU countries and the CEE countries we did find a significant difference.[13] Whereas the correlations look completely random inside the group of EU members, as well as between the EU countries and the group of CEE countries, the correlation coefficients inside the latter group are all positive and on average clearly higher. This indicates that the CEE countries export and import a same range of products to and from the EU. This finding is confirmed by Lemoine (1994), which shows that the export structure of all the CEE countries (exclusive of Slovenia) is concentrated in a limited number of sectors, namely leather, clothing, building materials, glass, and iron and steel. The similarity between their export structures is even rising. Within the EU Portugal is again the country, which shows the highest correlation with the trade structure of Central and Eastern Europe. This again indicates that the CEE countries and Portugal are potential competitors.

4. COSTS AND BENEFITS OF CLOSER INTEGRATION WITH THE EUROPEAN UNION

We complete the picture with a comparison between the expected benefits and cost of closer integration with the EU. As a measure of the benefits, we used the importance of trade with the EU for the individual countries.[14] Closer integration will take away obstacles to trade. It will make trade less costly. Therefore, we can expect countries which trade intensively with the EU to gain more. As a measure of the costs of closer integration, we used the difference in trade structure with the average EU trade structure.[15] Closer integration requires a trade structure more or less similar to the EU average, because otherwise asymmetric shocks can hit the member countries through their different structures.[16] The bigger the difference is at this moment, the higher the adjustment costs will be. Figure 4 shows that the highest benefits are to be expected for the BLEU, the Netherlands and Ireland.[17]

Among the CEE countries, the highest benefits are to be expected for Slovenia and the combination of the Czech and Slovak Republics. These countries would also have the lowest adjustment costs. They are even lower than for Ireland, the Netherlands and Portugal. From the viewpoint of the trade structure, they are the prime candidates among the CEE countries for closer integration with the EU. This is confirmed in the Table 5, where we ranked the countries according to the benefits and costs, after normalising them by setting the maximum value of both benefits and costs equal to 100.

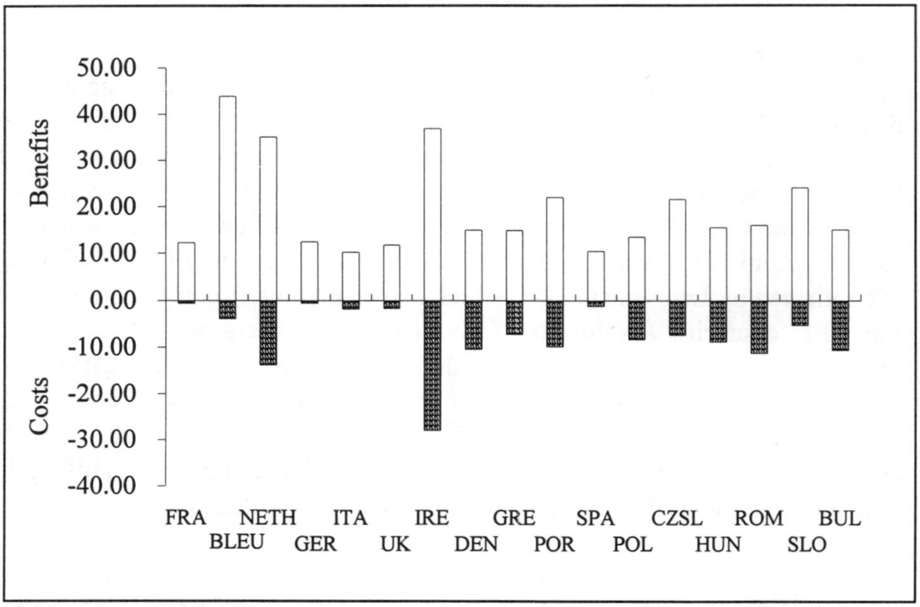

Figure 4. Benefits and costs of closer integration with EUR12

Table 5. Benefits and Costs of Closer Integration with the EU

	Benefit		Cost		Benefit/cost
BLEU	100.00	GER	2.40	GER	13.89
IRE	84.05	FRA	2.32	FRA	12.02
NETH	79.92	SPA	4.15	BLEU	7.15
SLO	54.96	UK	5.97	SPA	5.73
POR	50.17	ITA	6.47	UK	4.48
CZSL	49.21	BLEU	13.98	ITA	3.59
ROM	36.48	SLO	18.91	SLO	2.91
HUN	35.27	GRE	25.67	CZSL	1.88
BUL	34.27	CZSL	26.24	NETH	1.62
DEN	34.06	POL	29.64	POR	1.42
GRE	33.86	HUN	31.57	GRE	1.32
POL	30.78	POR	35.29	HUN	1.12
GER	28.31	DEN	37.08	POL	1.40
FRA	27.93	BUL	37.86	DEN	0.92
UK	26.76	ROM	40.15	ROM	0.91
SPA	23.75	NETH	49.34	BUL	0.91
ITA	23.25	IRE	100.00	IRE	0.84

The column to the right of the table shows the ratio of normalised benefits over normalised costs. This is a ratio, which is to be interpreted relative to the other countries. It shows that for Germany the relative benefits of closer integration will be almost fourteen times as large as the relative adjustment costs. For Slovenia and the combined Czech and Slovak Republics, the relative benefits are also higher than the relative adjustment costs. They are ranked above the following EU member countries: the Netherlands, Portugal, Greece, Denmark, and Ireland. Among the Eastern European countries they once more present themselves as the best candidates for closer economic integration.

NOTES

1 The definition of the correlation coefficient can be found in the statistical annex.
2 For the countries that recently joined the EU this is also the case for Austria and Sweden (86 and 78 respectively). Finland is a clear outliner with a correlation coefficient of only 34.
3 This concerns the following SITC categories: 01, 02, 03 and 29 (meat and preparations, dairy products and birds, eggs, fish and preparations, crude animal and vegetable materials n.e.s.), and 33 (petroleum and products). Two other categories showing above average exports are 28 (metalliferous ores and scrap), and 75 (office machines and ADP equipment).
4 SITC categories 01, 02, 03, and 82.
5 SITC categories 65 and 67. Below average exports are also found for categories 64 and 66 (paper and paperboard, non-metal mineral manufactures n.e.s.).
6 Using two-digit NACE codes the correlation coefficients of the Netherlands, Denmark and Ireland rise considerably. Except for the Netherlands the difference with the first group of countries stays large nevertheless.
7 The Baltics would clearly form a separate group if they were included, but the official data on the commodity composition of their trade is dominated by re-exports of Russian raw materials, and was therefore not presented here.
8 Sensitive products are calculated here according to the definition given in Neven (1994). This includes the products identified as sensitive under the general liberalisation regime in the Europë agreements, as well as those specified in special protocols for CECA iron and steel products, MFA textiles products, and agricultural products. This brings to bear the following list of sensitive products: live animals, meat, dairy products, fishes, cereals, fruits and vegetables, textile fibres, other raw materials, coal and coke, thread and textile, iron and steel, other metal products, motor vehicles, furniture, clothing, and shoes.
9 In this regression Slovenia was not included however, as no comparable data was available.
10 The ILO defines economically active population as all persons of either sex who furnish the supply of labour for the production of economic goods and services as defined by the UN systems of national accounts and balances, during a specified time-reference period. This means all persons who fulfil requirements for inclusion among the employed or unemployed are included. Not included are students, housewives, and retired persons wholly dependent upon others.
11 For the Netherlands the correlation coefficient rose from 66 to 73. For the other EU-members the changes were minimal. For the CEE countries the correlation decreased when only considering manufactures, although only considerable for Hungary, Bulgaria and Romania.
12 Using NACE codes this is only true for Ireland. For the new EU-members the correlation coefficient is also above 90 percent.
13 See Tables 7, 8, and 9 in the appendix.
14 This was calculated as (exports + imports) / 2 as a percent of GDP.
15 This was calculated as (the export correlation coefficient with the EU - 1) times 100, weighted by the ratio of exports to the EU and GDP. The use of these weights to assess the costs of integration has been neglected in previous studies. In those studies it is generally accepted that the potential benefits of integration depend on the openness of a country. The more a country trades, the more gains of reduced transaction costs there will be. However, the same is true for the costs of adjustment. If a country trades a lot, but in products very different from the average, the adjustment costs of getting the trade structure more in line

with the average trade structure will be high. The argument that small countries will gain more from integration because they are generally more open is therefore very misleading. When taking into account adjustment costs the potential net benefits could be higher for large countries.

16 See Gros, D. and Thygesen, N. (1992), Chapter 7.

17 Among the new EU members the highest benefits are to be expected for Austria. As their adjustment costs are also among the lowest, the potential net gain for Austria is quite high. For Finland the picture looks very different. Their adjustment costs are to be expected to be high. Their benefit/cost ratio is the lowest among the 15 current EU members.

18 Source: Wonnacott and Wonnacott (1979), Figure 5-9, p. 161.

REFERENCES

Ariff, M., and Hill, H., 1985, Export-oriented industrialisation: The Asian experience, Allen and Unwin, New York.

Balassa, B., 1979, "The changing pattern of comparative advantage in manufactured goods", *The Review of Economics and Statistics*.

Bank of Slovenia, 1994, *Monthly Bulletin*, May 1994.

Brenton, P., Gros, D., 1995,"Trade between the European Union and Central Europe: An economic and policy analysis", *CEPS Working Document,* No. 93, March 1995.

EBRD, 1994, Transition report, October 1994.

Eurostat, Comext database.

Gros, D., Thygesen, N., 1992, European Monetary Integration, Longman, London.

ILO, 1994, *Bulletin of labour Statistics*, (1 + 2).

ILO, 1993, Yearbook of Labour Statistics.

IMF, 1993, International Financial Statistics Yearbook.

Lemoine, F., 1994, "CEEC Exports to the EC (1988-1993): country differentiation and commodity diversification", *CEPII Document de Travail*, No. 94-15, December 1994.

Neven, D., 1994, "Trade liberalization with eastern nations. How sensitive?", *CEPR Discussion Paper*, 1000, July 1994.

UN, 1993, Yearbook of International Trade Statistics.

Wonnacott, R.J., and Wonnacott, T.H., 1979, Econometrics, John Wiley and Sons.

World Bank, 1994, World Development Report 1994.

APPENDIX

Correlation Coefficients

The correlation coefficient is defined as follows:

sum $((X_i-X)*(Y_i-Y))/\text{sqrt}(\text{sum}(X_i-X)^2*\text{sum}(Y_i-Y)^2)$

with:

X = average of the percentage distribution of the intra-EU imports

X_i = percentage of SITC category i in intra-EU imports

Y = average of the percentage distribution of imports into the EU by one member country

Y_i = percentage of SITC category i in imports into EU from one member country

sqrt = square root

Correlation coefficients might have a stochastic component (e.g. because of measurement error). Table 6 shows approximate lower and upper bounds of 95 percent confidence intervals for correlation coefficients calculated on a sample of 70 observations.[18] This corresponds to the sample used in this paper.

This table shows that with a coefficient of 0.85 the lower bound is 0.75. This means that the coefficients for France, Germany, the BLEU, the UK, Italy, and Spain are all quite robust. We can say with 95 percent confidence that the trade structure of these countries is very similar to the average EU structure. The lower figure for the Netherlands (66 percent) does not necessarily mean that the Dutch trade structure is that different from the EU average. The upper and lower bounds are 78 and 47 percent, respectively. In this range it is difficult to make strong inferences. For all the other countries with low correlation coefficients, it is clear, however, that their trade structure cannot be similar to the EU average.

Table 6. 95 percent Confidence Intervals around the Correlation Coefficient

Correlation coefficient	lower bound	upper bound
0	-25	25
5	-20	29
10	-15	34
15	-10	38
20	-5	42
25	0	46
30	5	50
35	11	54
40	17	59
45	23	62
50	29	66
55	35	70
60	41	73
65	47	77
70	55	80
75	61	84
80	68	87
85	75	90
90	83	94
95	91	97
100	100	100

Revealed comparative advantage indices (see: Balassa (1979), and Ariff, and Hill (1985)):

1. The net exports/total trade ratio

This ratio is calculated as the ratio of exports minus imports of a certain product in one country over the sum of exports and imports of the same product in the same country, times 100. The ratio is bounded by the values - 100 and +100. When this ratio is positive the country is a net exporter of the product concerned. This can be interpreted as an indication of the comparative advantage the country has for this product.

2. the export specialisation ratio

This ratio is calculated as follows. The numerator is the ratio of exports of product i from country j over the European exports of this product. The denominator is equal to the ratio of total exports from country j over total European exports. The ratio is bounded by zero and infinity. When the ratio is equal to one this means the country has a normal export performance for the product. When it is equal to two it performs twice as well as it does on average on the EU market. An export specialisation ratio above one is thus also an indication of a comparative advantage the country has for the product concerned. This index takes into account global differences between countries concerning their trade behaviour and environment. A country which heavily promotes exports and restricts imports may show a high net exports index for a wide range of products. This will say nothing about the relative performance of the sectors within the country. The export specialisation index on the other hand will reveal this.

The two ratios do not always lead to the same conclusion concerning the existence of a comparative advantage. It is thus advisable to compare both ratios. When both ratios indicate the possibility of a comparative advantage we can be more certain that this is indeed the case.

Table 7. EU Correlation Coefficients

STD	EU12	BLEU	FRA	GER	ITA	SPA	UK	NETH	DEN	IRE	POR	GRE
EU12												
BLEU	24											
FRA	27	7										
GER	44	-1	9									
ITA	26	8	-27	-13								
SPA	34	21	8	-29	29							
UK	42	-10	3	29	-6	7						
NETH	14	18	-26	-14	-17	-2	11					
DEN	-8	-11	6	-16	-21	-8	9	6				
IRE	1	3	27	-3	-21	-12	-2	9	47			
POR	27	2	-1	-18	25	41	-7	-2	16	17		
GRE	14	-16	18	-10	-10	31	-5	3	17	-5	28	

Table 8. Central and Eastern European Correlation Coefficients

	EUR12	SLO	CZE	HUN	POL	ROM	BUL
SLO	-2						
CZE	16	53					
HUN	13	42	62				
POL	20	51	72	46			
ROM	6	51	55	59	60		
BUL	23	36	61	46	77	53	

Table 9. Central and Eastern Europe and the EU Members, Correlation Coefficients

	SLO	CZE	HUN	POL	ROM	BUL
BLEU	4	-2	-12	10	6	8
FRA	13	9	12	27	-5	27
GER	-15	-14	-26	-11	-20	-13
ITA	28	8	4	-1	30	-7
SPA	20	31	21	27	8	30
UK	-9	8	-2	-8	-23	-21
NETH	-20	12	28	-1	2	8
DEN	25	18	33	11	19	8
IRE	10	5	1	8	1	16
POR	35	49	25	39	26	38
GRE	1	14	41	29	13	36

Note: These 3 tables contain the correlation coefficients (as defined in the statistical annex) between the values of net exports to the EU as percent of total trade with the EU.

Chapter 4

Fiscal Consolidation in the Central European Countries and European Monetary Union

PAUL DE GRAUWE AND VLADIMIR LAVRAČ

In order to accede to EMU, the Central European countries will have to satisfy the Maastricht convergence criteria. In this chapter we concentrate on the fiscal convergence criteria and analyse the trends in fiscal policies and their sustainability. Although the emphasis will be on fiscal convergence it will not always be possible to separate this from convergence in other fields, in particular in the field of inflation and interest rate convergence. (For a more general discussion of the Maastricht convergence criteria, see P. Backé, Chapter 7 in this book).

1. THE RECENT CONVERGENCE PROCESS

The convergence process in the Central European countries has been quite spectacular. This is vividly demonstrated in Figure 1 which shows the budgetary deficits in 1993 and 1997 in the CE-countries. We have also added the inflation rates, as these are the other major convergence criteria. The points shown in the elliptic area are the budget deficits and inflation rates (in 1997) of the 11 EU countries that will start EMU in 1999. We observe a significant movement towards the required Maastricht norms in all CE-countries from 1993 to 1997. This movement is the most spectacular for Poland and the Slovak Republic. We also note that the countries which had an unfavourable budgetary position in 1993 (Hungary, Poland, Slovak Republic) significantly reduced their budget deficits and have come close to the 3 percent norm (Poland actually reached it in 1997). The other two countries, Slovenia and the Czech Republic, which had a favourable fiscal position in 1993, experienced a slight deterioration in 1997, although they remain within the Maastricht norm of 3 percent.

It is interesting to mention that the Maastricht Treaty is not at all rigid about the fiscal deficit norm. According to article 104 c, a country can have a budget deficit exceeding the reference value (3 percent) provided "the ratio has declined substantially and continuously and reached a level that comes close to the reference value". A visual inspection of Figure 1 allows us to conclude that all CE-countries satisfied the Maastricht budget deficit criterion in 1997, as formulated in article 104 of the Treaty.

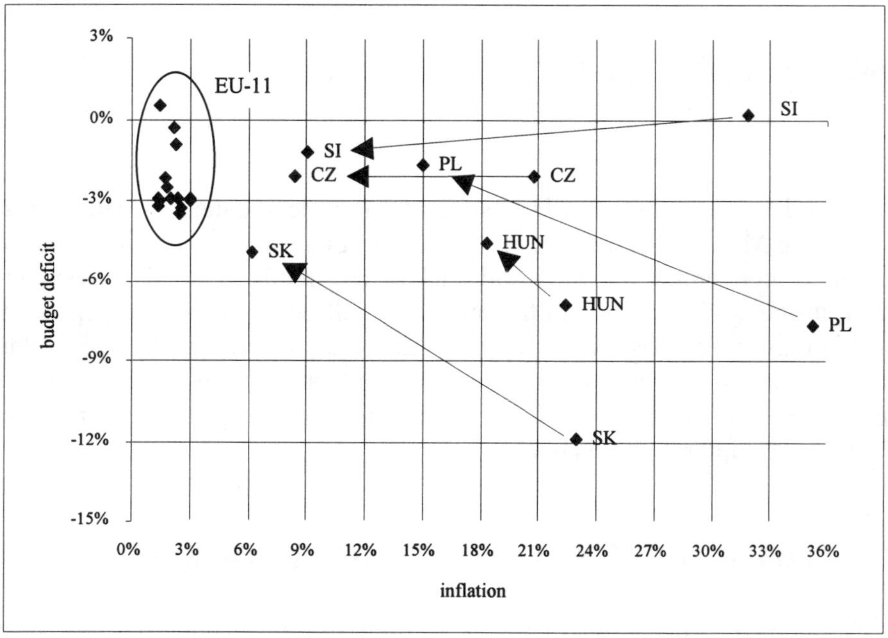

Figure 1. Inflation and budget deficit in Central European countries (1993-1997)

Note: The points located in the ellipse are the observations for the 11 EU-countries who will start EMU in 1999. The observations relate to 1997.
Source: IMF, World Economic Outlook, 1998.

The same cannot be said about the inflation rates. Here the Maastricht Treaty allows for little flexibility. The inflation rate of a candidate country should not exceed the average inflation rate of the three countries with the lowest levels plus 1.5 percent. According to this rule, none of the CE-countries satisfied the inflation convergence criterion in 1997, despite the significant progress achieved during 1993-1997. Presumably, once EMU starts, the reference value for inflation will be the average inflation in the euro-area. This will not affect very much the distance that will still have to be travelled by the CE-countries to achieve the inflation norm.

The other Maastricht fiscal criterion is the debt to GDP ratio. According to the Treaty, this ratio should not exceed 60 percent. If it does, it should be "sufficiently diminishing and approaching the reference value at a satisfactory pace" (article 104 c). How do the CE-countries perform? We try to find an answer in Figure 2, where we present the debt to GDP ratios of the CE-countries and the eleven EU-countries that will start EMU in 1999. The most striking aspect of this figure is that the CE-countries as a group have done much better than the EU-11 countries. In the latter group of countries only two (France and Luxembourg) had a debt to GDP ratio of less than 60 percent in 1997. Of the nine countries with a debt to GDP ratio exceeding 60 percent, six had seen this ratio increase recently, and one (Belgium) had reduced it but at a pace which keeps it far from approaching the 60 percent. Thus, more than half of the EU-11 countries that were accepted into EMU, did not satisfy one of the Maastricht convergence criteria.

Compared to this record, the prospects for satisfying the debt to GDP criterion looks promising in the CE-countries. As can be seen from Figure 2, only one country (Hungary) had a ratio exceeding 60 percent in 1997.

To conclude, it appears that the achievement of budgetary convergence in the CE-countries will be relatively easy. In 1997, the CE-countries had reached the Maastricht budgetary criteria. The only remaining issue is whether the underlying fiscal policies are sustainable, so that at the moment the decision about EMU-membership will be made these countries will still satisfy the budgetary criteria.

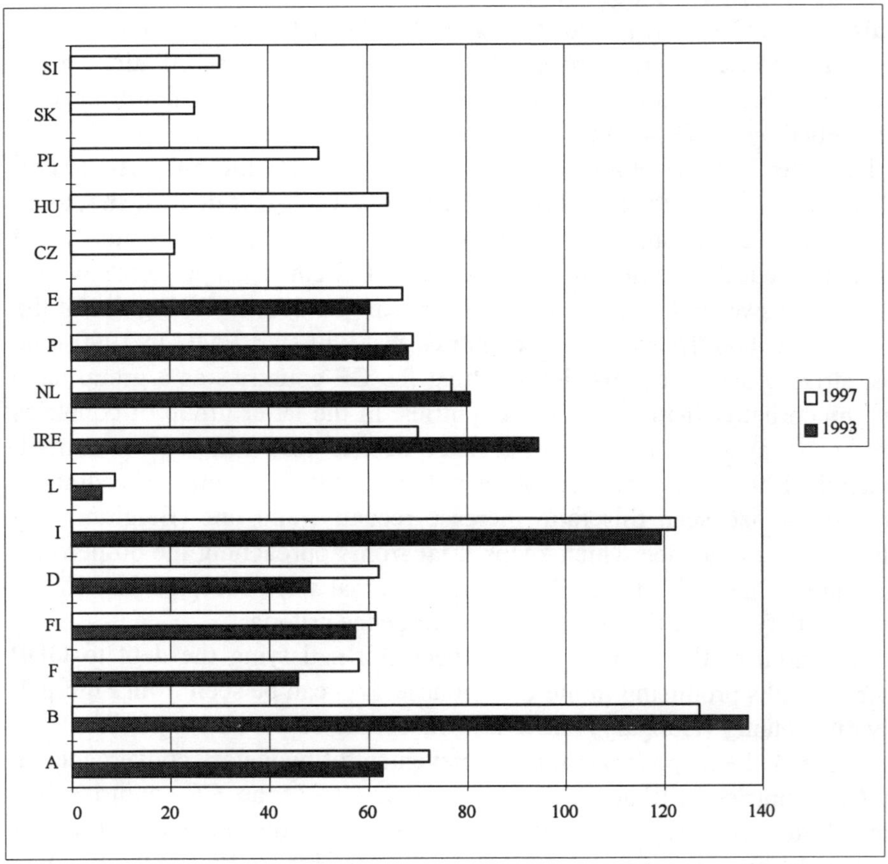

Figure 2. Debt to GDP ratio in EU-11 and Central European countries (in percent)

Source: IMF, World Economic Outlook, 1998 and European Commission, European Economy, 1998.

2. THE SUSTAINABILITY OF THE FISCAL CONVERGENCE IN THE CENTRAL EUROPEAN COUNTRIES

The issue of sustainability of fiscal policies is a difficult one. In its most general form sustainability refers to a policy stance that will allow the government to continue to service its debt in the future. In this sense sustainability means that fiscal policies should be such that the government remains solvent.

This is not a fully satisfactory definition, however. The reason is that sovereign nations have an (almost) unlimited power to tax their citizens, and therefore can, if they are willing to bear the cost, almost always ensure the continued service of the debt. This brute fact was aptly demonstrated by the Ceaucescu-regime in Romania which did not hesitate to drive its citizens into near-starvation so as to ensure the continued service of the debt. Conversely, sovereign nations that have the ability to service their debt, may still decide to default if their governments perceive this to be a politically attractive option. As a result, it is extremely difficult to give a quantitative content to sustainability of government debts and deficits.[1]

Here we will define sustainability in a practical sense. We formulate it in the form of a question: Will the present fiscal programs in the CE-countries make it likely that at the moment of entry in the EU (say between 2002 and 2005) the government deficits and debt levels will satisfy the Maastricht convergence criteria? This is basically the question of whether the present deficit and debt levels in the CE-countries can be sustained during the next five years.

In order to answer this question we have to concentrate on a number of variables that will influence future budgetary outcomes. Here we concentrate on two factors, the rate of economic growth and macro-economic stability.[2]

2.1 Economic Growth Prospects

In Figure 3 we show the rates of economic growth in the CE-countries during the second half of the 1990s. (The figures for 1998 and 1999 are projections made by the European Commission and should be handled with care). It appears that on the whole the growth prospects of CE-countries look relatively favourable in the short- and medium term. The country that may experience the greatest uncertainty in this respect is the Slovak Republic which is experiencing a growth slowdown while it still had the largest budget deficit of the CE-countries in 1997. The Czech Republic which had still not recovered its economic growth rates that prevailed prior to the currency crisis of mid-1997, has a strong advantage in that its budget deficit has remained low despite the crisis of 1997. The other CE-countries appear to be on a strong path of economic growth, and should not face budgetary problems resulting form a significant decline in economic growth.

An important issue that arises here, however, is the question of whether the growth rates themselves are sustainable. In order to answer this question it is useful to look at the current account positions of these countries. This is done in Figure 4, where we show the trade balances as a percent of GDP. As can be seen, the trade deficits in the CE-countries are quite large. There is a consensus today, however, that with the present levels of long term capital flows, these trade deficits are sustainable.[3] It is unclear, however, whether this conclusion holds for Poland which has seen a sharp deterioration of its trade balance position. This deterioration is expected to continue into the near future. As a result, Poland may be forced to take corrective action. This could then temporarily reduce the growth rate of output and negatively affect the budget balance. Apart from the case of Poland, one can conclude that the trade deficits of the CE-countries should not impede further economic growth. On the contrary, they are the counterpart of large capital inflows that increase the growth potential of these countries. This conclusion, however, is predicated on the assumption that macro-economic stability can be maintained. We analyse this issue in the next section.

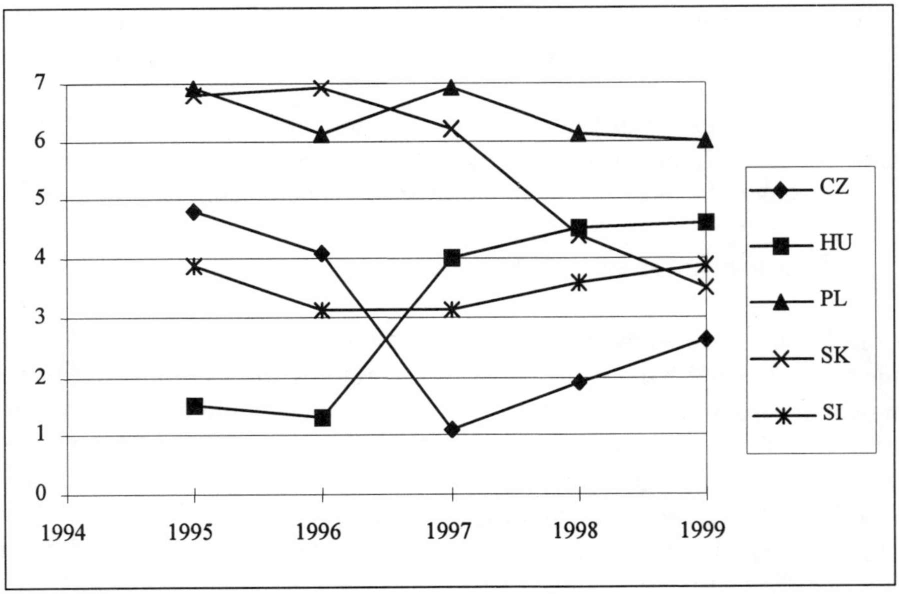

Figure 3. Gross domestic product, real (percent change)

Source: European Commission, European Economy, 1998.

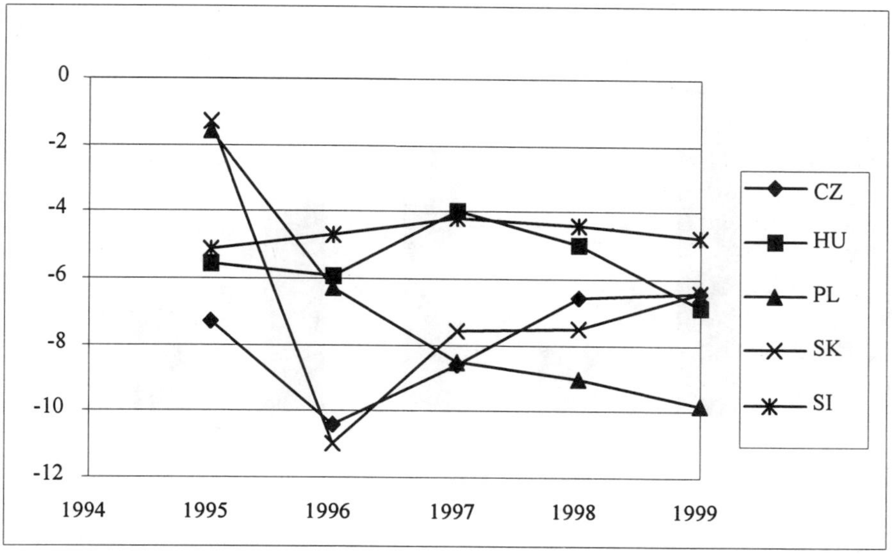

Figure 4. Trade balance (percent of GDP)

Source: European Commission, European Economy, 1998.

2.2 Sustainability of Economic Growth

After the declines in output observed in the early 1990s, most CE-countries have recovered sharply and are now experiencing healthy levels of economic growth. In principle, these growth rates should be sustainable. A prerequisite for sustainable growth, however, is macro-economic stability. This has been demonstrated recently by the Czech currency crisis and the ensuing macro-economic instability in that country. All this contributed to a sharp decline in the Czech growth rate. Are future currency crises likely in CE-countries that could jeopardise economic growth and retard the process of fiscal convergence?

The question is important but also very difficult to answer. Recent research has identified a number of factors that can lead to currency crises, which in turn affect macro-economic stability.[4] Here we concentrate on one such factor, i.e. the real exchange rate. As stressed by G. Tullio, Chapter 5 in this book, CE-countries have experienced strong real appreciations of their currencies between 1993 and 1997. We show these real appreciations in Figure 5.

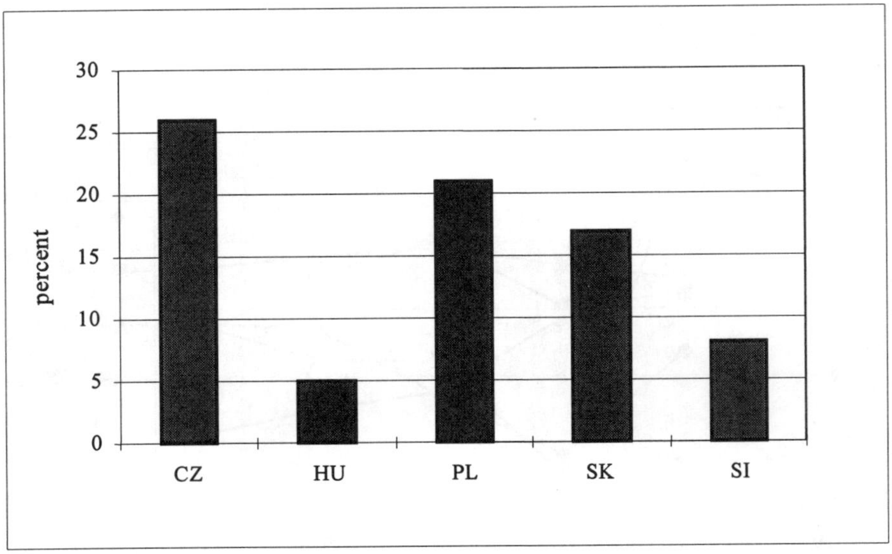

Figure 5. Cumulative real appreciation from 1993 to 1997, 1st quarter (in percent)

Source: G. Tullio, Chapter 5 in this book.

Undoubtedly, a significant part of the real appreciations of the currencies of the CE-countries is related to the high productivity growth rates experienced by these countries. These productivity induced real appreciations do not endanger macro-economic stability. But, as the Czech currency crisis demonstrates, another part of the real appreciations could be the result of exchange rate policies that have produced an overvaluation of the currencies. These overvaluations are then caused by a combination of high domestic inflation and an exchange rate peg that does not fully compensate for these high domestic inflation rates. Over time, these exchange rate policies produce an increasing overvaluation of the currency, which in turn hurts competitiveness and slows down exports. Again, the Czech crisis of 1997 illustrates the nature of this problem. The Polish economy (anno 1998) may be facing a similar problem. We observe that the zloty has appreciated by more than 20 percent in real terms and that the trade account deficit has increased sharply. All these are danger signs indicating that these policies may be unsustainable.

Although the CE-countries have significantly reduced their inflation rates, the latter continue to be much higher than the inflation rates of the EU-counties (see Figure 1). This creates a risk of increasing overvaluation of the CE-currencies. The risk arises because CE-countries find themselves in a dilemma situation. In order to reduce their inflation rates, they can tighten the exchange rate peg. If credible, this allows the CE-countries to "import price stability" from the EU-countries. If not fully credible, or if the domestic inertia in the inflation rates is high, this can lead to increasing overvaluation of the domestic currency. The pegging arrangement then becomes increasingly unsustainable and can trigger a currency crisis.

An alternative policy stance is to allow the exchange rate to accommodate for the differential between the domestic and the foreign inflation rates. This policy stance will avoid the build-up of an overvaluation of the currency, at the price of slowing down the process of disinflation.

Some middle road exchange rate policy should be possible. This consists in allowing for a partial accommodation of the inflation differential, thereby supporting domestic disinflationary policies (see G. Tullio, Chapter 5 in this book). The price paid for this approach is a gradual decline in the rates of inflation. The advantage is that it minimises the risk of a currency crisis which generates macro-economic instability and jeopardises economic growth and budgetary consolidation.

We conclude that conditional on a gradual disinflation, CE-countries should be able to maintain macro-economic stability. If they succeed in doing so, the success in fiscal consolidation achieved in 1998 could be sustained so that these countries can take the budgetary Maastricht hurdle.

NOTES

1 See Perotti, Strauch, and von Hagen (1997) for an analysis of these issues.
2 There are surely other important factors. For a survey, see IMF (1998), Chapter 5.
3 See European Commission (1998), Supplement C. See also IMF (1998), Chapter 4: Financial Crises: Characteristics and Indicators of Vulnerability.
4 For an overview see IMF (1998), Chapter 4. See also Sachs, Tornell and Velasco (1996).

REFERENCES

European Commission, 1998, *European Economy*, Bruxelles, April 1998.

IMF, 1998, World Economic Outlook, Washington, D.C.

Perotti, R., Strauch, R., and von Hagen, J., 1997, Sustainability of Public Finances, *CEPR Discussion Paper*, No. 1781, November 1997.

Sachs, J., Tornell, A., and Velasco, A., 1996, Financial Crises in Emerging Markets, *NBER Discussion Paper*.

Chapter 5

Exchange Rate Policy of Central European Countries in the Transition to European Monetary Union

GIUSEPPE TULLIO

1. INTRODUCTION

This paper analyses two questions. First, the paper deals with the question of whether joining the European Monetary Union (henceforth EMU) is a desirable goal for the five Central European countries (henceforth CE-5)[1]: Poland, Hungary, the Czech Republic, the Slovak Republic and Slovenia. It discusses in particular the risks of joining EMU too early. The answer to this first question forces us to look at some very long run aspects of the transition process, in particular the likelihood of the occurrence of asymmetric shocks. Joining EMU is neither a necessary nor a sufficient condition for joining the European Union (henceforth EU); in fact not even being part of the Exchange Rate Mechanism (henceforth ERM) of the European Monetary System is a necessary condition as shown by the experience of Greece for the whole period during which it was an EU member and of the UK for most of the period[2]. Therefore it is legitimate to keep the objective of joining the EU separate from the desirability of joining EMU.

Second, after reviewing critically past exchange rate policies of CE-5 countries in the light of the conflicting objectives of using the exchange rate as a nominal anchor for inflation and avoiding excessive losses in competitiveness, it addresses the question of which exchange rate policy would best serve their interests in the future in the light of their stage of development and of their intended goal to join the European Union. These countries have all signed between 1991 and 1995 Association Agreements with the EU and in September 1997 four of them (all except the Slovak Republic) have been invited by the EU to start negotiations of entry[3]. The intention is to aim for admission by about the year 2002.

These five countries are characterised by strong cultural links with the EU, geographical proximity, a history of industrialisation started well before Communist regimes seized power (unlike Russia) and a structure of production and trade which is rapidly moving towards the average of the EU. These countries have also in common the fact that since the fall of Communism they have already made significant progress in transforming their economies, in privatising them and in achieving some degree of macroeconomic equilibrium. Despite the understandable desire on the part of these countries to establish very close links with Western Europe there are strong arguments in favour of postponing the entry into EMU well beyond 2002 and some (admittedly weaker) reasons to doubt that joining EMU is a desirable long term goal. In the remainder of this paper I will take it for granted that EMU will start on time by January 1 1999, even though according to the Maastricht Treaty the euro will not fully replace national currencies until mid 2002.

The paper is structured as follows. In Section 2 I discuss in broad lines the exchange rate policies that the CE-5 countries should follow in the next years during the transition to EMU. In Section 3 I discuss the risks and costs of joining EMU too early. In Section 4 I will discuss some inherent defects of EMU and some economic problems of the EU, especially of Continental Western Europe, which are not likely to be resolved rapidly. The bigger are the inherent defects of EMU and the economic problems of the EU the less desirable it will be for the CE-5 to join EMU and the better it is to adopt a "wait and see" attitude like the United Kingdom. Section 5 concludes.

2. A SUGGESTED EXCHANGE RATE POLICY FOR THE PERIOD OF TRANSITION TO EMU

2.1 A Brief Overview of Exchange Rate Policies Followed so far by CE-5 Countries.

Before presenting suggestions for the future I briefly discuss the exchange rate policy followed by the CE-5 countries. Their exchange rate policy has been characterised so far during the transition by large differences between countries, by frequent changes in regime and in some cases, notably in the case of the Czech Republic and the Slovak Republic also by an excessive rigidity of the exchange rate system chosen.

After large initial depreciations of the domestic currencies the CE-5 countries chose very different systems. The Czech Republic and the Slovak Republic opted for virtually fixed exchange rates with very narrow bands (+/- 0.5 percent for the former and +/-1.5 percent for the latter) until early 1996. In January 1996 the band was widened to +/-3 percent for the Slovak currency and in February it was widened to +/- 7.5 percent for the Czech one. However, in February 1997 a reversal of capital flows started for the Czech Republic. It led to a sharp fall of the Czech crown within the band, until at the end of May 1997 the fixed exchange rate system had to be abandoned. From 1992 to the 1997 foreign exchange crisis, the exchange rate policy of the Czech Republic can be classified as stable despite the change in May 1993 from a peg to a five-currency basket to a peg to a two-currency basket (the DM with weight equal to 65 percent and the US$ with weight equal to 35 percent). The same holds for the Slovak Republic where the basket was changed in July 1994 with the new weights being 60 percent for the DM and 40 percent for the US$. These two countries used more than any other in the group the exchange rate as a nominal anchor to lower inflation and it should not be a surprise that in February 1997 inflation was much lower in the Czech Republic and in the Slovak Republic than in Poland and Hungary. Table 1 shows the February 1997 inflation rates in the CE-5 countries along with the exchange rate regime in effect for most of the transition period.

At the other extreme Slovenia opted for a flexible exchange rate system from the very first moment the tolar was introduced (October 1991). As appropriate for a small country the exchange rate was, however, managed by monetary authorities. The anchor role for inflation was played in Slovenia by monetary policy and by the control of monetary aggregates. The exchange rate policy of Slovenia can be considered as a success, as witnessed also by the low inflation reached by early 1997 (Table 1).

Poland and Hungary followed a less clear-cut exchange rate policy. Poland pegged at first the exchange rate to the dollar (from January 1 1990 to May 16 1991), then to a basket of five currencies (from May 17 1991 to October 14 1991). On October 15 1991 a pre-announced crawling peg was introduced with daily devaluations (initially 9 zloty per day). The peg was fixed in terms of the same basket of five currencies. The monthly rate of devaluations was successively reduced from 1.8 percent to 1.2 percent. The band was widened from +/-2 percent to +/-7 percent from the central rate. In August 1993 the currency was devalued by 7.4 percent.

Hungary adopted initially an exchange rate regime of discretionary devaluations, which was replaced in March 1995 by a pre-announced crawling peg. The basket to which the forint was pegged was initially composed of two currencies (the DM and the US$ with weights equal to 50 percent each). The margins were set at +/-2.25 percent. In May 1994 the ECU was substituted for the DM with a weight of 70 percent and the weight of the dollar was correspondingly reduced to 30 percent. Large devaluations occurred in August 1994 (8 percent) and in March 1995 (9 percent) along with smaller ones. After March 1995 the adjustable peg was substituted with a crawling peg with daily changes.

Both Poland and Hungary followed an "unstable" exchange rate policy with too frequent changes in regime. Too frequent changes in regime and devaluations damage the credibility of the exchange rate, do not allow the exchange rate to become an anchor for inflationary expectations and lead to higher inflation. With regard to the initial years of transition the exchange rate policy followed by Poland and Hungary was not unsuccessful. It allowed to redirect their trade towards the West by safeguarding the competitiveness of their exports in Western markets, it contributed to avoiding excessive current account deficits and it allowed a reduction of inflation from very high levels. However, especially after 1994, the exchange rate policy followed by these two countries showed its limits in helping to reduce inflation to more acceptable levels. In terms of inflation performance even Russia is at present doing better than Hungary and Poland. In July 1997 consumer price inflation was 14.9 percent in Poland, 18.1 percent in Hungary (Table 18) and 14.7 percent in Russia.

Does this criticism to Poland and Hungary imply that the Czech example described above is the one to follow? Clearly not, because an excessive rigidity of the nominal exchange rate leads to unsustainable losses in competitiveness, large current account deficits, capital flights and eventually to a foreign exchange crisis. Before and after the crisis erupts high real interest rates have to be used to sustain the currency and a sharp slowdown in economic growth follows. The Czech and Thai crises of the first half of 1997, the Mexican 1995 crisis and the Italian crises of 1992 and 1976 are examples of what happens if the government sticks for too long to a fixed nominal exchange rate which has become unrealistic.

Table 2 shows the current account deficits of some countries, which experienced a major foreign exchange crisis. The current accounts refer to one and two years before the crisis occurred, except for Italy in 1992 where they refer to the year of the crisis and to the year before, because the collapse of the currency occurred late in the year (September 1992). In the three most recent episodes the current account deficits in the year before the crisis were all in excess of 7.5 percent of GDP. In Mexico the current account deficit of 1981 was an astonishing 16.1 percent. The current account deficits in the two Italian episodes were instead much smaller. However, Italy is a large country and this implies that a small deficit in percent of GDP is a large number in billions of dollars. In addition in the 1970s international capital mobility was much smaller (foreign financing was less available). Another difference between the first four and the bottom two episodes is that in the bottom two the governments reduced economic growth much below its long-run potential also before the crisis erupted by adopting severe macroeconomic measures in the useless attempt to avoid devaluation (see the third column of Table 2).

Current account deficits are explained by internal demand growth compared with the main trading partners and by unfavourable developments in competitiveness. In most of the crises episodes considered in Table 2, including the Czech episode of 1997, a significant appreciation of the real exchange rate had been allowed to occur in the years preceding the crisis thus contributing to worsen the current account position and to endanger thereby the credibility of the existing exchange rate parity.

Table 3 presents the 1996 current account deficits of the CE-5 countries. Except Slovenia, which recorded a balanced current account, all other countries in the group had substantial deficits ranging from 3.9 percent of GDP for Hungary to 10 percent for the Slovak Republic. The real appreciation of the exchange rates of the CE-5 countries in the first quarter of 1997 with respect to 1993 is given in the second and third columns of Table 3. The Czech Republic, Poland and the Slovak Republic experienced large real appreciations with respect to the DM and the lira, the currencies of their main trading partners.

Figure 1 (a and b) shows the dynamics of the nominal exchange rates of the five currencies with respect to the DM and Figures 2-4 (a and b) and Table 4 show the real bilateral exchange rates with respect to the DM, the US dollar and the Italian lira. From 1993 to the first quarter of 1997 the Czech crown appreciated by 26 percent in real terms with respect to the DM, the currency of the Slovak Republic appreciated by 17 percent and the Polish zloty by over 21 percent. The real appreciation with respect to the US$ and the lira was only marginally smaller. In conjunction with the data on the current accounts (see Tables 2, 3 and 18) it is no wonder that the Czech and the Slovak Republics were the two countries where the foreign exchange crisis of 1997 was the most severe. The currencies of the least hit countries, Hungary and Slovenia, had appreciated by 5 and 8 percent respectively.

With current account deficits above 7.5 percent of GDP and a large real appreciation it is not difficult to predict that a foreign exchange crisis will sometime occur and that the likelihood is very high that a George Soros will appear on the horizon "trying to kick doors to see if they open", as Rudiger Dornbush put it in a newspaper interview in June 1997. One crucial aspect in the episodes of financial crises are namely the large capital inflows attracted by high domestic nominal interest rates and a stable currency which are suddenly withdrawn once negative expectations start developing. In the case of the Czech Republic net capital inflows reached 8.5 percent of GDP in 1994 and peaked at an astonishing 16.6 percent in 1995[4]. No exchange rate system is capable of completely shielding a country from large speculative capital flows. However, a fixed nominal exchange rate the defence of which is carried too far can aggravate the intensity of the crisis or even cause one where none would have occurred in the presence of sufficient exchange rate flexibility. Capital controls are helpful in stemming capital flights and at times even in avoiding the crisis altogether whatever the exchange rate regime but in the long run they interfere with the optimal allocation of real and financial resources worldwide.

The lesson to be learned from the Czech 1997 episode and from the other episodes described above is that excessive real appreciations of the exchange rate, and excessive and prolonged current account deficits should be avoided, where I would consider as excessive or at least dangerous any current account deficit above 4 percent of GDP, even if most of the deficit is caused by imports of investment goods. The exchange rate system should therefore be flexible enough to avoid these deficits and yet to provide the maximum anchor against inflation. All the CE-5 countries could have chosen an exchange rate policy striking a better balance between these two objectives. The example they should have followed and the one I advice them to adopt from now on is the one chosen by Russia since July 6 1995.

2.2 The Example to Follow: Russia's Exchange Rate Policy since July 1995

In July 1995 Russia moved from flexible exchange rates to a so-called exchange rate corridor similar to the one adopted by Israel in 1991. A band of +/-300 roubles per dollar around the central rate of the rouble with respect to the dollar was set and announced. The width of the band was about +/-6 percent at the time of the reform; now it is about +/-5 percent. The Central Bank is committed to keep the market exchange rate (now about 5850 roubles per dollar) within the band. The band has a positive slope, which is announced at the end of each year for the calendar year ahead. It is important that the corridor be announced for long periods ahead: one year preferably to six months. Notice the difference with the case of Poland throughout the period and with Hungary after March 1995 where the central rate was changed on a daily or monthly basis.

Returning to Russia, the slope of the corridor is set in such a way as to allow for a nominal depreciation of the central rate, which is less than the inflation targeted for the year ahead. Hence a real appreciation of the exchange rate is incorporated into the system even if actual inflation turns out to be equal to targeted inflation[5]. For instance for December 1997 target inflation is 12 percent and the announced slope of the corridor is 8 percent, which implies a real appreciation of the rouble with respect to the dollar. If actual inflation should turn out to be higher than planned the real appreciation will also be higher.

The fact that the slope is not indexed to past inflation is important because slippages in inflation do not get validated ex-post and this is crucial for expectation formation. The slope has been declining through the years as targeted inflation has come down, yet so far the corridor still has a positive slope in order to slow down the real appreciation of the rouble as inflation in Russia is still significantly higher than in the US. There is some discussion about the possibility of flattening the corridor to a zero slope for 1998, but I feel it may be too early.

Figure 5a and 5b show the corridor of the rouble for the years 1996-97. Fig. 5b shows also the market exchange rate in the second half of 1996. Three possible trajectories of the exchange rate are shown. As the market exchange rate entered 1997 at the lower (appreciated) end, if the market rate moves in the course of 1997 all the way to the upper bound, the nominal depreciation will be about 13 percent and the real depreciation about 3.5 percent (assuming Russian inflation on target and US inflation at 2.5 percent). If the market rate moves towards the lower bound, the nominal depreciation will be about 7 percent and the real appreciation of the rouble about 2.5 percent.

Whether the width of the band is set in absolute terms like in the case of Russia or as percentage deviation from the central rate is not important.

The introduction of the corridor has had very powerful stabilising effects on inflation, inflationary expectations, on the demand for roubles and de-dollarisation in Russia. This is proven by the occurrence of structural breaks in the econometric estimates of several behavioural relationships for Russia[6].

I advice a similar exchange rate policy for the CE-5 countries because it strikes a reasonable balance between the useful role that the exchange rate can play as an inflation anchor and the need for exchange rate flexibility to avoid excessive real appreciations and the accumulation of excessive current account imbalances. For the CE-5 countries defining the corridor in terms of an average of the DM and the dollar may be more appropriate than defining it in terms of the dollar alone for obvious reasons. Once chosen and announced the exchange rate policy should never be changed in the course of the year and the changes from one year to the other should be made within the framework of the policy. In this sense reasonable changes in the slope and/or in the width of the band are possible and if thoughtfully devised can contribute to the increase in the credibility of the exchange rate system and to the further stabilisation of inflationary expectations.

The exchange rate policy followed so far by Poland and Hungary has been similar to the one proposed here only in the initial phase of high inflation when the exchange rate was playing an important role as an anchor for inflation. After 1994/95 this role has been missing. The policy followed by the Czech Republic and the Slovak Republic has been too rigid and the one followed by Slovenia has not benefited from the anchor role for inflation which a system like the exchange rate corridor could play.

The introduction of a Russian-like corridor presents an additional advantage for CE-5 countries. As time goes by and macroeconomic stabilisation of these countries proceeds, the basket of the DM or ECU and the dollar can be changed to the euro, the slope can be flattened to zero, the band adapted to ERM (EMS) rules and CE-5 countries can first voluntarily shadow the euro, as Austria has done for many years with the DM, and later enter formally into the ERM. An adjustable peg with the DM and a flat slope are what characterises the ERM. Hence the proposal made here will guarantee a very smooth transition towards entry into the ERM and towards EMU[7]. However, in the next section I shall present arguments against introducing too early excessive rigidity in the exchange rate and in favour of thinking twice before formally joining the ERM and three times before joining EMU.

3. SHOULD CE-5 COUNTRIES JOIN EUROPEAN MONETARY UNION AND IF YES HOW SOON?

In this Section and the next I will argue that it is in the best interest of CE-5 countries to aim at joining EMU towards the end of the catching-up process which is likely to last at least 20 years. I argue this on the basis of three sets of arguments: a) the likelihood of asymmetric shocks arising from the transformation process itself (in the CE-5 countries and in Russia and the Balkans) (Section 3.1) b) considerations of optimal trade strategies for the CE-5 countries, (Section 3.2) c) some inherent defects of EMU which suggest that countries which still have a choice should adopt a “wait and see“ attitude, like the United Kingdom and to wait “until the time is ripe”(Section 3.3).

3.1 The Process of Catching-Up and Possible Implications for Exchange Rate Policy Derived from the Theory of Optimum Currency Areas

The theory of optimum currency areas asks what are the conditions under which two or more countries should form a monetary union and forego the exchange rate instrument to adjust external imbalances. The main message of the theory is that in the case of asymmetric (macroeconomic) shocks hitting the two countries forming a monetary union, adjustment can be very costly in the absence of high labour mobility and downwards wage flexibility.

Transition is not a smooth process. It is very likely to cause asymmetric shocks of the type that according to the theory of optimum currency areas should lead a country to opt to stay our of a monetary union. I therefore look first at the catching-up process of CE-5 countries and I also ask if they have the chance to reach the level of GDP per capita of the EU and if yes how long it may take.

Table 5 shows the 1995 GDP per capita of the CE-5 countries in relation to average GDP per capita in the EU. With the exception of Slovenia whose GDP per capita stood at 42 percent of EU average, the gap is enormous for all countries which are applying for accession. In 1995 Poland's and the Slovak Republic's GDP per capita were only 14 percent of EU GDP, Hungary's 19 percent and the Czech Republic's 20 percent. For Turkey, the Baltic States, Bulgaria and Romania the gap is even larger. Except for Slovenia, the gaps are so large that an average geometric growth rate of over 10 percent per year is required for all CE-5 countries to close the gap in 20 years. Table 6 shows the required growth rates of GDP per capita for different initial and final conditions. Even under the most pessimistic assumption that it will take 20 years to reach 40 percent of EU GDP, the growth rates of Poland and the Slovak Republic will have to be around 7.5 percent and those of Hungary and the Czech Republic close to 6 percent. In interpreting Table 6 one should keep in mind that the figures presented are mechanical calculations and that the speed and extent of catching-up will be endogenously determined by the economic policies pursued, including exchange rate policy.

In order to shed some light on the issue of whether the catching-up is likely to be fast and full, we compare in the next tables the 1937 structure of production and the 1937 investment in human capital of Poland, Hungary and Czechoslovakia with those of Western countries. Table 7 shows that in 1937 Hungary and Czechoslovakia had a share of industry in GDP equal or higher than those of Italy and Portugal, although they were significantly lower than in Germany and Belgium. Table 8 shows that in 1937 the share of agriculture in GDP was lower in Czechoslovakia than in Italy and Portugal. In Portugal it was the same as in Hungary. If a high share of agriculture can be interpreted as a sign of "backwardness" then Italy and Portugal were more backward than Czechoslovakia, and Portugal as backward as Hungary.

Tables 9 and 10 look at investment in human capital. Table 9 shows that in 1937 secondary school enrolment in the Eastern countries was on average lower than in the West, but in all Eastern countries it was higher than in Spain and Portugal. By 1989 the gap between East and West had widened sharply to the advantage of the West. In 1989 also the number of students in universities in the East was much lower than the number in the West (less than half), with the gap being larger than for secondary school enrolment.

Two conclusions emerge from Tables 7-10. First, in 1937 the degree of industrialisation and secondary school enrolment in Poland, Czechoslovakia and Hungary fell well within the range observed in Western European countries, although both tended to be on the side of the Southern European countries rather than the Central Western European ones. Second, regarding investment in human capital from 1937 to 1989 the East lost a lot of ground with respect to Western Europe.

On the basis of the tables just discussed one can perhaps conclude that full catching-up with Southern European countries is a distinct possibility. It is more difficult to envisage a full catching-up with Central and Northern Western Europe. But it is safe to say that it will take at least two decades and that the speed of the process and the end-result depend on how wise the economic policies chosen will be.

Economic growth of the magnitude mentioned above does not proceed smoothly, as it requires large structural and sectoral changes and increasing specialisation for markets which are becoming more and more global. As resources are being reallocated to new sectors it could be dangerous for CE-5 countries to fix too rigidly, or even worse, forever the exchange rate with the euro. A non-smooth process of transformation implies that country-specific supply and demand shocks occur. They are inherently asymmetric since they will not hit Western Europe. The theory of optimum currency areas suggests that the exchange rate tool should not be given up.

High labour mobility and high wage flexibility can help offsetting asymmetric shocks. However, in the case of a negative shock hitting one CE-5 country high labour mobility would help adjustment and solve the unemployment problem but would reduce the population in the country, its GDP and maybe also its long run growth potential as those who leave are often the most dynamic, hard-working and risk-loving. High labour mobility is therefore not a panacea. In addition there is the real danger that, like in the former East German territories the aspirations of the workers and the people lead after the union is formed to a too rapid adjustment of wages towards West German levels and this introduces in itself an asymmetric negative shock, unemployment and emigration.

Rather than high downwards wage flexibility, which is the one required to cope with asymmetric shocks, CE-5 countries may therefore easily experience during the transition a high upwards wage dynamics. Let's assume that joining the EU and/or EMU will increase the aspirations of workers and citizens in CE-5 countries for more rapidly rising incomes than the countries can afford on the basis of past productivity growth. This is an asymmetric shock of the most dangerous kind. If there is only such a small risk arising from joining the EU, then joining EMU should be postponed by many years. It is prudent to wait until the catching-up process is virtually complete. Such a perverse effect was at work in the former territories of East Germany and the disastrous consequences of German reunification and monetary union for these former territories and for Germany as a whole are in front of the eyes of all.

Another type of asymmetric shock is very likely to arise from the transformation and catching-up the process not of the CE-5 countries themselves but of Russia and the Balkans. Any shock originating in these areas will affect CE-5 much more than Western Europe. The proximity of Russia and the Balkans is therefore another reason for not fixing exchange rates too early. Even though trade with these countries has now fallen the CE-5 countries should not forego forever the benefits of exporting to markets which will record very high growth rates in the future. The CE-5 countries will therefore be subject from time to time to shocks originating in these countries[8]. According to the theory of optimum currency areas if labour mobility and wage flexibility are not high enough the exchange rate can play a useful role in shielding these countries from the shocks originating in Russia and the Balkans. The conclusion is again not to tie one's hand too early.

Later contributions to the theory of optimum currency areas have shown that the costs of adjustment are higher in the absence of a sizeable Federal Government which is able to compensate regional income setbacks with increased expenditures in the region and reduced tax revenues from the region. The EU will not be able to perform this role of compensating asymmetric shocks well into the next millennium as its budget is very modest in relation to EU GDP and is not expected to increase in the future. In 1997 spending of the EU is expected to be around 1.22 percent of EU GDP (of which 0.56 on agriculture and 0.43 on structural funds) and is expected to remain at these levels until 2006. On the contrary from 1993 to 1996 US Federal expenditures amounted to about 22-23 percent of US GDP.

Table 11 shows the ratio of US federal expenditures to GDP from 1993 to 1996. It is therefore clear that the EU will not be able to perform this shock absorbing function for many years to come. This shortcoming of EMU could be compensated by greater flexibility in the national budgets of the members in case of negative economic shocks causing downturns in activity. But the Stability pact signed in 1996 by the EU members goes exactly in the opposite direction as it limits budget deficits to 3 percent also after the start of EMU. We shall discuss the consequences of this pact in the section on the inherent defects of EMU (Section 4.1).

3.2 Optimal Trade Strategies: Why Put too Many of Your Eggs in One Basket?

Another reason not to join EMU too soon has to do with optimal trade strategies: it is dangerous to specialise too much in the production for EU markets and risk of not being able to compete in markets outside the EU which will also be the fastest growing ones. It follows that competitiveness in markets outside the EU will remain important and will become even more important as time goes by. As the exchange rate policy of the euro with respect to the dollar, the rouble and the Asian currencies cannot be predicted in advance[9], it is better for CE-5 countries not to "tie one's hands" by joining EMU too early.

The CE-5 countries have been remarkably fast in redirecting their trade away from the former Soviet Union towards Western Europe. Tables 12-16 show for each country the destination of exports and the origin of imports from 1989 to 1995. During this period Poland increased its exports to Germany from 14 percent of total exports to 40 percent. Its exports to Italy more than doubled from 2 to 5 percent, while those to Russia fell from 21 to 6 percent. For Hungary the re-direction of exports has also been remarkable. Hungary's share of exports to Germany grew from 12 to 29 percent and the one to Russia fell from 25 to 6 percent. The Czech Republic exported in 1995 37 percent of its exports to Germany (the Slovak Republic 24 percent) and only 2 percent to Russia (3 percent for the Slovak Republic). Slovenia exported 29 percent of its exports to Germany, 13 percent to Italy and 8 percent to France as opposed to only 4 percent to Russia.

Two considerations suggest themselves. First, this impressive redirection of trade shows how dynamic these countries have been. Their growing exports to Western Europe have certainly contributed significantly to their quick recovery after the initial years of transition and have allowed them to absorb faster the shock arising from the collapse of trade with the former Soviet Union. The sharply devalued exchange rate in the first years of transition has, however, contributed significantly to this development. This suggests that the exchange rate is an important tool for economies in transition and that it should not be abandoned for many years to come since transition is not yet over and the catching-up with Western Europe is still in its inception. Second, the sharp reduction of exports to the former Soviet Union may be only partly caused by the collapse of the economy there. First, even though output in Russia collapsed by about 50 percent and no recovery is in sight yet, import penetration by Western producers has increased very rapidly reaching 60-90 percent of consumption for some categories of goods. Second, politics and psychology may play a more important role in determining the direction of trade than one normally believes. Since sooner or later Russia will start growing rapidly, much more rapidly than the EU, the fall in exports by the CE-5 countries to Russia may have gone much too far. A legitimate question for the governments of the CE-5 countries is therefore whether in the long run it is right to favour so much exports to the EU and neglect other markets, which are much more promising in terms of long run growth prospects.

Table 17 shows the growth rates of GDP per capita of a number of countries from 1997 to 2001, as predicted by the World Bank. It is clear that Western Europe and the industrialised world will be the slowest growing areas of the world with the possible exception of Africa. The implications of this for trade policy and exchange rate policy are clear and do hardly require an explanation: do not invest excessively in conquering EU markets at the neglect of more promising ones in the long run and keep your hands relatively free for as long as you can as far as exchange rate policy is concerned. I am not saying that CE-5 countries should not join the EU, nor that they should not join EMU in the very long run. I am only saying that there are good reasons not to hurry and that joining EMU may not be the best of all possible worlds, not even in the long run.

3.3 Other Reasons not to "Tie One's Hands" too Soon

Two more reasons why it is prudent for the CE-5 countries not to give up the exchange rate instrument too soon are:

a) macroeconomic adjustment is still incomplete. Table 18 shows inflation and public sector deficits in the CE-5 countries. Inflation refers to July 1997 and is measured year on year while the deficit refers to 1996. In general CE-5 countries did satisfy already in 1996 the 3 percent Maastricht criterion for the deficit or came very close to satisfying it (see Hungary). Instead, they are far from satisfying the Maastricht inflation criterion. Reducing inflation too rapidly may be more costly than for industrial countries. High levels of investment are crucial for economies in transition especially in the early stages and too restrictive monetary policies generally hit investment more than other aggregate demand components. Furthermore, economies in transition require more relative price changes which are easier if inflation is above 2 percent, the Bundesbank target for inflation which will probably carry over to the whole of the EMU after 1998. The reason is that otherwise the prices of some goods and services may have to fall in absolute terms. For the sake of completeness it should be pointed out that joining EMU will allow countries in which productivity grows more rapidly than elsewhere in the union to have higher inflation without endangering current account developments and the long run participation in the union. As suggested by Balassa's model (Balassa, 1964), the higher inflation is simply an "equilibrium" phenomenon resulting from higher productivity growth, higher economic growth, and the catching-up. Assuming for a moment that the CE-5 are already members of EMU, higher inflation in the CE-5 will, however, increase average inflation in EMU and to the extent that the European Central Bank continues to aim at an inflation target of 2 percent for the whole union, participation of the CE-5 countries will impart a deflationary bias on the whole union. Although inflation is still too high in CE-5 countries, macroeconomic adjustment could probably be completed in 3-4 years, so this is not an argument against joining, it is only one for waiting.

b) EMU's success is far from certain. As latecomers, CE-5 countries have the easy option to wait and see how it performs and to follow the UK and Denmark's prudent attitude.

I conclude this section with the advice that it is better to wait at least 15 years before joining EMU. This conviction is based on the likelihood of the occurrence of asymmetric shocks originating at home and on optimal trade strategies to maximise economic growth. The exchange rate corridor proposed in section 2 leaves enough flexibility to cope with unforeseen economic developments at home and abroad and to manage the catching-up process more smoothly, while allowing the exchange rate to play to a sufficient degree the role of anchor for inflation.

In the next section I shall focus on some inherent defects of EMU and the economies of the EU which may be important in deciding if and how soon newcomers will want to join.

4. EUROPEAN MONETARY UNION IS NOT PERFECT AND THE EUROPEAN UNION IS NOT HEAVEN ON EARTH

This section will focus on three aspects of EMU. First, the lack of flexibility of national fiscal policies arising from the signing of the so-called stability pact which limits the deficits at 3 percent after the beginning of EMU. Second, the deflationary bias of macroeconomic policies in Continental Europe in the last several years which will certainly continue until all of 1998 and may well continue thereafter. Third, whether EMU will really lead to higher growth in the union and under what conditions.

4.1 The 3 Percent Maastricht Budget Deficit Criterion and the Stability Pact

At the end of 1996 the Heads of State of the EU signed in Dublin a stability pact for the period after the beginning of EMU. The 3 percent Maastricht budget deficit criterion is only an entry condition to be satisfied in 1997 and not beyond. The German government and the Bundesbank were worried that some countries would return to a high deficit policy after admission and were afraid that they would thereby destabilise financial markets in the union and increase the chances that the Union would bail them out. They were also afraid of risks of monetisation of these countries' debts by the European Central Bank.

While imposing sound public finance principles on spend-thrift governments is a good thing, there are dangers in the stability pact signed, because the 3 percent limit constrains anti-cyclical fiscal policies in case of an economic downturn. According to the pact, the deficit is only allowed to exceed 3 percent if the fall in GDP exceeds 2 percent, otherwise fines are imposed by the EU. This limit is quite severe, because a 2 percent fall in GDP is already a severe downturn. The pact is dangerous both in case of a negative asymmetric shock hitting one country and in the case of an EU-wide recession. The lack of a federal budget which could absorb regional shocks makes this danger more real.

Table 19 shows that from the peak of the cycle in 1988 to the trough in 1993 the UK experienced a swing in the budget deficit of 8.9 percentage points of GDP. Japan's deficit also changed by 8.9 percentage points from the peak of the cycle in 1991 to the trough in 1996. In France the swing in the deficit from 1990 to 1994 was 4.4 percentage points of GDP. In France the swing was smaller because the French government was constrained by the fixed exchange rate with the DM and by the desire to join EMU on schedule.

If such large swings in budget deficits were necessary to come out of a recession in the UK, and to come half-way out of it in Japan and France, imagine what would happen in the EU after EMU in case of a generalised fall in GDP between 1 and 2 percent. Paul De Grauwe has argued in the Financial Times that in order to impose fines a two third majority is needed in the European Council of Ministers and that especially in the case of a generalised recession this majority is not likely to be found so that the pact may remain a dead letter. Still the pact represents a severe psychological and political barrier to sound anti-cyclical fiscal policies. The stability pact is a strait-jacket and may lead to disaster, should a significant negative macroeconomic shock occur in the whole EU or in individual members. The only possible way to overcome the dangers posed by the strait-jacket of the stability pact is that all EU members aim at budget surpluses of 3-4 percent at the peak of the business cycle, which is very unlikely to happen, although it would be very good for national savings.

4.2 Too Tight Monetary and Fiscal Policies and the Overvaluation of Western European Currencies

In the last 5-6 years monetary policy in Continental Western Europe has been quite restrictive. After the expansionary phase of 1990-1991, which followed the German reunification, and the acceleration of inflation in West Germany to almost 5 percent in 1992[10], the Bundesbank slowly regained its grip on the monetary reins. Despite the fall in nominal interest rates in the last two years to very low levels by historical standards (the discount rate in Germany is 2.5 percent and the 10-year government bond yield about 5.5 percent), they remain high in real terms if one considers the high level of unemployment, the lack of domestic sources of growth and the overvaluation of the DM. This state of affairs is certainly going to continue in 1998 and may well continue after January 1st 1999 as the European Central bank will be keen to establish its reputation and keen to show that it is not second to the Bundesbank.

Also fiscal policy has been everywhere restrictive as countries were trying to reduce the public sector deficit in order to satisfy the condition of the Maastricht Treaty. The attempt by all EU member countries eager to join EMU to simultaneously adjust fiscal imbalances has only made the reduction of deficits more difficult by reducing economic growth in the area. This state of affairs bears some resemblance with the policies followed by Continental Western Europe in 1930-1932 when pro-cyclical fiscal policies were being followed as economic activity was falling.

The consequences of Maastricht could have been a lot more severe in the absence of a significant stimulus coming from exports to the areas of the world were growth was very solid: the US, the UK, the Tigers in East Asia and many countries in Latin America. Even the CE-5 countries, which are small by the standards of Germany, France, and Italy, gave a significant contribution to the growth rates of the latter in 1995 and 1996. For instance, imports by the CE-5 grew by about 40 percent in real terms in 1996 and before the Czech crisis erupted were expected to grow by a similar amount in 1997. Table 20 shows that the shares of exports of Germany, Italy, and France to the CE-5 countries were rather small in 1996: 5.9 percent for Germany, 3.8 percent for Italy and 1.9 percent for France. The table shows also the contribution of imports by the CE-5 countries from Germany, Italy, and France to the growth of the latter. The increase of German exports to CE-5 countries accounted for a high share of German nominal GDP growth: almost 9 percent. The same holds to a lesser extent for France, for which 3.3 percent of the growth of nominal income was accounted for by rising exports to the CE-5 countries. For Germany this amounts to a 0.13 percentage points contribution to the 1.4 percent growth rate in 1996.

Another problem for the economies of Continental Western European countries is the excessive overvaluation of the Deutsche Mark with respect to the other world currencies (US dollar and yen). This carries with it an excessive overvaluation also of the French franc and exarcebates the problem of high labour costs and of the competitiveness of EU products in world markets. Germany and France are trying to regain the lost competitiveness of their products by deflating their economies. Firms are firing workers to increase productivity[11].

According to a 1996 study of the US Federal Reserve System on absolute labour costs and productivity in industry in the major seven industrial countries of the world (the so-called G-7), the DM was overvalued by about 50 percent with respect to the dollar in 1995 and the French Franc by somewhat less. Absolute Canadian and US labour costs were the lowest of the G-7. The 26 percent nominal depreciation of the DM with respect to the dollar since 1995 has adjusted about half of the overvaluation of the DM. This state of affairs is very unfortunate for Europe as the North American, Latin American and East Asian markets are and will remain the most dynamic of the world.

The cause of this excessive overvaluation of EU currencies is the restrictive monetary policy pursued by the Bundesbank since the end of 1991 and the attempt by all EU countries to satisfy the Maastricht inflation and interest rate criteria, which is bringing about a convergence of inflation towards 1.5-2 percent, much too low a rate for economies which have to undergo rapid structural change and substantial changes in relative product and factor prices. Unemployment in Germany is close to 11 percent of the labour force, a historical peak. In the territories of the former East Germany unemployment is much higher and the economy was growing in the first half of 1997 less than in the western part of the country. This is a dismal performance for an economy, which has barely started the transition.

Monetary policy in Western Continental Europe should boldly compensate for the negative effects on the economy arising from the restrictive fiscal policy pursued in the name of Maastricht and the euro. Japan and the US had to keep real short term interest rates at around zero for several years in the early 1990s to return with a lag to acceptable rates of economic growth and Japan is still struggling to make the recovery sustainable. Real interest rates with one-year maturity in Western Europe range from 1.5 percent in Germany to 5 percent in Italy. The current account of the EU is about in balance only because the very slow growth of aggregate demand compensates for the overvaluation of their currencies. At full employment, and unchanged exchange rates, the current account deficit of the EU would be large.

4.3 Will European Monetary Union Cause Higher Economic Growth in the European Union?

EMU is likely to have some positive effects on economic growth in the union, but these effects are likely to be very small. Probably the biggest positive effects will come from the reduction of risk premia on interest rates in formerly higher inflation countries and from a more efficient and competitive banking and financial system. Both will increase the level of GDP rather than the long run rate of economic growth.

A recent study by Daveri and Tabellini (1997) shows that the sharp increase in taxation of labour which has occurred in Western Continental Europe in the last three decades or so has significantly increased unemployment and significantly reduced the rate of economic growth. In 1960, North America, Australia, the UK and Japan had a much lower taxation of labour and a much lower ratio of total tax revenues to GDP. In addition, the increase in taxation between 1960 and 1995 was much less pronounced. This explains, according to Daveri and Tabellini, why they have much less unemployment and why, other things being equal, their rates of economic growth have been higher than in Western Continental Europe. The channels which lead to these effects are the following: high taxation of labour leads to shifting forward of taxation, this increases labour costs, which in turn leads to a reduction in the demand for labour by the private sector. The capital-labour ratio increases and the marginal product of capital falls. This in turn leads to lower economic growth. These channels were well known also by Smith and Ricardo (Tullio, 1987, 1989).

The degree of shifting forward of taxation depends on how highly workers value public expenditures because this determines their willingness to accept a reduction in the after tax wage. There is evidence that in Western Europe the degree of forward shifting of taxes on labour income has increased with the level of taxation (for evidence on Germany see Tullio et.al., 1996).

Table 21 taken from the above mentioned study of Daveri and Tabellini shows that in the second half of the 1960s effective tax rates on labour income averaged in a group of Continental Western European countries 31.9 percent, while they were only 17.5 percent in the other group of countries. By the second half of the 1990s the tax rates had grown to 46.5 percent in the European group and to 25.9 percent in the Anglo-Saxon-Japanese group. Table 22 contains the ratios of total government revenues to GDP. In 1995 in the European group the ratio was 50 percent of GDP and in the Anglo-Saxon-Japanese one it was 36 percent.

The message from the study of Daveri and Tabellini is clear: a reduction in the effective taxation of labour would reduce unemployment and lead to higher growth in Western Europe. So what is missing from the Maastricht conditions and the stability pact is a condition on the size of government and the degree of taxation of labour incomes. Unless Europe takes bold action on this front, growth will not exceed 2 percent on average and unemployment is here to stay. Table 23 shows unemployment rates in the two groups of countries in 1995. Since then they have gone up in the European group and come down sharply in the Anglo-Saxon world.

Continental Western European countries have too high taxation also in relation to the East Asian Tigers, Latin America, and the former Soviet Union. For the latter group, the unweighted average of government revenues to GDP was 23.8 percent in 1995 (Table 22). Once also the countries of the former Soviet Union will have solved their main economic imbalances and assuming they reach some degree of political stability, and I have no doubt that Russia will make it, where do you think an increasing share of world real investment is likely to be located? Certainly not in Western Continental Europe.

In Sections 4.1, 4.2 and 4.3 I have tried to explain why Europe is not bound to grow so much in the future: deflationary policies (Sections 4.1 and 4.2) will be coupled with too slow reductions in the level of taxation (Section 4.3). Western Europe is trapped in a vicious circle of too high government expenditure, too powerful lobbies favouring high expenditures at the expense of tax payers, too high taxes, too rigid labour markets, too centralised wage setting, too strong labour unions, too inflexible labour costs, too slow redesigning of the welfare state, too many distortions (disincentives to save, work and invest) caused by high and inefficient government expenditures and by taxation. The governments of the EU and in particular Germany have started the painful adjustment of the share of government expenditure to GDP and of labour costs and company taxation. The question is whether they will be able to proceed fast enough in view of the level of labour costs and the rapid economic changes occurring elsewhere in the world.

I wish to make three more points. First, I do not mean to say that the EU is doomed to stagnation. It is only doomed to lose economic power in relation to all other areas of the world with the exception of Africa and the Middle East. The Harvard historian Paul Kennedy maintains that the decline of nations depends on their economic growth relative to other areas. The UK did not stop growing since the middle of the last century, it just grew less than the US, Germany and Japan. After over 100 years the cumulated effects of even small yearly differences in growth rates can be enormous. Second, the fall of the Berlin wall, by opening up Eastern Europe and Russia to the world markets has "disturbed" the "cosy" world in which Western Europe was living, with Japan and the US relatively far away and with a strong degree of protectionism in sensitive sectors like agriculture, textiles, steel, automobiles and services. The trade agreements with CE-5 countries, the Baltic States and several countries in the Balkans and eventually their inclusion in the internal market, the signing of the Uruguay Round and the globalisation of markets will lead to drastic consequences which in my opinion are not yet fully understood by many politicians in the EU. Third, the long run effects of the globalisation of markets and of the fall of the Berlin wall on the EU are not necessarily negative; on the contrary, international trade theory and the well known gains from trade point in theory to rather substantial positive net effects. But trade theory is based on the assumptions of perfectly functioning markets and perfectly flexible factor prices and this is exactly where my pessimism comes from. I fear that the EU economy and political process is not flexible enough to allow it to reap all the potential benefits from these changes in the world economy. Rigidities in Western Europe will lead to an uneven distribution within the EU of the gains from trade and to faster growth than otherwise in the East.

5. SUMMARY AND CONCLUSIONS

This paper has dealt with the costs for CE-5 countries of joining EMU before the transition process and the process of catching-up towards GDP per capita levels of the EU is almost completed. It also looks at the optimal exchange rate policy, which should be adopted by these countries during the transition.

In Section 2 I first review some episodes of financial crisis across the world, then look at the current account developments, internal demand growth, and competitiveness in the CE-5 in the run-up to the 1997 Czech and Slovak financial crisis. I also analyse the exchange rate policy of CE-5 countries from about 1992 to the present. I show that they chose very different trade-offs between the anchor role of the exchange rate and the need to avoid excessive real appreciations of the exchange rate. The Czech and the Slovak Republics have chosen to favour the anchor role, which has led to excessive rigidity of the nominal exchange rate and to the foreign exchange crisis of 1997. Poland and Hungary have changed the exchange rate regime too often, have devalued too frequently and have not succeeded in using the exchange rate as a nominal anchor, except in the early phases of transition when inflation was very high. Especially since 1995 they seem to be living without a nominal anchor. Slovenia has been more successful in reducing inflation by relying on internal monetary aggregates as an anchor. However, considering the instability of money demand in countries where currency substitution is very important and the problems caused to monetary management by large capital inflows and outflows, it is better not to rely solely on internal anchors.

I maintain that all CE-5 countries should have adopted an exchange rate corridor, whose main characteristics are: its announcement in advance for a whole year, a positive slope, an implicit appreciation of the real exchange rate, no ex-post validation of inflation slippages, a relatively large band and sufficient flexibility of the exchange rate within the band during the year and from year to year in adapting the corridor to new circumstances without changing the regime. It's not too late to adopt such a regime and I strongly advise all of them, including Slovenia, to do so.

In Section 3 I look at the distance the CE-5 countries will have to cover if they want to reach levels of GDP per capita close to the ones of the EU. I show that this distance is huge, except for Slovenia, and I argue that it will take at least two decades to close the GDP gap. I also argue that the catching-up process will not be smooth and that frequent asymmetric shocks in relation to the EU economies are possible. These shocks will arise from the transformation process itself in the countries considered and in other countries like Russia and the Balkans. An example could be domestic wages running ahead of productivity growth because of the strong aspirations of workers generated by entry into EU. This is an argument for not joining EMU before 2010-2015. Considerations of optimal trade policy in an increasingly global world also suggest not to tie the exchange rate too soon to the euro forever by joining EMU.

Section 4 looks at some inherent defects of EMU and one structural problem of the economies of Western Continental Europe. The problems of EMU are the lack of fiscal flexibility to deal with economic crises and the deflationary bias of monetary and exchange rate policy. The lack of fiscal flexibility has its root in too small a federal (EU) budget and in the "stability pact" signed in 1996. The structural problem affecting the economies of Western Continental Europe is excessive taxation of labour. Economic growth in the EU will remain dismal because I do not expect sufficiently rapid changes in the degree of taxation of labour and in the size and efficiency of governments. CE-5 countries may find more stability by linking their economies tightly to the EU, but their catching-up may be better served by not neglecting too much commercial ties with the economically much more dynamic parts of the world (East Asia, the former Soviet Union, the Anglo-Saxon world and Latin America).

NOTES

1 These countries are also called the Visegrad countries.
2 The UK participated in the ERM only from the end of 1990 to September 1992, while it has been a member of the European Union since 1973.
3 Estonia and Cyprus have also been invited.
4 See Oldrich Dedek, Chapter 8 in this book.
5 Actually this is not always true. If at the beginning of the year the market exchange rate is close to the lower (appreciated) end of the band and depreciates sufficiently within the band in the course of the year, a real depreciation can nevertheless occur. See below.
6 See for instance Wyplosz, Grafe and Kirsanova (1996), Tullio and Ivanova (1997).
7 One significant difference between a corridor with a flat slope and the ERM is that the corridor policy is up for review every calendar year, while in the ERM the central rate can be changed only at the discretion of the Finance Ministers of the EU and that a change in the central rate is usually a traumatic event.
8 In addition, shocks can propagate also through channels other than trade flows.
9 However, some clues as to the future exchange rate policy of the euro will be offered in Section 4.2.
10 The increase in nominal wages in 1992 was over 10 percent, also because of a sharp increase in the degree of forward shifting of labour taxes, see Section 4.3 and Tullio et.al. (1996).
11 By the way, this is the policy followed in the last years also by Argentina which fixed the peso to the dollar in 1991 and, having since then lost competitive margins, is now adjusting the whole economy to the exchange rate instead of adjusting the exchange rate to changed economic conditions at home with disastrous consequences for unemployment.

REFERENCES

Balassa, B., 1964, "The purchasing power parity doctrine: a reappraisal", *Journal of Political Economy*, Vol. 72.

Cheasty, A., and Davis, J. M., 1996, "Fiscal Transition in Countries of the Former Soviet Union: An Iterim Assessment" *IMF Working paper*, June 1996.

Daveri, F., and Tabellini, G., 1997, Unemployment, growth and taxation in industrial countries, University of Brescia and IGIER, May 1997.

De Grauwe, P., 1989, International Money: Post-War Trends and Theories, Oxford University Press, Oxford.

De Grauwe, P., Micossi, S., and Tullio, G., 1996a, Inflation and Wage Behaviour in Europe, Oxford University Press, Oxford.

De Grauwe, P., 1996b, "Inflation Convergence During the Transition to EMU" in: Inflation and Wage Behaviour in Europe, De Grauwe, P., Micossi, S., and Tullio, G. (eds.), Chapter 7, Oxford University Press.

De Grauwe, P., 1996c, *Financial Times*, December 12, 1996.

De Grauwe, P., and Aksoy, Y., Chapter 2 in this book

Dedek, O., Chapter 8 in this book.

Dornbusch, R., Goldfajan, I., and Valdes, R., 1995, "Currency crises and collapses", *Brooking Papers on Economic Activity*, 2, 1995.

Kennedy, P., 1988, The rise and fall of the great powers, Unwin Hyman, London.

Lavrač, V., Stanovnik, P., 1995, "Monetary policy under a flexible exchange rate in Slovenia", *Banking Newsletter, Special Issue*, The Bank Association of Slovenia, Ljubljana.

Mundell, R., 1961, "The theory of optimum currency areas", *American Economic Review*, Vol. 51.

Tullio, G., 1987, "The long run implications of the increase in taxation and public debt for employment and economic growth in Europe", *European Economic Review*, Vol. 31, April 1987.

Tullio, G., 1989, "Smith and Ricardo on the Long-Run Effects of the Increase of Government Expenditure, Taxation and Public Debt: Is their theory relevant today?", *History of Political Economy*, Vol. 21, 4, Summer 1989.

Tullio, G., Steinherr, A., and Busher, H., 1996, "German Wage and Price Inflation before and after Unification" in: Inflation and Wage behaviour in Europe, De Grauwe, Micossi, Tullio (editors), forthcoming, Oxford University Press, Oxford.

Tullio, G., and Ivanova, N., 1997, "The demand for money and currency substitution in Russia during and after hyperinflation, 1992-1996", RECEP, Moscow, November 1997, unpublished paper.

Wyplosz, C., Grafe, C., and Kirsanova, T., 1996, "Pocket Model of the Russian Macroeconomy", *RECEP Working Paper*.

APPENDIX

Table 1. CE - 5 Countries; Exchange Rate System and Inflation

Countries	Exchange Rate System, from 1992 until May 1997	Consumer price inflation, February 1997
Czech Republic	fixed rate	7.3
Slovak Republic	fixed rate	6.0
Poland	frequent changes in regime and devaluations	17.3
Hungary	frequent changes in regime and devaluations	18.8
Slovenia	flexible rate	8.4

Source: IMF, IFS Monthly; The Economist.

Table 2. Current Account Deficits and Financial Crises, Selected Episodes

Countries and year of crisis	Current account deficits in % of GDP		GDP growth 1 year before	Real exchange rate appreciation vs. US dollar or DM[c] during last three years before the crisis
	2 years before	1 year before		
Czech Rep. (1997)	-2.7	-8.2	4.1	18.80 %
Thailand (1997)	-7.6	-7.5	6.7	6.36 %
Mexico (1995)	-6.5	-7.8	3.5	10.15 %
Mexico (1982)	-10.8	-16.1	7.9	-22.43 %
Belgium (1982)	-4.1	-4.2	3.9	-5.00 %
Italy (1992)	-2.1[a]	-2.4[b]	0.9[c]	3.29 %
Italy (1976)	-3.9	-0.3	-3.7	11.53 %

a) 1991
b) 1992
c) During the last three years before the crisis, except for Italy (1976) where the appreciation refers to the last 18 months. With respect to the DM for European countries and to the US dollar for non-European ones.
Sources: IMF-IFS Yearbook; IMF-IFS Monthly statistics; The Economist.

Table 3. CE-5 Countries; Current Account Deficits, Real Appreciation and Internal Demand

	Current account deficit in % of GDP, 1996	Real appreciation from 1993 to 1997-Q1		Real[a] internal demand growth 96 on 95 w. r. to Germany[b]
		w. r. to DM	w. r. to lira	
Poland	-6.3	21.34	18.75	9.2
Hungary	-3.9	4.87	1.73	-3.9
Czech Rep.	-8.2	25.88	23.43	6.2
Slovak Rep.	-10.0	16.97	14.23	n.a
Slovenia	-0.0	7.93	4.89	2.8

a) Final internal demand growth 1996 on 1995 with respect to Germany for each CE-5 country is calculated by subtracting demand increase in Germany from demand increase in each CE-5 country.
b) Final domestic demand increase in Germany in 1996: 1.1 percent.
Sources: OECD - Economic Outlook.

Table 4. Cumulated Real[a)] Appreciation of CE-5 Currencies with Respect to DM, US Dollar, Lira, from 1993 to 1997 - 1st Quarter (1993 = 100)

	DM	US Dollar	Lira
Poland	78.66	81.06	81.25
Hungary	95.13	98.03	98.27
Czech Rep.	74.12	76.39	76.57
Slovak Rep.	83.03	85.56	85.77
Slovenia	92.07	94.88	95.11

[a)] Computation based on consumer price indices.
Sources: IMF-IFS Monthly Statistics; The Economist.

Table 5. GDP per capita as Percent of EU Average and Percent of Labour Force Employed in Agriculture, 1995

	GDP per capita	Percent of labour force in agriculture
EU average	100	5.3
Poland	14	26.9
Hungary	19	8.0
Czech. Republic	20	6.3
Slovak Republic	14	9.7
Slovenia	42	7.1
(unweighted) average	21.8	11.6
Romania	7	34.4
Bulgaria	7	23.2
Turkey	14	53.0[a)]
(unweighted) average	9.3	36.8
Estonia	11	13.1
Latvia	8	18.5
Lithuania	5	23.8
(unweighted) average	8	18.5

[a)] 1993
Source: The Economist, July 19, 1997.

Table 6. Required Growth Rates of GDP per capita to Reduce the Gap with the EU by 2018[a] (20 years)

Initial GDP per capita	Final GDP per capita as % of EU average in 20 years			
as % of EU average	40	60	80	100
5	12.9	14.9	16.3	17.4
10	9.4	11.4	12.9	14.0
15	7.4	9.4	10.8	11.9
20	5.9	8.0	9.4	10.5
40	2.5	4.5	5.9	7.1

[a)] The assumed average geometric growth rate for the EU average from 1997 to 2018 is 2.5 percent.

Table 7. Share of Industry in GDP/NNP, Selected Countries, 1937 and 1989

	1937	1989
Poland	52[a]	52.4
Hungary	31	37.3
Czechoslovakia	35[b]	68.8
(unweighted) average	39.3	52.8
Germany	50	38.1[c]
France	36[d]	29.3
Italy	31	33.9
UK	36[e]	36.8
Belgium	46[f]	30.2
Netherlands	35[g]	28.9
Spain	35[h]	35.3
Portugal	32[i]	38.1
(unweighted) average	37.6	33.8
US	30	29.0[j]

a) 1950-54
b) 1935-37
c) West Germany, 1991- East Germany: 77.5%
d) 1938
e) England and Wales only
f) 1948-49
g) 1938-39
h) 1954
i) 1953-54
j) 1987

Source: World Bank, World Tables, 1995, The John Hopkins University Press, Baltimore and London and B. R. Mitchell, International Historical Statistics: Europe 1750-1988, MacMillan, London.

Table 8. Share of Agriculture in GDP/NNP, Selected Countries, 1937 and 1989

	1937	1989
Poland	35[a]	12.9
Hungary	31	13.7
Czechoslovakia	24[b]	10.1
(unweighted average)	30	12.2
Germany	16	1.3[c]
France	22[d]	3.5
Italy	29	3.5
UK	4[e]	1.9
Belgium	9[f]	2.2
Netherlands	8[g]	4.3
Spain	22[h]	4.8
Portugal	31[i]	6.2
(unweighted) average	17.6	3.4
US	10	2.0[j]

a) 1950-54
b) 1935-37
c) West Germany, 1991 - East Germany: 10.4%
d) 1938
e) England and Wales only
f) 1948-49
g) 1938-39
h) 1954
i) 1953-54
j) 1987

Source: World Bank, World Tables, 1995. The Johns Hopkins University Press, Baltimore and London and B. R. Mitchell, International Historical Statistics: Europe 1750-1988, MacMillan, London.

Table 9. Secondary School Enrolment in Selected Countries, 1937 and 1989[a]

	1937	1989
Poland	0.6	4.8
Hungary	0.8	4.7
Czechoslovakia	0.9[b]	5.5
(unweighted) average	0.8	5.0
Germany	1.4	9.7[c]
France	1.2	9.6
Italy	1.7	9.1
UK	1.1	7.5
Belgium	1.0	7.7[d]
Netherlands	1.8	8.4
Spain	0.5	12.4
Portugal	0.5	5.5
(unweighted) average	1.1	8.7

a) In percent of population
b) 1935
c) East Germany: 8.5
d) 1990

Source: B. R. Mitchell, International Historical Statistics; Europe 1750-1988, MacMillan, London and Statistisches Bundesamt, Vierteljahrsheft zur Auslandsstatistik, 4,1992.

Table 10. Students Enrolled in Universities in Selected Countries, in Percent of Population, 1989

Poland	1.3
Hungary	1.0
Czechoslovakia	1.2
(unweighted) average	1.1
East Germany	1.6
West Germany	2.8
France	2.8
Italy	2.4
UK	2.1
Belgium	2.7[a]
Netherlands	2.9
Spain	3.0
Portugal	1.7
(unweighted) average	2.5

[a)] 1989

Source: Statistisches Bundesamt, Viertelsjahrsheft zur Auslandsstatistik, 4, 1992.

Table 11. US Federal Government Expenditure (billions of US dollars)

Year	Federal expenditure	GDP	Federal expend. in % of GDP
1993	1491.9	6553.0	22.76
1994	1532.2	6935.7	22.09
1995	1598.5	7253.8	22.03
1996	1667.0	7576.1	22.00

Source: IMF-Government Finance Statistics; IFS-Monthly

Table 12. Poland, Trade Flows

	(a) - Exports to[a]						
	1989	1990	1991	1992	1993	1994	1995
Germany	14.16	25.11	29.43	31.34	36.36	35.67	39.52
Italy	2.30	2.95	4.09	5.52	5.23	4.96	4.91
France	2.43	3.22	3.78	3.63	4.19	3.99	3.57
UK	6.48	7.12	7.10	4.30	4.31	4.54	4.00
US	2.80	2.76	2.48	2.35	2.90	3.44	2.72
Japan	1.40	0.81	0.57	0.51	0.34	0.22	0.18
Other Ind. Countries	18.28	22.72	25.76	20.71	21.45	22.19	19.98
Russia	20.79	15.27	10.97	5.48	4.56	5.42	5.56
Developing Countries	31.35	20.02	15.81	26.16	20.76	19.57	19.56
Total	100.00	100.00	100.00	100.00	100.00	100.00	100.00
	(b) - Imports from[b]						
	1989	1990	1991	1992	1993	1994	1995
Germany	15.73	20.11	25.53	23.89	28.07	27.47	26.63
Italy	4.14	7.47	4.46	6.90	7.79	8.41	8.54
France	3.12	3.01	3.62	4.43	4.26	4.51	4.78
UK	4.64	5.64	3.97	6.64	5.75	5.27	5.17
US	1.36	1.62	2.26	3.43	5.18	3.90	3.92
Japan	1.36	2.30	1.61	2.10	1.75	1.62	1.64
Other Ind. Countries	22.34	23.56	26.25	22.12	23.08	23.64	23.16
Russia	18.09	19.83	14.11	8.50	6.74	6.73	6.74
Developing countries	29.22	16.46	17.19	21.99	17.38	18.45	19.42
Total	100.00	100.00	100.00	100.00	100.00	100.00	100.00

a) In percent of total exports.
b) In percent of total imports.
Source: IMF Direction of Trade Statistics.

Table 13. Hungary, Trade Flows

(a) - Exports to:[a]	1989	1990	1991	1992	1993	1994	1995
Germany	11.870	20.213	27.466	27.688	25.296	28.036	28.666
Italy	4.651	5.887	7.731	9.506	8.300	8.105	8.520
France	2.367	2.697	2.928	3.196	3.580	3.050	4.026
UK	1.819	2.039	2.075	1.994	2.359	3.050	3.044
US	3.298	3.555	3.239	3.196	4.347	3.993	3.212
Japan	1.847	1.160	1.764	0.913	0.999	0.824	0.599
Other Indust. Countries	15.204	17.256	22.215	22.304	21.092	20.509	20.441
Russia	24.994	20.244	12.033	13.084	13.996	6.924	6.398
Developing Countries	34.650	26.949	20.549	18.119	20.031	25.509	25.094
Total	100.000	100.000	100.000	100.000	100.000	100.000	100.000
(b) - Imports from:[b]	**1989**	**1990**	**1991**	**1992**	**1993**	**1994**	**1995**
Germany	15.884	23.361	21.828	23.46	21.498	23.558	23.433
Italy	3.332	4.048	7.498	6.276	6.054	7.039	7.880
France	2.183	2.053	2.752	3.048	3.366	3.051	9.944
UK	2.184	2.122	2.544	2.886	2.583	2.373	3.077
US	2.499	2.644	2.698	2.904	4.036	1.842	3.111
Japan	1.587	2.099	2.833	2.373	2.785	1.571	2.190
Other Indust. Countries	18.756	20.777	25.728	24.757	24.504	22.364	26.038
Russia	22.053	19.069	14.347	16.752	20.925	16.014	11.882
Developing Countries	31.522	23.827	19.772	17.544	14.249	22.188	12.445
Total	100.000	100.000	100.000	100.000	100.000	100.000	100.000

a) In percent of total exports.

b) In percent of total imports.

Source: IMF Direction of Trade Statistics.

Table 14. Czech Republic, Trade Flows

(a) - Exports to:[a]	1993	1994	1995
Germany	31.65	34.74	37.15
Italy	5.15	4.72	4.26
France	2.26	2.41	2.45
UK	3.47	3.01	2.57
US	2.13	2.36	2.30
Japan	0.59	0.67	0.60
Other Ind. Countries	17.39	16.56	15.71
Russia	3.53	2.08	2.29
Developing Countries	33.83	32.77	32.67
Total	100.00	100.00	100.00
(b) - Imports from:[b]	**1993**	**1994**	**1995**
Germany	29.41	35.09	36.44
Italy	4.92	5.39	5.94
France	3.40	4.24	4.32
UK	3.10	3.60	3.88
US	2.94	1.86	1.62
Japan	1.53	0.78	0.63
Other Ind. Countries	20.65	18.19	17.28
Russia	9.59	8.59	9.26
Developing Countries	24.46	22.26	20.63
Total	100.00	100.00	100.00

a) In percent of total exports.
b) In percent of total imports.
Source: IMF Direction of Trade Statistics.

Table 15. The Slovak Republic, Trade Flows

(a) - Exports to:[a]			
	1993	1994	1995
Germany	22.57	25.06	24.46
Italy	5.03	6.76	6.24
France	2.01	2.33	2.83
UK	0.08	1.58	1.23
US	1.63	2.59	1.41
Japan	0.16	0.16	0.29
Other Ind. Countries	12.32	13.27	11.19
Russia	4.23	3.82	3.33
Developing Countries	51.97	44.43	49.02
Total	100.00	100.00	100.00
(b) - Imports from:[b]			
	1993	1994	1995
Germany	16.92	21.43	21.51
Italy	5.55	6.44	5.37
France	1.76	2.15	3.30
UK	0.32	1.21	1.19
US	0.59	0.72	0.58
Japan	0.25	0.16	0.15
Other Ind. Countries	13.85	13.39	11.51
Russia	18.63	12.49	12.81
Developing Countries	42.13	42.01	43.58
Total	100.00	100.00	100.00

a) In percent of total exports.
b) In percent of total imports.
Source: IMF Direction of Trade Statistics.

Table 16. Slovenia, Trade Flows

	1993	1994	1995
(a) - Exports to:[a)]			
Germany	29.10	32.25	29.26
Italy	12.22	13.50	13.10
France	8.54	8.58	7.66
UK	2.39	3.04	2.05
US	3.49	3.63	3.44
Japan	0.40	0.26	0.84
Other Ind. Countries	11.98	12.18	11.80
Russia	4.79	4.63	3.70
Developing Countries	27.09	23.92	28.65
Total	100.00	100.00	100.00
(b) - Imports from:[b)]	1993	1994	1995
Germany	24.76	23.54	23.88
Italy	15.97	17.07	20.76
France	7.94	8.16	7.27
UK	1.56	1.75	1.98
US	2.86	2.67	1.26
Japan	1.90	1.70	0.49
Other Ind. Countries	17.16	9.65	18.77
Russia	3.30	2.23	1.26
Developing Countries	24.55	33.23	24.33
Total	100.00	100.00	100.00

a) In percent of total exports.
b) In percent of total imports.
Source: IMF Direction of Trade Statistics.

Table 17. 1996 GDP per capita in US $, and GDP Growth Rates

	in $, 000	in % of US	average growth of GDP 1980-95	95-96	97-2001[a]
US	28.5	100.0	2.4	2.1	2.5
Germany	28.7	100.7	2.0	1.7	2.0
France	26.5	93.0	1.9	1.9	2.0
Italy	21.2	74.4	2.0	1.9	2-3
UK	19.7	69.1	1.9	2.3	2-3
Poland	3.5	12.3	0.2	6.5	4-6
Hungary	4.3	15.1	0.4	1.2	4-6
Czech R.	5.3	18.6		4.5	4-6
Brazil	4.7	16.6	2.5	3.5	3.5-4
Russia	3.0	10.5		-4.5	4-6
Indonesia	1.2	4.0	6.3	8.0	7.5-8
China	0.6	2.2	9.8	10.0	8.0
India	0.4	1.3	5.5	6.1	7.0

a) World Bank forecasts and own forecasts.
Source: J. P. Morgan, World Financial Markets.

Table 18. The Visegrad Countries: Key Macroeconomic Indicators

	Inflation, July 1997	Public sector deficit, 1996	Current account deficit, 1996	Real GDP growth, 1996
Poland	14.9	-2.5	-1.0	6.1
Hungary	18.1	-3.3	-3.9	1.0
Czech Rep.	9.4	-0.1	-8.2	4.1
Slovak Rep.	6.0[a]	-1.3	-10.0	6.9
Slovenia	8.4[a]	0.0	0.0	3.5

a) February 1997

Source: J.P. Morgan, World Financial Markets, Third Quarter 1997.

Table 19. The Anti-cyclical Role of Public Sector Deficits

	JAPAN		UK		France	
	Deficit[a]	GDP[b]	Deficit	GDP	Deficit	GDP
1988	-1.5	6.3	-1.0	5.0	1.7	4.5
1989	-2.5	4.8	-0.9	2.2	1.2	4.3
1990	-2.9	4.8	1.2	0.4	1.6	2.5
1991	-3.0	4.3	2.6	-2.0	2.2	0.8
1992	-1.5	1.3	6.1	-0.5	4.0	1.3
1993	1.4	-0.2	7.9	2.2	6.1	-1.5
1994	3.5	0.5	6.0	3.8	6.0	2.7
1995	5.3	0.4	5.0	2.7	4.1	2.7
1996	5.9	2.1	5.4	2.1	3.7	1.7
Change in deficit from peak to trough:						
	+8.9[c]		+ 8.9[d]		+ 4.4[e]	

a) In percent of GDP

b) Real growth rate

c) 1991-1996

d) 1988-1993

e) 1990-1994

Sources: Bank of Italy, J.P. Morgan, World Financial Markets.

Table 20. Contribution to GDP Growth of Additional Exports to CE-5 Countries

Year	Exports to CE-5 in % of total exports			Contribution to GDP growth[a)]		
	Germany	Italy	France	Germany	Italy	France
1994	4.44	2.93	1.23	2.69	2.09	1.06
1995	5.18	3.33	1.41	5.09	2.64	1.47
1996	5.87	3.77	1.86	8.90	1.06	3.25

Source: for the period 1993-1995, Direction of Trade, IMF; for 1996, OECD, Monthly Statistics of Foreign Trade.

a) Nominal increase in exports to CE-5 in percent of nominal increase in GDP.

Table 21. Effective Tax Rates on Labour Incomes

Country/Year	1965-1970	1986-1991
Belgium	30.5	47.7
France	33.9	45.7
Germany	30.5	41.7
Italy	26.1	41.4
Netherlands	36.1	51.8
Sweden	34.3	50.9
(unweighted) average	31.9	46.5
Australia	11.7	18.2
Canada	17.1	29.2
Japan	16.0	27.5
UK	22.6	25.7
US	20.1	28.9
(unweighted) average	17.5	25.9

Source: Daveri and Tabellini, "Unemployment, growth and taxation in industrial countries" unpublished paper, University of Brescia and IGIER Bocconi, 1997.

Table 22. Government Revenues in percent of GDP, 1995

Belgium	50.8	Armenia	14.2
France	48.9	Azerbaijan	19.0
Germany	46.0	Belarus	43.7
Italy	45.1	Estonia	41.2
Netherlands	48.1	Georgia	5.0
Sweden	58.7	Kazakhstan	16.0
		Kyrgyz R.	15.0
(unweighted) average	49.6	Latvia	36.0
		Lithuania	23.5
Australia	34.3	Moldova	17.7
Canada	42.4	Russia	27.0
Japan	32.0	Tajikistan	14.0
UK	37.6	Turkmenistan	9.0
US	31.3	Ukraine	41.3
		Uzbekistan	35.0
(unweighted) average	35.5		
		(unweighted) average	23.8
Poland	31.4		
Hungary	49.0		
Czech Republic	35.8		
Slovak Republic	48.0		
Slovenia	46.7		
(unweighted) average	42.2		

Source: Eurostat and IMF.

Table 23. Unemployment Rates in Selected Countries

	1996[a]	July 1997
Belgium	13.8	13.7[b]
France	12.4	12.5
Germany	10.4	11.5
Italy	12.1	12.4[c]
Netherlands	7.1	5.9
Sweden	8.0	9.1[b]
(unweighted) average	10.6	10.8
Australia	8.6	8.7
Canada	9.7	9.0
Japan	3.4	3.4
UK	7.5	5.5
US	5.4	4.8
(unweighted) average	6.9	6.3

a) Average of the year.
b) Not seasonally adjusted.
c) April 1997.
Source: J.P. Morgan, World Financial Markets and The Economist

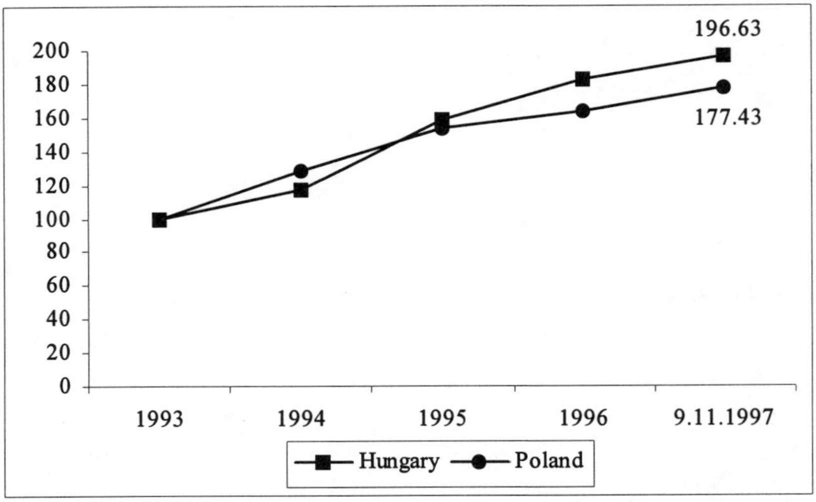

Figure 1a. Nominal exchange rates with respect to the DM, 1993 = 100; Hungary and Poland

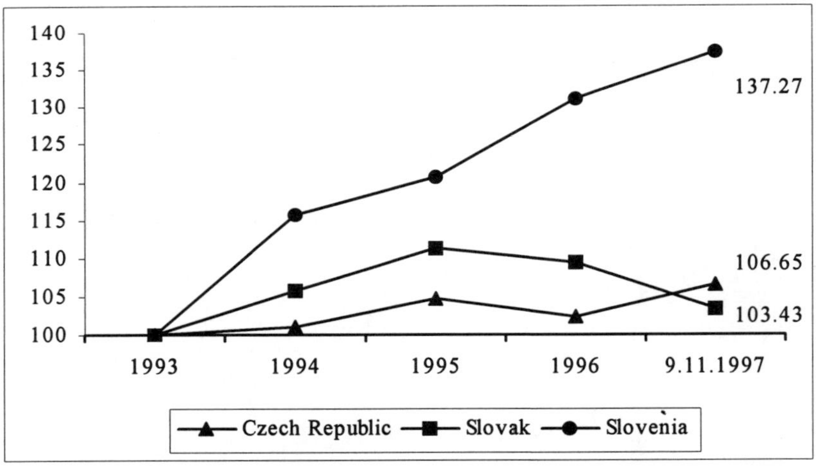

Figure 1b. Nominal exchange rates with respect to the DM, 1993 = 100; Czech Republic, Slovak Republic, and Slovenia

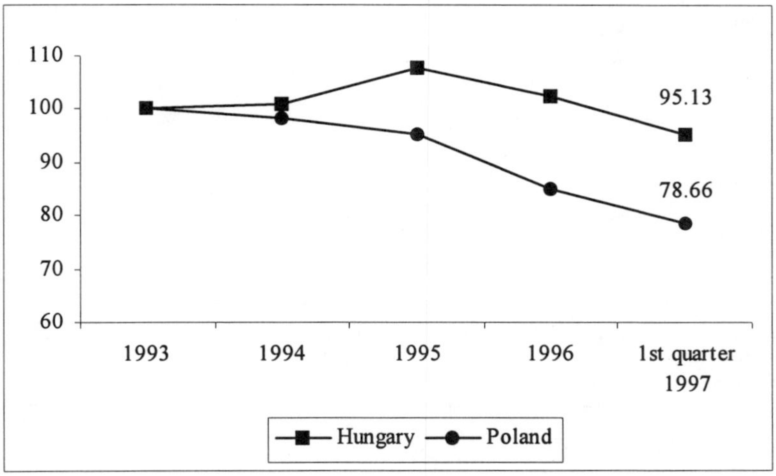

Figure 2a. Real exchange rates with respect to the DM, 1993 = 100; Hungary and Poland

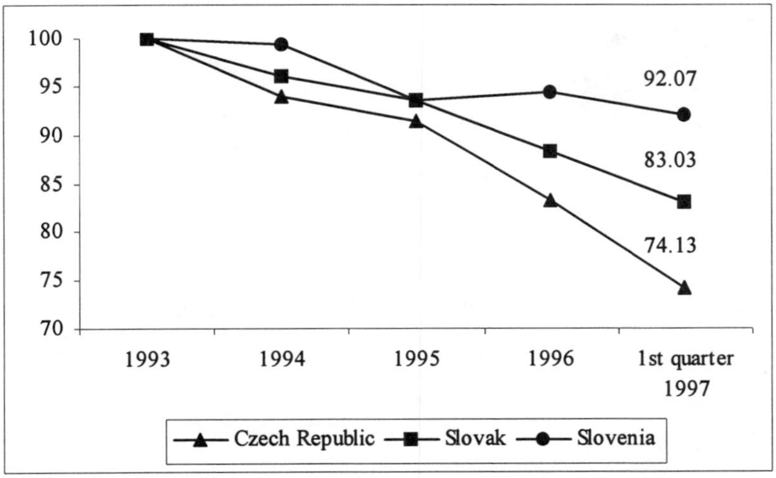

Figure 2b. Real exchange rates with respect to the DM, 1993 = 100; Czech Republic, Slovak Republic, and Slovenia

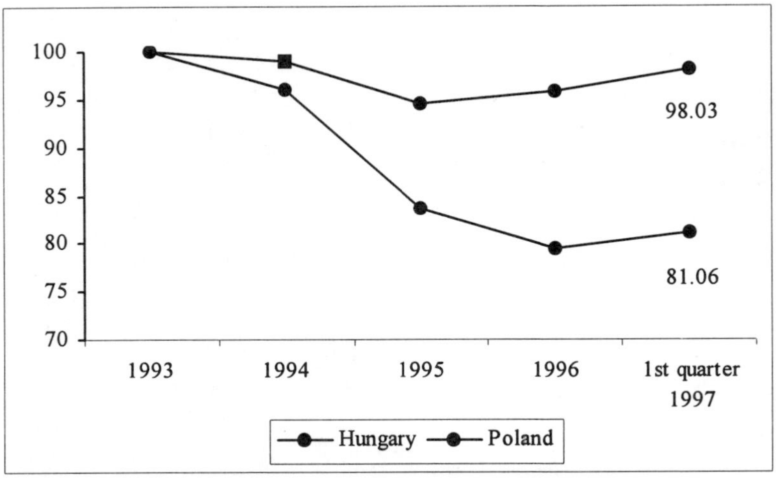

Figure 3a. Real exchange rates with respect to the US dollar, 1993 = 100; Hungary and Poland

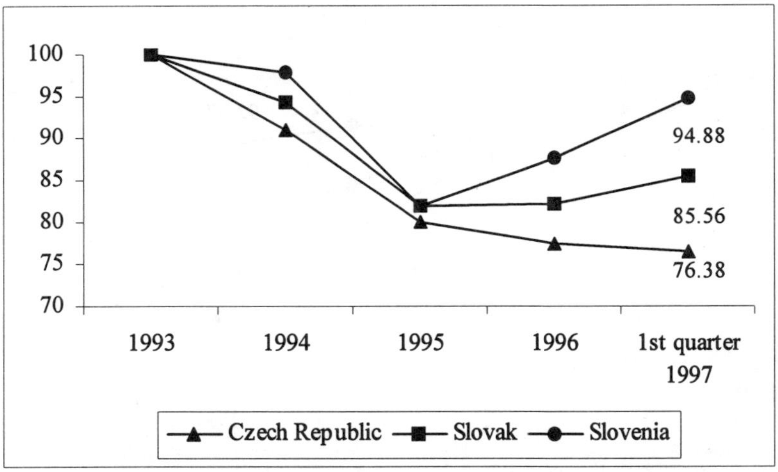

Figure 3b. Real exchange rates with respect to the US dollar, 1993 = 100; Czech Republic, Slovak Republic, and Slovenia

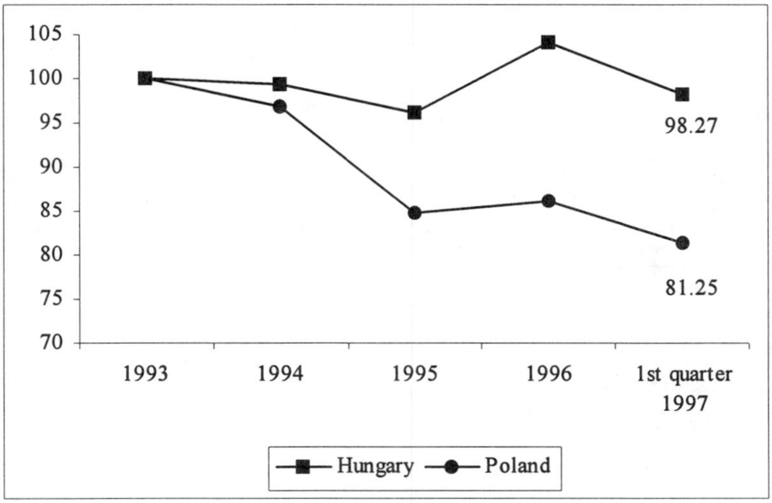

Figure 4a. Real exchange rates with respect to the Italian lira, 1993 = 100; Hungary and Poland

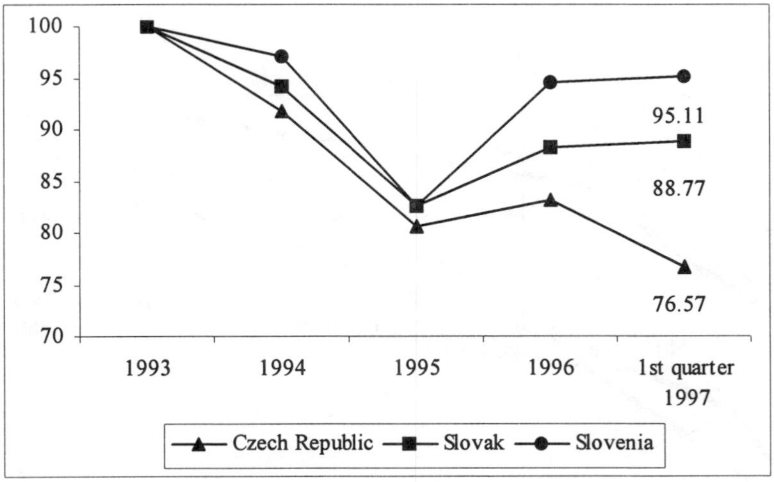

Figure 4b. Real exchange rates with respect to the Italian lira, 1993 = 100; Czech Republic, Slovak Republic, and Slovenia

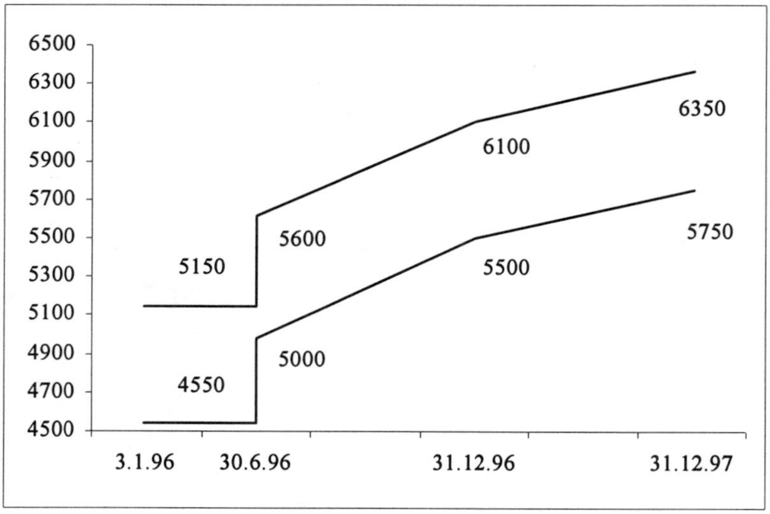

Figure 5a. Russia, exchange rate corridor, 1996 - 1997

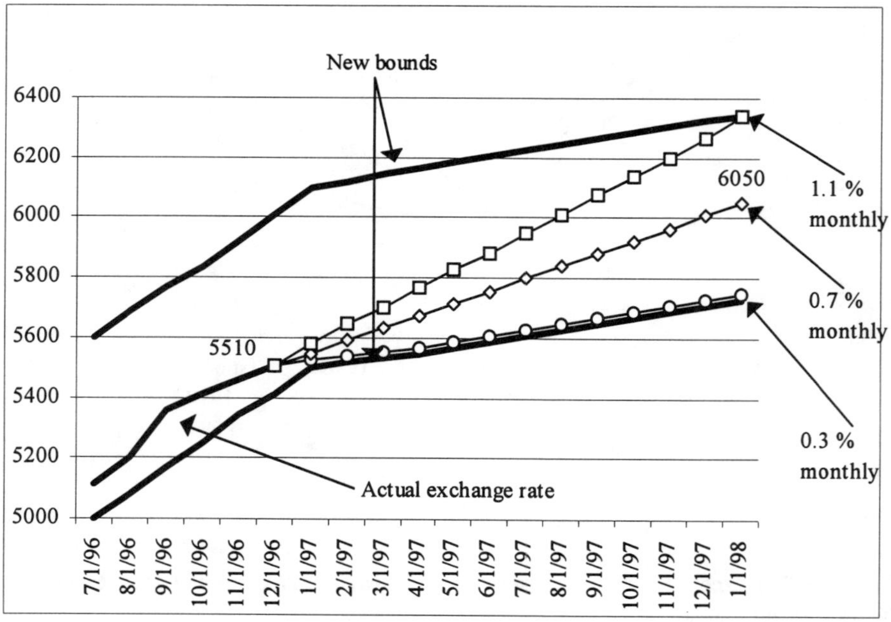

Figure 5b. Russia, exchange rate corridor, 1997

Chapter 6

Inclusion of Central European Countries in the European Monetary Integration Process

VLADIMIR LAVRAČ

1. INTRODUCTION

The present state of the European monetary integration process can be characterised as a period of intensive preparations for the creation of European Economic and Monetary Union (EMU) and for the transition to a single currency. European Union (EU) member countries and EU institutions seem firm in their decision to proceed with the EMU according to the timetable agreed upon in Maastricht. EMU is almost certainly starting in 1999, at least for a group of best performing EU member countries. Presently, the efforts of the EU member countries are concentrated on achieving requested macroeconomic stability, as defined in the Maastricht convergence criteria.

On the other hand, the Central European countries (CE countries) are among the most successful economies in transition, and - individually or as a group - natural first candidates for a full membership in the EU, when its Eastern enlargement becomes a reality. Since they aim at a full EU membership, and this implies (more or less directly) inclusion in the European monetary integration, it can be assumed they are not a priori reluctant to give up their monetary sovereignty. It is up to the CE countries to ask themselves before joining the EMU about the expected costs and benefits. In particular, will they be able to correct their lower international competitiveness by other means than through exchange rate adjustments?

This paper aims at analysing the possibilities for the inclusion of the CE countries in the European monetary integration process. It analyses present and expected readiness of the CE countries to enter the European Monetary System (EMS) and to join the EMU and indicates some necessary adjustments in their monetary and exchange rate policies, which they should undertake while preparing themselves for the inclusion in the European monetary integration process.

The paper first overviews the relationship between the EU membership and the inclusion in the European monetary integration process. Next, the paper analyses the exchange rate regimes of the individual CE countries and compares them to the requirements of the EMS. As the requirements of the future EMU are embodied in the Maastricht convergence criteria, the paper addresses the question of how the CE economies comply with these standards.

2. RELATIONSHIP BETWEEN THE MEMBERSHIP IN THE EUROPEAN UNION AND THE INCLUSION IN THE EUROPEAN MONETARY INTEGRATION FOR THE CENTRAL EUROPEAN COUNTRIES

In the present period and at least until the turn of the millennium the CE countries will not be included in any institutional form of the European monetary integration. They can enjoy their full monetary sovereignty, meaning that they can have their own national currencies and lead independent monetary and exchange rate policies. The question is whether it makes sense to discuss possible strategies for the inclusion of the CE countries in the European monetary integration process already now, or are these considerations premature.

Under quite reasonable assumptions that a) the CE countries will still be interested in the EU membership, b) the EU will sooner or later decide for the Eastern enlargement and c) there will be the EMU with a single currency and/or the EMS at that time, it makes sense for the CE countries to closely monitor developments in the European monetary integration, to define their vision (inclusion in the EMS and in the EMU) and to formulate their strategy as to how to achieve this goal (when and how to make the necessary adjustments in their monetary and exchange rate systems and policies).

The term European monetary integration of course means monetary integration within the EU, with its mechanisms such as the EMS and the EMU. Other forms of regional economic integration in Europe, such as the EFTA or the CEFTA, which the CE countries established among themselves, are not relevant for this discussion, since they do not foresee any special forms of monetary integration among member countries, so that they can maintain their full monetary sovereignty.

The term CE countries in this paper include the following countries: The Czech Republic, Slovakia, Poland, Hungary and Slovenia. This is the standard classification (see The Economist, 1995), although other definitions are possible.

As the CE countries are for the time being not included in the European monetary integration, developments in the EMS and preparations for the transition to the EMU influence them only indirectly. Fluctuations of the exchange rates in the EMS affect competitiveness of the CE exports in the individual EU markets and domestic prices of their imports from there. Preparations of the EU members for the EMU and their efforts to meet the Maastricht convergence criteria have the impact on macroeconomic stability and economic activity in these countries, which is important for the CE countries, having in mind high shares of their trade with the EU.

In formulating their vision and strategy regarding inclusion in the EMS and in the EMU, CE countries can have two alternative approaches. One approach is to start from the assumption that they wish to integrate into the EU, the sooner the better. The decision for the EU is taken as given, and that more or less directly implies the decision for the inclusion in the EMS and in the EMU. As the CE countries signed the Association agreements with the EU and formally applied for a full EU membership, this seems to be the realistic approach in the CE countries.

The other possible approach is more theoretical. By identifying and analysing the necessary adjustments in their monetary and exchange rate systems and policies, which the future inclusion in the EMS and in the EMU requires, the CE countries could assess expected costs and benefits of their inclusion in the European monetary integration process. Only if net benefits are expected, the inclusion in the EMS and in the EMU makes sense, and vice versa. These monetary considerations per se, taken outside the context of wider economic and political interests for the EU membership, would then represent a strong argument in favour or against the integration of these countries in the EU in general. Since such cost-benefit analysis of monetary integration is very demanding even for the EU countries (see M. Emerson, 1992), it can safely be assumed that the CE countries rather used the first approach.

Membership in the EU in principle assumes the inclusion in its monetary integration mechanisms, although in practice this does not necessarily apply to all countries or immediately. The experience has demonstrated that an individual EU member country can be a non-member of the EMS, if it is not monetarily mature enough (Greece), can join almost immediately (Austria) or later and even "temporarily" opt out of the EMS (UK, Italy). More or less the same can be said about the EMU. Only those EU member countries that will demonstrate required monetary and fiscal "maturity" (as defined by the Maastricht convergence criteria) would be admitted to the EMU. On the other hand, some countries reserved the right not to participate in the EMU (UK, Denmark).

It should be concluded that the membership of the CE in the EU implies their obligation to participate in the EMS and in the EMU, but the timing of their admission is rather flexible. The candidate must first undertake the necessary adjustments and reach a certain monetary "maturity", lest it should detrimentally influence the process of the European monetary integration as a whole. On the other hand, the possibility that a CE country would apply for a full EU membership and then unilaterally opt out of its monetary integration process would look very odd and would be highly improbable.

In fact the candidate countries are expected to accept the whole *acquis communautaire* in the field of EMU at the time of their accession to the EU. The Copenhagen summit, which defined the EU accession criteria, declared that candidate countries have to share the aim of monetary union, although they do not have to fulfil the Maastricht convergence criteria at the time of EU accessions or even before that. In practice this means that the CE countries will not be in a position to opt out of the EMU. Adherence to the goals of EMU is considered to be an obligation from the membership in the EU for the candidate countries (see Daviddi and Ilzkovitz, 1996).

The Association agreement with the EU does not foresee any obligations of the CE countries with respect to monetary integration. On the contrary, membership in the EMS and in the EMU is open only to full members of the EU. Association agreements include successive liberalisation of financial services and of capital flows between the associated countries and the EU, which may have some impact on the actual autonomy of their monetary policy, but they do not interfere with the monetary sovereignty of the associated countries. On the other hand, non-member countries, with or without an association agreement, can approach the European monetary process only informally, unilaterally and functionally. They can only adjust their monetary and exchange rate systems and policies to the requirements of the EMS and the EMU, thereby preparing themselves for the future institutional inclusion in the EMS and in the EMU, when they become full members of the EU.

3. ARE THE CENTRAL EUROPEAN COUNTRIES READY FOR THE INCLUSION IN THE EUROPEAN MONETARY SYSTEM?

In this part of the paper some characteristics of the monetary and exchange rate systems and policies of the CE countries are compared to the requirements of the EMS in order to determine how they are presently compatible with the EMS rules and to identify the necessary adjustments which will have to be undertaken before joining the EMS.

Here we assume that the EMS will still exist and that it will have (when the CE countries join the EU) more or less the same characteristics as presently. Of course, in reality, this is far from certain. The EMS may, after the transition to the EMU (which we also assume is not questionable) remain the same, go back to the narrow bands of fluctuations of 2.25 percent, completely disappear, or fundamentally change its rules, perhaps even in the direction that it would admit non-members of the EU (serious candidates, such as the CE countries). Some authors (Heinemann, 1995) offer convincing arguments in favour of an early inclusion of the CE countries in the EMS.

After the Dublin summit the features of the future ERM (the so-called ERM II) are now more clearly defined. The new exchange rate mechanism, ERM II, should replace the present ERM as from 1 January 1999. Membership would continue to be voluntary. ERM II will be based on central rates, defined vis-à-vis the euro, which will be at the centre of the system. The standard fluctuation band will be relatively wide, like the present one. Interventions at the margins will in principle be automatic and unlimited, with very short-term financing available. It should be ensured that any adjustment of central rates is conducted in a timely fashion so as to avoid significant misalignments (Ecofin Council, 1996).

However, for analytical reasons it is useful to assume that the EMS will stay such as it is in the foreseeable future (with wider bands of fluctuations of 15 percent to each side of the central rates) and that the CE countries will have to join the EMS first, regardless of whether they enter the EMU later. The CE countries should therefore compare themselves with the requirements of the present EMS.

The most important element of the EMS is its exchange rate mechanism (ERM). Other elements of the EMS are less important and the CE countries would not have much trouble complying with them. There are no formal and transparent criteria, which would enable an outside country to assess whether it is suitable for a membership in the EMS. The entry of a new candidate depends more from judgement (assessment of its monetary maturity).

However, by comparing their monetary and exchange rate systems and policies to those of the EMS members and to the EMS rules, the CE countries can at least vaguely asses how close are they to the EMS and how they should adjust to it.

This paper focuses on the exchange rate systems and policies of the CE countries in comparison with the ERM requirements. The explicit analysis of their monetary systems and policies is beyond the scope of the paper. However, a quick assessment would be the following: Some basic prerequisites for a sound monetary system and policy have been established in the CE countries (independent central bank, internal and later also external current convertibility of the currency, market-oriented instruments of monetary policy, targeting of monetary policies, use of nominal anchors) but others are still missing (healthy banks, developed financial markets, competitive interest rates).

The ERM is basically the system of fixed exchange rates among the currencies of the member countries. Its basic determinants are the central rates, bands of fluctuations around them and occasional realignments of currencies. These characteristics remained the same even after the 1992-1993 crises, when intervention band was widened to 30 percent in total. In that band, which is according to the Western standards really wide, currencies are in fact free to float, which gives the member countries more freedom in conducting their monetary and exchange rate policies and gives the ERM some characteristics of a quasi-floating exchange rate system.

The CE countries have chosen very different exchange rate regimes since the beginning of the transition process, covering practically the whole spectrum between the fixed and floating exchange rates. On the one side there are those who decided for a fixed exchange rate (the Czech Republic, Slovakia) and on the other side those who opted for a floating exchange rate (Slovenia). Other regimes, like an adjustable peg or a crawling peg fall in between the two, although formally they can be viewed as a version of a fixed exchange rate system.

The rules of the ERM require that a member country maintains a fixed exchange rate (the official exchange rate of its currency is determined in terms of the ECU; bilateral central exchange rates towards other member currencies are fixed on the basis of the ECU exchange rate) and intervenes to keep it within the permissible band of fluctuations. Realignment of the exchange rate is in principle possible, but it is the result of the collective decision in the ERM and is not a discretionary right of a member country. It is implicitly assumed that realignments should not be too frequent and too large. How do the exchange rate systems and policies of the CE countries comply with these rules? (A useful description of the exchange rate regimes of the CE countries can be found in Hochreiter, 1995, Krzak, 1995 and Oblath, 1995).

The Czech Republic: After substantial initial devaluations in 1990-1991 the currency was pegged to a five-currency basket, which was changed in May 1993 to a two-currency basket (65 percent mark, 35 percent dollar). Narrow band of fluctuations of 0.5 percent to each side was used until February 1996, when it was widened to 7.5 percent. The exchange rate remained fixed without devaluations throughout the period.

Slovakia: After separation in 1993 the exchange rate was pegged to a five-currency basket. In July 1994 the basket was changed (60 percent mark, 40 percent dollar). The narrow band of fluctuations of 1.5 percent to each side was in January 1996 widened to 3 percent. Except for 10 percent devaluation in July 1993, the currency remained stable without further devaluations.

Poland: After sharp initial devaluation, the exchange rate was pegged to the dollar. From October 1991, a crawling peg regime with daily devaluations, based on a basket of five currencies was introduced. Monthly rates of devaluations were successively declining from 1.8 percent to 1.2 percent. The band of fluctuations was widened from 2 percent to 7 percent on each side of the central rate. In August 1993 there was a 7.4 percent devaluation of the currency.

Hungary: Adjustable peg regime was adopted at first. The intervention band stayed at 2.25 percent on each side throughout the period. In May 1994 the basket was changed (from 50 percent mark and 50 percent dollar to 70 percent ECU and 30 percent dollar). Minidevaluations were combined with maxidevaluations, such as 8 percent devaluation in August 1994 and 9 percent devaluation in March 1995. From then on, crawling peg with daily devaluations is used. The monthly rate of devaluations in the crawling peg regime declined from 1.9 to 1.2 percent.

Slovenia: The floating exchange rate regime was adopted from the introduction of the tolar in October 1991. It is a managed floating regime, where the exchange rate is in principle determined on the foreign exchange market, but the central bank intervenes at times quite heavily (and in some periods with sterilised intervention), mostly to prevent excessive real appreciation of the currency.

What are the possible lessons from the differing experiences of individual CE countries with their exchange rate regimes? The majority of the CE countries opted for a fixed exchange rate regime of one kind or another. This decision was in line with a prevailing view in the IMF and in academic circles that a fixed exchange rate should be used in the CE countries as a nominal anchor in their price stabilisation efforts. Sharp initial devaluations were typically used before pegging the currency. The CE countries decided to peg their currencies to a basket rather than to a single major currency. This choice is more technical than fundamental in nature.

Later on, as the nominal exchange rate was fixed (or adjusted, discretionary in case of an adjustable peg or automatically in case of a crawling peg), while the domestic inflation persisted (although at a declining rate), their currencies appreciated in real terms and become substantially overvalued. In 1995 real appreciation of the CE currencies (measured as the change in the official exchange rate of the dollar deflated by the producer price index in industry, December/December) is estimated to be 11 percent for the Czech Republic, 12 percent for Slovakia, 13 percent for Poland, 3 percent for Hungary and 8 percent for Slovenia (Podkaminer, 1996).

In some of the CE countries, such as the Czech Republic and Slovakia, where the inflation rate declined substantially and reached the annual level of 8 percent and 7 percent (respectively) in 1995, the fixed nominal exchange rate proved to be sustainable, and the real appreciation manageable, although it put some pressure on the trade balance. However, in both countries there were (particularly due to large capital inflows) tendencies to switch to a more flexible exchange rate regime, which finally materialised in the widened intervention band. The other two countries, Poland and Hungary, were less successful in bringing down the inflation rate, which in 1995 is still at a relatively high level (22 percent and 28 percent annually). The exchange rate policy in Hungary, where the initial inflation rate was in fact lower than in other CE countries at the beginning of transition, was not very successful (Oblath, 1995). There was a switch in the exchange rate regime, monetary and fiscal policies were inconsistent with exchange rate regime, there were occasional major devaluations, which all seems to have contributed to the loss of credibility and to persistence of inflationary expectations.

On the other hand, Slovenia was the only CE country which opted for a floating exchange rate regime. It had no foreign exchange reserves after the dissolution of Yugoslavia, and the inflation rate was at a hyperinflationary level (more than 20 percent monthly). The floating exchange rate regime enabled internal convertibility immediately after the introduction of the new currency and a rather liberalised foreign exchange and trade regime was instituted. The floating regime was of course of a managed kind, but it was planned that the interventions of the central bank would be only minor and of a "leaning against the wind" kind.

However, due to the surprisingly favourable current account developments, as the exporters succeeded in redirecting their exports to the EU instead of to the disappearing Yugoslav or Eastern markets, the nominal exchange rate remained relatively stable. For longer periods it lagged behind the domestic inflation rate, so that domestic currency appreciated strongly in real terms and became, according to the purchasing power parity theory, seriously overvalued (Lavrač and Stanovnik, 1995). In addition to this, large private short-term capital inflows contributed to the excess supply on the foreign exchange market. The central bank had to intervene substantially to prevent further real appreciation of the domestic currency. Partly the intervention was non-sterilised and resulted in the accumulation of large foreign exchange reserves, and partly it was sterilised through the issuance of central bank's securities, so that the restrictive monetary policy of the central bank would not be endangered. The sterilisation operation proved to be costly and of a limited scope.

First, it exhausted the budget of the central bank. Its seigniorage revenue was used up in the sterilisation operations, so that continuation or even intensification of sterilisation would call for a budgetary transfer to the central bank, which would have to go through a parliamentary procedure. Second, by issuing its own securities, which had to be competitive on the market, the central bank was actually pushing up the interest rates, which on the other hand it was at the same time trying to bring down, as the level of interest rates was already very high. Third, by crowding out other securities, the sterilisation had a negative impact on the development of the emerging capital market in Slovenia.

The lesson from Slovenia might be that a floating exchange rate can also be the right solution, providing it is accompanied by responsible monetary and fiscal policies and by adequate institutions and instruments of the financial market, which can make central bank's intervention policy effective. Restrictive monetary policy, based on targeting the money supply, liberalised foreign exchange regime and continuously declining inflation rate contributed to the credibility of the central bank and to the declining inflationary expectations. The inflation rate declined from 93 percent in 1992 to 23 percent in 1993, to 18 percent in 1994 and to 9 percent in 1995. In 1996, it remained at the same level, slightly under 9 percent.

How the exchange rate regimes of the individual CE countries comply with the ERM rules? At first sight it appears that those countries that maintain fixed exchange rates are in a better position. Particularly those countries where the nominal exchange rate is unchanged for a longer period seem to be almost ready for joining the ERM. On the other hand, at first sight it would appear that Slovenia, which has a floating exchange regime, is still far away from the ERM.

Such a conclusion would be oversimplified and misleading. To be able to participate in the ERM, a currency must not only be stable (currency crisis must be avoided), but a fixed nominal exchange rate must be sustained for a longer period. If a nominal exchange rate is stable for a certain period, but domestic inflation substantially exceeds the average inflation in the EU and real exchange rates fluctuate widely, this could hardly be called an equilibrium situation. Real appreciation of the domestic currency may undermine the current account and, sooner or later, lead to corrections of the nominal exchange rate and, depending on expectations, perhaps even to currency crisis.

Therefore, the best candidates for an early inclusion in the EMS are at the moment most likely those CE countries, which have reached a single-digit inflation (the Czech Republic, Slovakia, Slovenia) and intend to follow the trend of lowering inflation further, till they reach the EU level. Transition from a floating to a fixed exchange rate regime in Slovenia would in that case represent no difficulty, but merely a technical issue. Inclusion of other CE (Poland, Hungary) which have a much higher inflation rate (more than 20 percent annually) in the EMS would not make much sense at the moment, since their currencies would have to be devalued too frequently for the EMS standards.

The conclusion is that the CE countries are not yet ready for the inclusion in the EMS, since their inflation rates are still too high. However impressive their nominal exchange rate performance may be, their real exchange rates do not guarantee that they could follow the ERM rules without too frequent devaluations of their currencies. Nevertheless, they are on the right way to be able to join the EMS in the near future.

Although the trend of disinflation in the CE countries in the years since the beginning of transition is encouraging, it may be particularly difficult to bring down inflation rate further, once it has reached the single-digit level. The costs of disinflation from lower levels are particularly high and may not be considered as a priority by policy makers. A moderate inflation can even be welcome, as it allows an easier adjustment of relative prices, which is not yet completed in transition economies (see Wyplosz, 1996).

4. ARE THE CENTRAL EUROPEAN COUNTRIES READY FOR THE INCLUSION IN THE EUROPEAN MONETARY UNION?

As the CE countries at the moment do not meet the requirements of the EMS, it is obvious that they are also not ready for joining the EMU yet. Conditions for entering the EMU are well known and are embodied in the Maastricht convergence criteria. It is interesting to see how the CE countries meet these criteria. The complete data on the fulfilment of the Maastricht convergence criteria for the CE countries are not available in official publications (such as EBRD, 1996 and European Commission, 1996), while unofficial estimates are incomplete or imperfect (Vujičić, 1995).

The most consistent estimates on the fulfilment of the Maastricht convergence criteria for the CE countries can probably be found in Backé and Lindner, 1996.

Table 1. Fulfilment of the Maastricht Convergence Criteria for the CE Countries in 1995

	Average inflation	Average long-term interest rates	Public sector deficit/GDP	Public debt/GDP
Reference value	2.7%	9.7%	3.0%	60%
Czech Republic	9.1%	app. 9%	(-) 0.6%	13%
Hungary	28.2%	app. 30%	2.9%	87%
Poland	27.8%	app. 22%	2.6%	58%
Slovakia	9.9%	app. 10%	1.6%	26%
Slovenia	12.6%	app. 12%	0.0%	31%

Source: Backé and Lindner 1996; for Slovenia Lavrač and Lavrač, 1996.

Table 1 does not include the fifth convergence criterion, the stability of the exchange rate, which of course has no quantified reference value. It only states that a currency should be inside the ERM, fluctuating within the normal limits and should not devalue against any other ERM currency on its own initiative for at least two years. The CE countries are non-members of the EU and as such are also non-members of the EMS and of its ERM. Therefore, they do not fulfil this criterion from the formal aspect in its narrow interpretation. Next test would be whether they maintain a fixed or a floating exchange rate system. By this standard Slovenia would be in the worst position, Poland and Hungary somewhere is the middle and the Czech Republic and Slovakia would be in the best position. Additional test could be whether the nominal exchange rates are actually stable, regardless of the exchange rate regime used. Again, the Czech Republic and Slovakia would be in the best position, since their nominal exchange rates are practically unchanged for several years. They would be followed by Slovenia, where the nominal exchange rate was relatively stable, by Poland and finally by Hungary. Finally, the issue of a longer-term sustainability of the nominal exchange rates could be raised, which should perhaps be the most important in the context of the future inclusion of these countries in the ERM. It can probably best be assessed by the level of the inflation rate. In this case, the best performing group consists of the Czech Republic, Slovakia and Slovenia, while Poland and Hungary lag somewhat behind. This line of thinking reveals the relativity of this convergence criterion, at least when applied to the CE countries, which makes its merely formal treatment rather questionable.

According to the Maastricht convergence criteria, the performance of the CE economies is rather good. Contrary to most of the EU members, the CE countries (except Hungary) do not have problems with meeting both fiscal criteria. On the other hand, contrary to most EU members, CE countries have problems with meeting the three monetary criteria. However, as the trends regarding the inflation rate in some of the CE countries (the Czech Republic, Slovakia, and Slovenia) are very encouraging, they could meet the Maastricht convergence criteria in the near future. For others (Poland, Hungary) it may take a little longer.

As the results in fulfilling the Maastricht convergence criteria are good in case of the CE countries, it has become quite fashionable to use and interpret them uncritically. It should be remembered what is their purpose in the first place. They are the criteria for the selection of those EU member countries, which will be able to join the EMU. Their purpose is to define the standards for sound monetary and fiscal policies, which should lead to a stable single currency and enable individual EMU members to participate in the EMU without using the exchange rate as an instrument of adjustment. (For a critical analysis of the Maastricht convergence criteria, see De Grauwe, 1994).

The CE countries use the Maastricht convergence criteria mostly for other purposes, primarily to demonstrate their readiness for the accession to the EU. The idea is the following: If they perform better then some of the EU members in such an advanced matter as is the EMU, it is logical that they are more than ready for the EU membership. There are three problems with this interpretation.

First, the EU members are forced to meet the Maastricht convergence criteria if they want to join the EMU. Nobody forces the CE countries to meet these criteria, they use them voluntarily. Nothing is wrong if they use them as standards for defining their own sound monetary and fiscal policies. However, criteria for the admission of the CE countries to the EU will be different.

Second, since the Maastricht convergence criteria apply to the third stage of the EMU, they assume that the EU member countries have already undertaken adjustments in the previous two stages. CE economies do not comply with all of the internal market requirements. For instance, they have not liberalised capital flows yet.

Third, the data for the CE countries are questionable. It is hard to get reliable official data on all the Maastricht convergence criteria and furthermore, even if they exist, their meaning may be different than in the case of the EU countries. Which government securities should be taken to calculate a long-term interest rate? Even if government bonds with 10-years maturity exist, their role is very different than in the case of the EU developed financial markets. Therefore, the role of the long-term interest rate itself is different and not comparable to that in the EU, so it should also be interpreted differently. More or less the same is true at least for the other two criteria - public debt and exchange rate behaviour.

5. CONCLUSIONS

In the present period and at least until the turn of the millennium the CE countries as non-members of the EU will not be included in any institutional form of the European monetary integration. An Association agreement with the EU does not foresee any obligations of the CE countries with respect to monetary integration. On the contrary, membership in the EMS and in the EMU is open only to full members of the EU. Non-member countries of the EU can approach the European monetary integration process only informally, unilaterally and functionally. They can only adjust their monetary and exchange rate systems and policies to the requirements of the EMS and the EMU, thereby preparing themselves for the future institutional inclusion in the EMS and in the EMU, when they become full members of the EU.

The CE countries would like to become full members of the EU as soon as possible. Therefore, they should also join the European monetary integration process and include in the EMS and/or EMU when the time comes. At the moment they are not yet ready for the participation in the EMS. Although some of them achieved remarkable progress in lowering inflation, their inflation rates are still too high for the EMS standards. Regardless of the exchange rate regime they practice, lowering of their inflation rates to the level near to the EU average is the right way of preparing themselves for the inclusion in the EMS.

Regarding their readiness to join the future EMU, the performance of the CE countries in meeting the Maastricht convergence criteria is, compared to the EU countries, better for the fiscal and worse for the monetary criteria, but even for the monetary criteria, trends are positive. However, the Maastricht convergence criteria should not be overemphasised and misinterpreted. Their purpose is to determine the readiness of the EU member countries to join the EMU and not to determine the readiness of the EU candidates for a full EU membership.

It should be pointed out that the data on the fulfilment of the Maastricht convergence criteria for the CE countries should only be used: (i) as a standard when drawing up the macro-economic stabilisation policy, (ii) in view of relatively favourable figures, for promotional activities, especially abroad, and (iii) as a guideline for the preparation for the future accession to the EMU. They cannot be used for other purposes as: (i) they are not the criteria for measuring the readiness for membership in the EU, (ii) are designed for EU member states, and imply integration in the European internal market, and (iii) the availability, quality and comparability of data on the fulfilment of these criteria is not the same in the CE countries as it is in EU member states.

REFERENCES

Backé, P., and Lindner, I., 1996, "European Monetary Union: Prospects for EU Member States and Selected Candidate Countries from Central and Eastern Europe", *Focus on Transition*, 1996/2, Österreichische Nationalbank, Vienna.

Daviddi, R., and Ilzkovitz, F., 1996, "The Eastern Enlargement of the EU: Major Challenges for Policies and Institutions of Central and East European Countries", *Congress of the EEA*, 21-24 August 1996, Istanbul.

De Grauwe, P., 1994, "The Economics of Monetary Integration", Oxford University Press, Oxford.

EBRD, 1996, Transition Report Update, EBRD, London.

ECOFIN Council, 1996, The Preparations for Stage III of EMU, Report by the ECOFIN Council to the European Council, 13 December 1996, Dublin.

Emerson, M., et.al., 1992, "One Market, One Money", Oxford University Press, Oxford.

European Commission, 1996, Report on Convergence in the EU in 1995, *European Economy, Supplement A*, Brussels.

Heinemann, F., 1995, "Central Europe and European Monetary Integration: A Strategy for Catching Up", *Intereconomics*, May/June 1995.

Hochreiter, E., 1995, "Necessary Conditions for a Successful Pursuit of a Hard Currency Strategy in an Economy in Transition", *Working Paper, Annual Meeting of the WEA*, San Diego, July 1995.

Krzak, M., 1995, "The Experience of East European Countries with Different Exchange Rate Regimes", The Vienna Institute for Comparative Economic Studies, Vienna.

Lavrač, V., and Lavrač, I., 1996, "Maastricht Convergence Criteria", *Slovenian Economic Mirror*, Institute of Macroeconomic Analysis and Development, 1996/11, Ljubljana.

Lavrač, V., and Stanovnik, P., 1995, "Monetary Policy Under a Flexible Exchange Rate in Slovenia", *Banking Newsletter, Special Issue*, Ljubljana.

Oblath, G., 1995, "Exchange Rate Policy and Exchange Rate Regimes: A Comparison of Experiences in Hungary and Some other Countries in Transition", *Working Paper, Conference "Macroeconomics of Transition"*, Budapest, June 1995.

Podkaminer, L., 1996, "Eastern Economies: Current Situation and Outlook", *The Vienna Institute Monthly Report*, No. 3, 1996, Vienna.

The Economist, 1995, *Central Europe, Survey*, London.

Vujičić, B., 1995, "Joining the EU: Open to debate", Banka International, December 1995.

Wyplosz, C., 1996, "Monetary Options for the 'Outs'", *Conference on Monetary Policy in Transition: Strategies, Instruments and Transmission Mechanisms*, Österreichische Nationalbank, 17-19 November, Vienna.

Chapter 7

Integrating Central and Eastern Europe into the European Union: The Monetary Dimension

PETER BACKÉ

1. INTRODUCTION

Over the last three years, preparations for a widening of the European Union to the East have reached a considerable momentum. In July 1997, the European Commission published Agenda 2000, a comprehensive package that „outlines in a single framework the broad perspectives for the development of the Union and its policies beyond the turn of the century, the horizontal issues related to enlargement, and the future financial framework beyond 2000 taking account of the prospect of an enlarged Union“. It also contains the Commission's opinions on the accession applications from ten Central and East European countries, namely Bulgaria, the Czech Republic, Estonia, Hungary, Latvia, Lithuania, Poland, Romania, Slovakia and Slovenia. After a decision of the European Council in Luxembourg in December 1997, accession negotiations with a number of candidate countries will presumably start in the spring of 1998.

Against the backdrop of progressing preparations for enlargement, the perspectives of Central and East European countries (CEE countries) for monetary integration have increasingly been discussed. The purpose of this paper is to look into the main points of this debate, with a focus on five advanced transition economies, namely the Czech Republic, Hungary, Poland, Slovakia and Slovenia. In order to lay the groundwork for the subsequent analysis, the study first puts the issue of monetary integration into the wider context of the CEE countries' quest for EU membership (section 2). This is followed, in section 3, by an examination of the prospects of the most advanced CEE countries for an eventual joining of Stage Three of Economic and Monetary Union (EMU). Section 4 sheds some light on the potential economic consequences an accession to the euro area would entail for the frontrunner transition countries. The main conclusions of the study are summarised in section 5. Given the broad range of unknowns about the future integration and enlargement process, the findings of this study are necessarily of a tentative nature and are very much determined by the set of assumptions upon which the analysis is based.

When scrutinising the prospects of the advanced CEE countries for joining the euro zone, one implicitly starts out from two assumptions: First, Stage Three of EMU will be implemented as envisaged. Second, at least some countries from Central and Eastern Europe have a concrete and realistic perspective for full integration into the European Union in the not too distant future.

Both of these assumptions seem to be fair and, in fact, they have become more likely recently. Still, it should be noted that while there is a clear timetable for the implementation of Stage Three of EMU, time horizons for a first wave of Eastern enlargement, let alone later rounds of EU widening, are fraught with considerable uncertainty. The following analysis takes account of this state of affairs by distinguishing between three (hypothetical) enlargement scenarios, namely, first, a best-case scenario assuming a first wave of Eastern enlargement occurring in 2002 or shortly thereafter, second, an intermediate scenario putting the date at 2005 and, third, a protraction scenario with an even later enlargement date.[1]

2. THE INTERPLAY BETWEEN ACCESSION TO THE EUROPEAN UNION AND JOINING STAGE THREE OF EUROPEAN MONETARY UNION

How does the issue of monetary integration and, in particular, the eventual inclusion of countries from Central and Eastern Europe into the euro zone fit into the overall integration endeavours of these states and, more specifically, into their preparations for membership in the European Union? In order to analyse the interplay between EU accession and a joining of the single currency area, it is useful to start out by juxtaposing the criteria for participation in Stage Three of EMU, as laid down in the Maastricht Treaty, with the set of conditions for EU membership, spelled out by the European Council in Copenhagen in June 1993. From such a comparison, the following picture emerges: The Maastricht criteria relate to stable prices, low long-term interest rates, healthy public finances as well as exchange rate stability within the framework of the European Union's exchange rate arrangements. In turn, the EU accession criteria set political standards, refer to the existence of a functioning market economy, the capacity to cope with competitive pressure and market forces within the Union and the candidate's ability to take on the obligations of membership, including the adherence to the *aims* of political, economic and monetary union. This leads to the conclusion that the two sets of criteria constitute two clearly distinct assortments of benchmarks: The Maastricht convergence criteria focus on *nominal* convergence, while the Copenhagen conditions are mainly about *real* and *institutional-legal* convergence.[2] The two criteria sets are interlinked in only one rather specific regard, namely by the obligation for applicant countries to share the objectives of EMU.

EU membership is the number one policy goal of all advanced CEE countries. Hence, preparing for the fulfilment of the Copenhagen criteria has top priority in the applicant countries' policymaking. In Agenda 2000, the Commission has made the Copenhagen criteria operational. In the individual country opinions, it has analysed to what extent the CEE countries live up to these benchmarks, taking into account information available by May 1997.[3] This has been complemented (except for the political realm) with a forward-looking approach, as the Commission has assessed what progress the applicant countries can be expected to make towards meeting the criteria over the medium term.[4] Taking corrective action on the weak spots identified in the avis would thus be the obvious underlying intention of any candidate country's EU (pre-)accession strategy. To this end, it would seem expedient to strengthen the functioning of the applicant country's market economy and to improve its competitive position with a view on smoothing the future incorporation into the EU internal market. Typically, this would relate to further developing and strengthening the financial sector, restructuring the enterprise sector, fostering competition, reforming public administrations, pension systems and health sectors as well as improving transport and communications infrastructure. Another obvious mainstay of such a strategy would be to lay a particular emphasis on intensifying, in a comprehensive manner, the adoption, implementation and enforcement of the Union's acquis; clearly, this also implies a major effort at building up the administrative and judicial capacity which is necessary for properly applying the whole range of EU norms.

EMU-related issues cut through both of these main areas, with three aspects being of special importance: the macroeconomic policy stance in general, monetary and exchange rate policies in particular, and institutional-legal matters. Monetary integration themes, thus, constitute a well-defined subset within the overall preparations for EU membership.

Several criteria for EU membership, in particular the obligation to adhere to the aims of Economic and Monetary Union in conjunction with the requirement to establish a functioning market economy and to build up the capacity to cope with competitive pressure and market forces within the Union, clearly indicate: Candidate countries have an obligation to pursue stability-oriented macroeconomic policies. Yet, the Copenhagen conditions do *not* imply that the CEE countries will have to meet the convergence criteria at the time of their EU accession or even before. Hence, fulfilling the Maastricht criteria is not a condition for joining the European Union. Indeed, at the current stage of transition, embarking on a fast-track move towards full financial convergence and, in particular, towards complete monetary convergence could prove counterproductive. Such a policy stance could distract the authorities' attention from the daunting challenge to iron out underlying structural weaknesses and/or lead to temptations to delay structural reforms (and liberalisation measures) which would have negative effects on financial indicators in the short term but are clearly important for the sustainability of the macroeconomic position in the medium to long run.[5] Also, such a strategy could possibly lead to uneven policy mixes and, in particular, to an overburdening of monetary and exchange rate policy. Both the postponement of structural reforms and lopsided combinations of policies - in particular, a disproportionately strong reliance on the exchange rate in fighting inflation - could, over the medium run, seriously impair the competitive position of a candidate country. An uneven and premature focus on financial convergence could thus lead to severe policy inconsistencies. In particular, such a posture could come into conflict with meeting the preconditions for EU membership at an early stage and, in the worst case, it could delay accession to the European Union.[6]

This leads to the conclusion that macroeconomic policies should center, as the European Council in Madrid in December 1995 put it, around "the creation of a stable economic and monetary environment", as one of "the conditions for the gradual, harmonious integration" of the candidate countries into the EU. In this vein, attention should concentrate primarily on qualitative improvements (rather than quantitative indicators), i.e. on the capacity to correct macroeconomic distortions with policies and instruments that are compatible with market mechanisms in general and EU rules in particular.[7] The Maastricht convergence criteria should be viewed, during the period leading to EU accession, as medium and longer-term points of reference for sound policymaking and not as short-run „operational“ targets.[8]

The inception of Stage Three of EMU will have some beneficial effects on the overall framework conditions for macroeconomic policymaking in the CEE countries primarily resulting from interest rate reduction and positive growth effects that are expected to be induced by the creation of the euro zone.[9] First, a decrease in interest rates resulting from EMU would reduce the interest service burden of the CEE countries, a factor that is important for countries with sizeable foreign debt.[10] Second, additional growth within euro zone countries due to monetary union will positively affect the demand for imports from the CEE countries. Given the fairly high sensitivity of the CEE countries' export performance to GDP changes in the EU, this effect could make a tangible difference for output developments in the transition countries in the medium run. Finally, the exchange rate risk in trade with the European Union, the main trading partner of the CEE countries, will become significantly less diverse through the introduction of the single currency.

Within the macroeconomic realm, advancing monetary integration within the European Union, and in particular the creation of the euro zone in 1999 will have specific policy implications for the CEE countries' monetary and exchange rate policies during the period to EU accession. Those countries that peg their currencies to baskets (Hungary, Poland, and Slovakia) will have to adjust these baskets.[11] This means replacing the Deutsche mark and, in the case of Poland, the French franc. Such technical adjustments could also offer an occasion for deliberations of a more strategic nature, namely to lower the USD share in the baskets or even to opt for an outright peg to the euro.[12] For Slovenia and the Czech Republic, the two vanguard CEE countries with a managed float regime,[13] there will be no direct need for changes as a consequence of the introduction of the euro. Nevertheless, the policymakers will have to tackle the basic issue of whether to switch - in the case of the Czech Republic: to return - to a fixed exchange rate system or to retain the float during the preaccession period. If the country opts for the former, questions of timing and regime design will have to be answered. Apart from exchange rate considerations, the euro will influence the management of official reserves held by the Central and East European central banks as well as foreign debt management.

EU accession will have further substantial ramifications for the monetary and exchange rate policies of the CEE countries. Upon joining the Union, their national central banks will participate, on a restricted basis, in the European System of Central Banks (ESCB), comprising the European Central Bank (ECB) and the national central banks (NCBs) of all EU member states. The CEE countries will be formally included into the EU-wide monetary policy dialogue, most importantly via the participation of their central bank governors in the meetings of the General Council of the ECB. It will be primarily through this body that monetary policies between euro and non-euro countries will be co-ordinated. In order to guarantee the effectiveness of monetary policy co-operation and, more generally, of overall macroeconomic policy concertation, the newly acceding member states will have to ensure that "monetary policy... be conducted with market-based instruments and… [that it] be 'efficient' in transmitting its impulses to the real economy".[14]

The room for manoeuvre in the exchange rate policy area will be limited for the newly acceding CEE countries, like for any incumbent EU Member State, as this policy field is a matter of common interest within the Community (Article 109 m TEU). The question here is whether the new member states will conduct and co-ordinate their exchange rate policies within or outside EU exchange rate arrangements.

From the inception of Stage Three of EMU, exchange rate relations between the euro area and non-participating EU countries will be governed by the Exchange Rate Mechanism 2 (ERM 2). This mechanism will rest on two pillars. Its principles and fundamental elements are spelled out in a resolution adopted by the European Council in Amsterdam in June 1997,[15] its operating procedures will be laid down in an agreement between the ECB and the NCBs of the member states outside the euro area. The prime characteristics of the mechanism are the following: Participation in ERM 2 will be voluntary; nevertheless, non-euro area countries "can be expected to join the mechanism". ERM 2 will be based on fixed but adjustable central parity rates of the participating currencies vis-à-vis the euro. There will be a standard fluctuation band of plus/minus 15 percent around the central rates of participating currencies, but formally agreed narrower bands will be possible. Intervention at the margins will in principle be automatic and unlimited, with very short-term financing available. However, the ECB as well as the participating NCBs can suspend intervention if it were to conflict with their prime objective of price stability. The flexible use of interest rates by central banks will be an important feature of the mechanism and there will be the possibility of co-ordinated intramarginal intervention.

The main intention of the ERM 2 is twofold: First, it is to ensure "the good functioning of the single market" which "must not be endangered by real exchange-rate misalignments, or by excessive nominal exchange-rate fluctuations between the euro and the other EU currencies, which would disrupt trade flows between member states". To avoid the former, realignments are to be conducted "in a timely fashion".[16] Second, it is to provide a framework for the convergence efforts of the member states outside the euro area.

From today's perspective, it appears sensible to assume that the basic institutional arrangement provided for by the ERM 2 will also be the framework of reference for the CEE countries upon their accession to the European Union.[17] There are two main reasons why the countries under review may opt for a participation in the ERM 2 from the outset of their EU membership. First, EU institutions and most member states will expect the acceding countries (just like incumbent EU countries which do not join the euro area from the outset) to participate in the mechanism. After all, the objectives to be achieved by the ERM 2 are equally valid both for incumbent member states and for newly acceding countries: Close and formalised exchange rate policy co-ordination between the euro area and the other EU countries is a vital precondition for the ultimate completion of an EU-wide monetary union and an instrumental flanking measure for a smooth working of the Community's internal market.[18] Agenda 2000 points into the same direction, though in a somewhat more general manner, not explicitly referring to the ERM 2: In the view of the Commission, the CEE countries "are expected to participate [upon accession] in an exchange rate mechanism and to avoid excessive exchange rate changes".[19]

Second, taking part in the ERM 2 will be in the economic self-interest of the CEE countries, as the balance of rights and obligations within the arrangement is more favourable than in the case of staying aside, even if necessary policy adjustments will need to be undertaken primarily by non-euro area countries. Participation in the ERM 2 should facilitate the moderation of nominal exchange rate changes of the countries outside the euro area and thereby provide a useful monetary framework for their convergence efforts.

Successful participation in an exchange rate arrangement is contingent on lasting exchange rate stability which, in turn, hinges on a sufficiently high degree of sustainable convergence of economic fundamentals. Given that the ERM 2 - resting on fixed but adjustable exchange rates and a wide standard fluctuation band - will be a reasonably flexible regime, the advanced CEE countries should, if they continue to pursue stability-oriented policies and structural reforms, be able to achieve a stage of convergence which would be satisfactory for joining and staying within the ERM 2 from the outset of their EU membership.[20] Apart from the disciplining effects of the ERM 2 itself, the multilateral policy co-ordination and surveillance schemes of Economic and Monetary Union, which will apply not only to euro-zone countries but - to a large extent - to the other EU member states as well,[21] will help to ensure that the economic and structural policies of these countries remain consistent with the requirements of participating in the Exchange Rate Mechanism. Among these schemes, in particular the convergence programs and the excessive deficit procedure can be expected to be instrumental.

Besides macroeconomic policy issues, a range of particular legal and institutional adjustment measures will be at the centre of specifically EMU-related activities within the overall preparations of the accession of Central and East European countries to the European Union. EMU embodies a set of institutional and legal provisions that pertain, in principle, to all EU member states no matter whether they are members of the euro zone or not. These provisions relate particularly to the fields of central bank independence, the maintenance of price stability as primary statutory objective of central bank policy and the prohibition of budgetary financing by central banks. A related issue is full currency convertibility, which constitutes both a precondition for joining the EU internal market and a main element of Stage One of Economic and Monetary Union.[22]

Detailed analyses on the current state of affairs with respect to these regulatory areas show that the most advanced transition countries have made major progress over past years.[23] Central bank independence, as understood by the Maastricht Treaty,[24] has been achieved to a large extent in the leading CEE countries. Price stability can be said to be the de facto prime objective of the central banks in the countries under review, although this has not been laid down unequivocally in all respective central bank laws. There is a clear awareness for the need to undertake the necessary legal changes in due time. Direct lending to government by central banks has been strictly limited in terms of amount and maturity. The goal of the advanced CEE countries is to prohibit any such lending by law in the medium term.[25] In the area of convertibility, the liberalisation of current account transactions was completed by all advanced CEE countries until end-1995. The Czech Republic, Hungary and Poland have made major progress liberalising invisible transactions and capital movements in the context of their accessions to the OECD in 1995/96. Slovakia and Slovenia can be expected to achieve a similar degree of currency exchangeability in the medium term.[26] Full or almost full liberalisation, based on broadly similar deregulation plans, is envisaged in all leading CEE countries by the year 2000.

In sum, the advanced transition economies are, by and large, well underway to adapting their regulations and institutional set-ups in the areas relevant to Economic and Monetary Union.[27] In a scenario of sustained soundness of macroeconomic policies and ongoing structural reforms, EMU-specific legal convergence should presumably not pose a major hurdle for the accession of candidate countries to the European Union.

3. WHEN WILL THE MOST ADVANCED TRANSITION COUNTRIES JOIN STAGE THREE OF EUROPEAN MONETARY UNION?

When assessing the prospective timeframes for an accession of the advanced transition countries to the euro area, two questions have to be answered: First, when will the CEE countries become eligible, from a legal point of view, to qualify for Stage Three of EMU and, second, when will candidate countries be economically ready to do so?

As for the eligibility for EMU qualification, the timing of the EU's first enlargement round to the East will be decisive - as EU membership is a necessary precondition for joining Stage Three of EMU. This may sound trivial but it is still worth being stated, as the idea of joining monetary union *before* accession to the EU has been floated at least in one of the candidate countries.[28] There is, however, no perceptible support within the Union for monetary integration to precede the other dimensions of EU integration and, above all, a full integration into the internal market of the Community.

A further constraint on the eligibility to qualify for EMU results from the convergence criteria. In this context, the exchange rate criterion has a specific bearing. Currently, this criterion requires a country's "observance of the normal fluctuation margins provided for by the Exchange Rate Mechanism of the European Monetary System, for at least two years, without devaluing against the currency of any other Member State" (Article 109 j [1] indent 3).[29] The Treaty on European Union is clear in that it demands formal "participation in the Exchange Rate Mechanism" (Article 109 j [1] indent 4), and most member states agree that actual exchange rate stability is not sufficient to fulfil this criterion. As EU membership is a precondition for joining the ERM, according to Community rules as they stand, a country can, from a legal point of view, in fact join Stage Three of EMU at the earliest two years after having acceded to the European Union.[30]

Economic readiness for EMU qualification is primarily associated with the candidate countries' actual fulfilment of the Maastricht convergence criteria. The dynamics of financial convergence hinges, in the first place, upon the economic and reform policies the candidate countries will follow during the years to come, but external framework conditions and, in particular, the stance the EU takes and will take vis-à-vis the candidate countries during the preaccession period will also play a tangible role. Since the beginning of transition, the most advanced CEE countries have made substantial progress towards macroeconomic stability. More specifically, a rather favourable picture has emerged, by and large, with respect to fiscal convergence, while - in general - monetary convergence has reached a considerably less advanced stage. General government balances have been kept in broad balance in Slovenia. The Czech Republic has recorded deficits in the order of 1 percent to 2 percent of GDP in recent years, while Poland has had deficits of around 3 percent of GDP. Hungary, in turn, brought down its formerly substantial public sector-borrowing requirement to somewhat more than 3 percent of GDP by 1996. In 1997, it recorded a deficit of 4½ percent of GDP, the increase being due to technical reasons. Slovakia's general government finances were balanced in 1995 but have deteriorated since. In 1996, a deficit of somewhat more than 1 percent of GDP was registered. A year later total expenditures surpassed revenues by more than 4 percent of GDP. Public debt-to-GDP ratios have been low in the Czech Republic, Slovakia and Slovenia, while in Poland and Hungary proportions have come down from high levels in the early 1990s to somewhat below 50 percent and 64 percent of GDP in 1997 respectively.

Inflation has been reduced to moderate but not yet to low levels in the advanced transition countries. In the Czech Republic, Slovakia and Slovenia, annual inflation rates were in the high single digits in 1996 and 1997, with no further progress towards price stability being made in 1997. In Poland and Hungary, inflation was higher - 15 and 18 percent in 1997 -, but continued to decline - by 5 percentage points in both countries in 1997. Typically, long-term interest rates are difficult to measure in the CEE countries, in particular if the long-term interest rate criterion of the Maastricht Treaty is taken as a yardstick. This results from the fact that none of the candidate countries has been in the position to issue 10-year fixed interest government bonds, which serve as reference bonds for establishing yield figures with respect to the interest rate criterion.[31] Applicability problems are even more pronounced with respect to the Maastricht exchange rate criterion, given the exclusion of non-EU members from exchange rate arrangements within the Union. As regards actual exchange rate stability, the vanguard CEE countries have made significant headway. These advances, though, have not always proved to be sustainable, as became evident in Hungary in 1994/95 when a substantial cumulative devaluation of the forint became unavoidable or in May 1997 in the Czech Republic when the fixed peg could not be maintained further and was replaced by a managed float.

Looking at future perspectives, several factors will make further substantial progress in the area of nominal convergence an arduous and presumably time-consuming undertaking. In the fiscal field, the focus is to be on assuring the sustainability of the consolidation achieved so far. To this end, there is a need to tackle existing structural problems, especially in the social security system (but also in other sectors like education). Further challenges relate to substantial prospective revenue losses from customs duties (in the wake of the reduction of tariffs and, in some cases, the phasing-out of import surcharges) as well as to potentially higher expenditures due to badly needed investment in infrastructure and environment, the costs of legal harmonisation and administrative preparation for EU membership as well as the need to eliminate financial sector weaknesses. Finally, in the wake of EU accession, the acceding countries will have to set aside substantial budgetary means to meet the co-financing requirements for EU transfers from the structural funds. Furthermore, in order to make accession fully acceptable socially, the need may arise to grant transient budgetary compensation to those groups of society, which will be most negatively affected by accession.

A significant further lowering of inflation will be a difficult task, given the persistence of several elements of cost-push inflation, the deep entrenchment of inflationary expectations, the limited scope for further fiscal tightening and potential monetary management problems resulting from capital inflows. Important cost-push factors relate to the still uncompleted liberalisation of regulated prices or their full adjustment to cost-recovery levels[32] and to nominal wage pressures, in particular if wages rapidly adjust to past inflation as a consequence of stiff inflation expectations.[33] Nominal devaluations of the exchange rate may increase inflationary pressures, both through cost and expectations channels. Imperfect competition and, generally, delays in enterprise and financial sector reform may also hamper disinflation. In the medium-term context of accession to the Community, the acceding countries will experience a substantial upward adjustment towards EU price levels for agricultural goods and food products (if the CEE countries are fully integrated into the EU's Common Agricultural Policy from the outset of their EU membership), although this may be counterbalanced by falling prices for other products. Moreover, inflation performance may be negatively affected by cost-push effects resulting from the adoption of the Community's social and environmental standards.

Progress at the inflation front will be decisive for a country's perspectives for moving towards low long-term interest rates and its ability to participate in the Exchange Rate Mechanism of the European Union. Bringing long-term interest rates in line with the Maastricht benchmark will require a country's overall convergence process to be perceived as sustainable by the financial markets. This also includes a positive assessment of a country's ability and readiness to react to potential asymmetric shocks in the future. Given current economic structures and the policy instruments and procedures in place in the CEE countries, the potential for country-specific disturbances is still substantial and the possibilities to respond to such shocks are as yet limited in several respects. This state of affairs can change only gradually, implying that interest rate convergence is still fairly far off for the candidate countries from Central and Eastern Europe.

This also suggests that even the most advanced CEE countries will, in all likelihood, need a certain degree of nominal exchange rate flexibility for some years to come, in order to retain (or regain) sustainable current account positions and to cope with potential or actual swings in capital flows (in the aftermath of the liberalisation of capital movements).

Furthermore, as the vanguard transition countries set out to move from moderate towards low inflation levels, the simultaneous meeting of the inflation and the exchange rate criteria may pose a policy dilemma. Regularly, these countries experience a real appreciation of their exchange rates which appears to correspond to a continuing appreciation of equilibrium real exchange rates due to the unfolding efficiency gains resulting from institutional reforms and structural change as well as due to greater capital mobility.[34] Real appreciation can either be taken through nominal appreciation or result from accepting higher inflation.[35]

Against this backdrop of obstacles and challenges, what time horizons could be considered realistic for the advanced CEE countries' meeting of the Maastricht convergence criteria? Under the assumption of appropriate economic and structural policies and the absence of major negative shocks, sustainable compliance with the fiscal criteria could be attainable within a period of up to five years. Monetary convergence appears to be a significantly more remote perspective; it could probably be achieved within seven to ten years. Convergence would tend to be faster in a best-case enlargement scenario and slower in a protraction scenario, as EU membership would increase the growth potential of the CEE countries and thus facilitate macroeconomic and structural adjustment.

In sum, the most likely answer to the question of when the most advanced candidate countries will qualify for Stage Three of EMU is: Presumably a few years after having become EU members. If EU membership comes in 2002/2003, the first country or countries from Central and Eastern Europe may join the euro zone in 2004/2005 and the others (or most of them) may follow during the second half of the next decade. In this scenario, the advanced transition economies would become economically ready for participation in the euro area once they are already eligible, from a legal point of view, to do so and, consequently, legal eligibility would not be a problem in the process of monetary integration of the advanced transition countries. Alternatively, an enlargement in 2005 would presumably imply a joining of the euro zone by the first country or countries from Central and Eastern Europe in 2007, thereby somewhat delaying EMU membership for a country or countries having achieved nominal convergence already around the middle of the next decade, but not for the other countries included in a first wave of an Eastern enlargement of the EU. In turn a protraction scenario in which enlargement takes place even later would most likely also slow down monetary integration between the EU and the advanced transition countries.

How does this assessment fit in with the positions and timetables of candidate countries on joining Stage Three of EMU? All of the most advanced transition countries base their EMU aspirations on a best-case scenario of their accession to the European Union, as they hope to join the Community in the year 2002. All advanced transition countries wish to accede to the euro area as soon as possible. Poland and Hungary have stated for some time that they envisage joining Stage Three of EMU only some time after their EU accession. Both countries have very similar target dates for joining Stage Three of EMU: They aim at acceding to the euro zone within 8 to 10 years.[36]

The Czech authorities have not set a specific target date for joining Stage Three of EMU, given the unclear timing of their accession to EU, but they have, until recently, declared their intention to meet the Maastricht criteria by the year 2000.[37] This target date has been in line with a perception that joining EMU will not necessarily have to come later than accession to the European Union and that a simultaneous joining of the EU and of the euro area may well be a viable option.[38] From the turn of 1996/1997, the Czech position has begun to change. Since then, not all government members have continued to fully share the view that the year 2000 is still a realistic time horizon for the fulfilment of the convergence criteria.[39] The recent move to a managed float, after massive pressures on the koruna, and the concomitant depreciation of the Czech currency has apparently contributed to a more general perception that the formerly announced target date is out of reach: In July 1997, central bank governor Tosovsky declared that the Czech Republic, "like other Central European reform countries", was interested in joining Stage Three of EMU in the course of its Western integration, but at the current stage achieving EU membership had top priority. Even if economic development were smooth and stable, it would take "a long time" before the Czech Republic and other euro zone candidates from Central and Eastern Europe would fulfil the Maastricht criteria.[40]

The Slovenian position, in turn, appears to be based on the perception that, in principle, three options may be available for the country, namely joining EMU either before, or at the time of or, alternatively, only after acceding to the EU. Slovenia has not adopted an explicit target date for joining the euro area but, similar to the earlier Czech stance, the country intends to fulfil the Maastricht convergence criteria by the year 2000.

In Slovakia, the position of the authorities is not fully uniform: While the prime minister stated in the fall of 1996 that the country would meet the Maastricht convergence criteria by the year 2000, this view is apparently not shared by all Slovak authorities.[41]

4. THE ECONOMIC CONSEQUENCES OF JOINING STAGE THREE OF EMU FOR CANDIDATE COUNTRIES: WHAT FACTORS WILL BE AT WORK?

The assessments of the economic consequences of EMU have shown a considerable degree of divergence, resulting from the fact that Economic and Monetary Union has no historic precedents. Any assessment is further complicated by the fact that costs and benefits cannot be easily offset against each other, as they are partly of a macroeconomic and partly of a microeconomic nature and as, moreover, both short-term and longer-term factors will be at work. The main effects of EMU on a country joining the euro zone[42] are

- reduced transaction costs (due to the cessation of currency exchange transactions and hedging costs),
- lower costs of financial services (due to increased competition within the financial sector),
- positive effects resulting from stable exchange rates, though paired with substantial initial adjustment costs for soft-currency countries and
- dynamic growth effects resulting from a more efficient allocation of capital (as a consequence of disappearing transaction costs) and increased accumulation of real capital (as a consequence of falling yields on financial capital).

How could these factors affect the growth potential of CEE countries joining Stage Three of monetary union?[43]

Typically, transaction costs are comparatively high in smaller and less developed member countries whose currency is not used much for intra-EU transactions. These characteristics relate well to the most advanced transition countries (perhaps, given its size, with the partial exception of Poland). Studies in Hungary have shown that transactions costs are extraordinarily high in that country,[44] and it is plausible that this holds true for other advanced reform countries as well. This is probably due to the ongoing transition process, and transaction costs will go down to more normal but still comparatively high levels as the transformation to a market economy moves on. By joining the euro zone, countries from Central and Eastern Europe could further reduce transaction costs significantly, thus reaping a tangible welfare gain.

Intensified competition in a country's banking sector as a consequence of joining the euro zone could lead to a lowering of interest rates, which in turn would stimulate investment and growth. How much interest rates would go down is difficult to predict even for incumbent EU countries.[45] Obviously, from today's perspective, it is virtually impossible to make a forecast of the impact of a candidate country's joining Stage Three of EMU on this country's interest rate levels. What can be said is that this impact will be influenced by the achievements in the field of financial sector reform, restructuring and competition in the sector when a country accedes to the euro zone. In general, progress in this area has been dynamic in most of the advanced transition economies and one may expect further substantial improvements in the efficiency of financial intermediation in the vanguard countries over the next years.

By irrevocably fixing exchange rates, monetary union will do away with exchange rate turbulences within the single currency zone, turbulences which have tended to cause losses in output and employment, in particular in the EU hard-currency countries. On the other hand, giving up the exchange rate instrument would make the soft currency countries undergo fairly significant adjustment processes, which would have a perceptible negative growth impact for several years. Here again, it is close to impossible to estimate the size of these adjustment costs, because one cannot predict how actively the countries of Central and Eastern Europe will actually use changes in the nominal exchange rate as a policy instrument during the years before joining the euro zone. As judged against the backdrop of the benchmarks set by the inflation and interest rate criteria of monetary union, substantial adjustments will have to be undertaken already in the preparatory phase of joining the euro area.

In order to facilitate and speed up adjustment and to lower its cost, it will be important for the advanced reform countries to develop an institutional framework and a set of procedures which are conducive to ensure real wage flexibility at an early stage.[46] Appropriate co-ordination of macroeconomic policies will also have beneficial effects.

Turning to dynamic growth effects related to capital allocation and accumulation, there again is a fairly high degree of uncertainty about the magnitudes of associated additional growth potentials. Still, such effects appear to be more pronounced for countries which have not yet exploited their efficiency potential fully - a feature which is and will, for quite some time, be characteristic of countries from Central and Eastern Europe.

In a longer-term perspective these dynamic effects are the most important ones, suggesting a positive contribution to growth for all euro zone members. In the short to medium run, for soft-currency countries, adjustment costs may compensate or even overcompensate the gains from the reduction of transaction costs and the lowering of interest rates.

Other aspects which will influence the economic performance of the advanced transition countries as a consequence of joining Stage Three of EMU are first, the determination of the conversion rates between the transition economies' national currencies and the euro and, second, the issue of potential country-specific economic disturbances. As to the latter, the main questions are: Will future euro zone countries from Central and Eastern Europe likely be exposed to asymmetric shocks and, if so, what adjustment mechanisms will these countries have at their disposal to adjust to such shocks? In general, the likelihood of asymmetric shocks will probably diminish over time for the countries of Central and Eastern Europe.[47] Nevertheless, for contingency reasons, it would be helpful to have appropriate wage determination mechanisms in place in order to contain potential adjustment costs, all the more so as cross-border migration is not a viable alternative: The readiness to migrate does not seem to be very pronounced in the advanced transition countries and, even if it were, incumbent EU member states would very much dislike such an adjustment response. Thus, setting up appropriate wage formation mechanisms could help mitigate EMU-related adjustment costs on two accounts, namely those initial costs that result for soft-currency countries from doing without nominal exchange rate changes and costs related to potential future asymmetric shocks.[48]

5. CONCLUSIONS

This study has looked at the monetary dimension of integrating the advanced CEE countries into the European Union. The main conclusions of the study are:

First, at the current stage, it would seem expedient for candidate countries from Central and Eastern Europe to base their integration efforts on comprehensive EU accession strategies. Efforts should focus on strengthening market-economy mechanisms and improving competitive positions as well as on legal harmonisation, thereby tackling the weak spots identified in the Commission's opinions on the CEE countries' membership applications. EMU-related issues constitute a fairly specific subset of themes within the overall preparations for EU membership, with three aspects being of special importance: the macroeconomic policy stance in general, monetary and exchange rate policies in particular, and institutional-legal matters.

Second, under the assumption of appropriate economic and structural policies and the absence of major negative shocks, the vanguard transition countries may reach sustainable fiscal convergence within a period of up to five years. Monetary convergence appears to be a significantly more remote perspective; it could probably be achieved within seven to ten years. From a legal point of view, joining Stage Three of EMU is possible at the earliest two years after attaining EU membership. If, in a best-case scenario, the most advanced transition countries accede to the European Union in 2002/2003, the first CEEC or CEE countries may join the euro zone in 2004/05 and the others (or most of them) could possibly follow during the second half of the next decade.

Third, the joining of the euro zone will affect the CEE countries' growth potential in several ways. Transaction costs will presumably be reduced significantly, thus implying a tangible welfare gain. Intensified competition in the banking sector could lead to a lowering of interest rates, which in turn would stimulate investment and growth. The irrevocable fixing of exchange rates will eliminate output losses in hard-currency countries stemming from exchange rate turbulences, but also make the soft-currency countries undergo fairly significant adjustment processes with a perceptible negative impact on growth for several years. From today's perspective, it is hardly possible, though, to estimate the size of the two latter effects for future euro zone members from Central and Eastern Europe. Much the same is true of dynamic growth effects, the most important effects in the longer run. Still, such effects seem more pronounced for countries, which have not yet exploited their efficiency potential fully and thus presumably also for the CEE countries. Appropriate wage determination mechanisms will be instrumental in mitigating the potential costs of participating in the euro zone.

NOTES

1 For the preconditions for an early first round of EU enlargement to the East and for the problems related to further waves of Eastern widening see Backé and Lindner (1996).
2 Parameters that relate to real convergence (and, in particular, competitiveness) are also included in the Maastricht Treaty, but only as secondary criteria assisting an assessment of the sustainability of financial convergence.
3 For a detailed review of the central bank related issues of the opinions see Horváth et al. (1997).
4 As for the political criteria, the Commission's assessment is solely based on the situation prevailing in early summer 1997.
5 In this context, one could think of areas like pension reform, continual (rule-based) adjustment of utility prices in line with cost-recovery levels, enterprise reform or the liberalisation of the capital account.
6 The question of what time horizons could be considered realistic for the advanced CEE countries' meeting of the Maastricht convergence criteria will be scrutinised in greater detail in section 3 which examines the prospects of the most advanced CEE countries for an eventual joining of Stage Three of EMU.
7 See also Pearce (1995).
8 See Backé and Lindner (1996) as well as European Commission (1997), section 3.3 of the opinions.
9 For a more detailed discussion of the effects of Stage Three of EMU see section 4.
10 See statement of the Hungarian central bank (*Reuters*, December 24, 1996).
11 Those advanced transition countries that have opted for a peg have typically linked their national currencies to a basket (with the exception of Poland, which had a USD peg in the early phases of transition). Apart from this common feature, exchange rate regimes have differed between individual peg countries in three main respects, namely as to the kind of the peg, the width of fluctuation bands and the composition of baskets. First, Poland and Hungary have had a crawling peg regime since 1991 and 1995 with preannounced monthly devaluations rates of 1 and 1.1 percent respectively. Slovakia, in turn, has retained the fixed peg it had taken over from former Czechoslovakia, and the exchange rate has been nominally stable since mid-1993. Second, Hungary has a relatively small intervention band of plus/minus 2.25 percent; the Polish and the Slovak bands are wider (both plus/minus 7 percent). Third, the Hungarian basket contains a 70 percent DEM and a 30 percent USD share. In the Slovak basket, the Deutsche mark has a weight of 60 percent and the U.S. dollar a 40 percent share. The Polish basket, in turn, is composed of five currencies (45 percent USD, 35 percent DEM, 10 percent GBP, 5 percent FRF, 5 percent CHF). For recent changes of the band and the baskets see Radzyner and Riesinger (1996) and Backé and Lindner (1996).
12 See Radzyner and Riesinger (1996), Backé and Lindner (1996).
13 Slovenia opted for a managed float in 1991 when it reached monetary sovereignty and has maintained this regime since. The tolar's nominal depreciation has remained limited since 1991. Until recently, the Czech Republic sticked to the fixed peg that had been in place in former Czechoslovakia. In May 1997, the koruna came under massive pressure, eventually rendering the fixed peg unsustainable and giving way to a managed float. After losing 10 percent of its value against the DEM when the floating regime was introduced, the Czech koruna has been largely stable in nominal terms against the German currency (although so far at the price of high interest rates, which may not be sustainable in the longer run).
14 European Commission (1997). The key to improve the efficiency of monetary policy is further financial sector reform. In this context, the Commission sees a particular need to

strengthen the competition in the banking sector, to go ahead with bank privatisation, to proceed with the development of financial markets and to solve the bad-loan problem in the banking sector.

15 European Council Amsterdam (1997), Annex II.

16 European Council Amsterdam (1997), Annex II.

17 This is not to imply that any future change in the mechanism is necessarily ruled out; clearly, the ERM 2 will be open to modifications in the light of practical experience. However, even if there are alterations, the main principles of the arrangement will in all likelihood remain untouched which, in turn, limits the scope for change basically to details. In particular, it is hard to see how the ERM 2 could be made tangibly more flexible without, at the same time, impairing its role to limit exchange rate fluctuations (which could endanger the functioning of the single market). In the same vein, intervention asymmetries can barely be watered down, while at the same time preserving the ECB's objective of price stability. Hence, at the present stage, the only reasonable working assumption is that the mechanism's basic elements will stay in place for the foreseeable future.

18 This position is also reflected in the principles of the ERM 2, as defined in Amsterdam ("Member states with a derogation can be expected to join the mechanism.") In the case of the CEE countries, incumbent member states could refer to one of the Copenhagen criteria in order to support their position, namely to the obligation to adhere to the aims of Economic and Monetary Union as a condition for EU membership.

19 European Commission (1997). In the individual country opinions, there is a further reference to exchange rate policy co-ordination within „a mechanism yet to be decided". Apparently, the Commission has found it premature to specifically mention the ERM 2 in Agenda 2000 and there are good reasons for the Commission's cautious wording: The principles, objectives and main characteristics of the ERM 2 were approved only very shortly before Agenda 2000 was finalised and the mechanism's operating procedures are still to be laid down. Thus, the future acquis in the exchange rate policy field has not been fully established and the specified features have been determined only very recently. Furthermore, as mentioned above, some features of the ERM 2 might be developed further in the period up to a first round of Eastern enlargement. Finally, none of the incumbent member states (nor any of the applicant countries) have formally adopted elaborate positions on the exchange rate arrangements after enlargement, while the ECB (which will have a key role to play in these matters) has not yet been set up. Against this backdrop, it appears perfectly sensible for the Commission to have maintained, in Agenda 2000, a relatively low profile on the issue.

20 Participation in the ERM 2 will alter the exchange rate regimes of the CEE countries in several ways. Changing parity rates will no longer be possible unilaterally, but will require common consent. The latter is also true for the setting of initial parity rates. Intervention constraints will change. Still existing baskets will be replaced by a peg to the euro and there will be no room for crawling pegs. Slovenia and the Czech Republic will have to give up their floating regimes, at the latest when joining the ERM 2.

21 EMU policy co-ordination and surveillance provisions, as laid down in the Maastricht Treaty, have been complemented by the Stability and Growth Pact. This pact is primarily about ensuring budgetary discipline in future euro zone countries (and thus mostly applicable only to member states participating in Stage Three of EMU), but it will also provide for a strengthened surveillance and co-ordination of budget positions and for a speedier and more clearly defined excessive deficit procedure pertaining to all EU member states (for details see the Resolution on the Stability and Growth Pact, European Council

Amsterdam (1997), Annex I). As regards the surveillance regulations of the Maastricht Treaty, the array of sanctions of the excessive budget procedure will remain limited for non-euro zone countries; however, the liberalisation of capital movements in the context of EU accession will in any case provide a strong incentive for fiscal prudence.

22 The first phase of EMU, which was approved by the European Council in June 1989, focused primarily on two areas, namely on the liberalisation of capital movements and on an enhanced co-ordination of the economic, financial and monetary policies of the EU countries.

23 For central bank independence, including direct central bank lending to government, see Radzyner and Riesinger (1997); for convertibility issues see Backé (1996). See also European Commission (1997) and Horváth et al. (1997).

24 Article 107 TEU states that "neither the ECB, nor a national central bank, nor any member of their decision-making bodies shall seek or take instructions from Community institutions or bodies, from any government of a Member State or from any other body."

25 It should be noted however that a draft amendment to the Slovak central bank law, adopted by the government in the fall of 1997, would, if accepted by parliament, curb the bank's independence and raise the limit on central bank financing of the budget.

26 In fact, since late 1996, Slovakia has taken some measures to further liberalise capital account transactions, in particular inward capital movements.

27 This assessment would have to be qualified for Slovakia, if there were a setback in central bank legislation or in any other of the EMU-related legal approximation areas.

28 At the European Council meeting in Dublin in December 1996, Slovenia's Prime Minister Drnovšek said that "Slovenia will do its best to join monetary union as soon as possible, perhaps even before full EU membership" (*Slovenia Weekly*, January 11, 1997).

29 For countries joining the euro zone after 1999, the exchange rate criterion will relate to the ERM 2.

30 In order to remove this specific constraint, it has been proposed, in the academic discussion, to change the Union's rules so as to render possible a participation of the most advanced transition economies in the ERM *prior* to EU accession (see Bofinger 1996). However, judging from past experience with European monetary integration, prospects for putting such a proposal into practice appear to be fairly low.

31 Nevertheless, the most advanced transition countries have made major headway in moving into longer government debt maturities, and in some countries five-year fixed interest state bonds have been issued. However, the secondary market for these securities still tends to be thin and fairly illiquid.

32 Typically, this is the case for the areas of energy and other utility services as well as rents. Progress already achieved towards a full adjustment or a liberalisation of these prices differs from applicant country to applicant country.

33 Furthermore, inflation performance may be negatively affected by attempts to increase (compressed) profit margins, especially if and when a country experiences a strong and sustained recovery of domestic demand. In addition, price levels may be pushed upwards as a result of changes in the systems of indirect taxes.

34 During the first years of transition, real appreciation also concurred with the gradual correction of the initial undervaluation that resulted from the drastic devaluations of most Central and East European currencies at the outset of transition. By 1996, this overshooting had been corrected, as real exchange rates for most advanced CEE countries roughly came to „the neighbourhood of equilibrium“ (see Halpern and Wyplosz 1996).

35 It is not quite clear what mechanisms interlink structural-institutional change and the real exchange rate in the transformation context. Standard adjustment mechanisms, as the Balassa-Samuelson effect, resting on above-average productivity gains in the tradables

sector combined with wage equalisation across sectors, or approaches based on different factor endowments (as put forward i.a. by Bhagwati), appear to have limited power to explain the evolution of the real exchange rate during the transition to a market economy. For a more detailed discussion see Rosati (1996) and also Grafe and Wyplosz (1997) who explore alternative potential linkages.

36 For Poland see Kolodko (1997), whose timetable was basically reaffirmed by Foreign Minister Rosati recently (see *vwd Mittel- und Osteuropa*, May 6, 1997); for Hungary see e.g. Surányi (1997).

37 In the case of the exchange rate criterion, the point of reference would obviously be a sufficient degree of actual nominal exchange rate stability. The same qualification appears to hold true for Slovenia (see below).

38 This suggests that, in the view of the Czech authorities, there is a chance for overcoming the legal obstacle with respect to the exchange rate criterion.

39 See e.g. statement of the former Industry and Trade Minister Dlouhy, who sensed that the cutting of inflation did not proceed successfully enough for the Maastricht requirement to be met by the end of the century (*CTK*, January 14,1997).

40 *Handelsblatt*, July 4, 1997.

41 See *Reuters*, September 28, 1996, October 16 and 30, 1996. In Estonia, the central bank governor announced in mid 1997 that the country would be ready to join the euro area in five years' time (*Reuters*, June 18, 1997). In most other CEE countries, the issue of a future accession to Stage Three of EMU has not entered the political agenda.

42 The following sections draw on Baumgartner et al. (1997) and, in particular, on section 3 of that report (Breuss 1997).

43 This paper concentrates upon scrutinising the effects on growth potentials resulting from an accession to the euro zone. This is not to say that joining Stage Three would not be attractive for the CEE countries for other reasons as well, considering that such a move would further improve credibility (thereby i.a. lowering possibly existing interest rate premia) and rid these countries of monetary management problems (e.g. related to capital inflows).

44 Inotai and Palánkai (1994).

45 Breuss (1997) assumes that interest rates will fall by 1 percentage point in all euro zone countries.

46 Experience so far with real wage flexibility has been divergent in the candidate countries: In several advanced transition economies, real wage growth outstripping productivity advances is one of the causes for the persistence of inflation and the problems at the external front. On the other hand, Hungary was in fact able to engineer a substantial lowering of real wages in 1995 and 1996, albeit under exceptional circumstances.

47 External shocks will presumably become less probable, as traded goods structures continue to converge with those of the core countries of the European Union and foreign trade links remain concentrated upon the Community. In the field of domestic shocks, there will no longer be asymmetric shocks from monetary policy (apart from initial variations due to the divergent functioning of monetary transmission mechanisms in individual countries) and shocks from fiscal policy will be less likely (as the excessive deficit procedure and the Stability and Growth Pact become fully applicable).

48 In fact, improving wage determination mechanisms will already be a must in the pre-EU accession stage, so as to foster the competitiveness of candidate countries.

REFERENCES

Backé, P., 1996, "Progress towards Convertibility in Central and Eastern Europe", *Focus on Transition*, 1 (1).

Backé, P., and Lindner, I., 1996, "European Monetary Union: Prospects for EU Member States and Selected Candidate Countries from Central and Eastern Europe", *Focus on Transition*, 1 (2).

Baumgartner, J., et.al., 1997, Auswirkungen der Wirtschafts- und Währungsunion, Österreichisches Institut für Wirtschaftsforschung.

Bofinger, P., 1996, "Vertiefung und Osterweiterung der Europäischen Union: Optionen für die Währungsunion der Zwanzig", *DIW Vierteljahresheft*, 65 (1).

Breuss, F., 1997, "Die gesamtwirtschaftlichen Auswirkungen der WWU in Modellsimulationen", *Baumgartner* (1997).

European Commission, 1997, Agenda 2000.

European Council Amsterdam, 1997, Presidency Conclusions.

Grafe, C., and Wyplosz, Ch., 1997, "The Real Exchange Rate in Transition Economies", *Paper presented to the Third Dubrovnik Conference on Transition Economies.*

Halpern, L., and Wyplosz, Ch., 1996, "Equilibrium Exchange Rates in Transition Economies", *IMF Working Paper,* No. 125.

Holzhacker, H., 1997, "Ab 2007 Euro vermutlich auch in Osteuropa", *Osteuropa Perspektiven*, April, 1997.

Horváth, Á., Dvorsky, S., Backé, P., and Radzyner, O., 1997, "EU Opinions - The Qualifying Round for Applicants", *Focus on Transition*, 2 (2).

Inotai, A., and Palánkai, T., 1994, "Magyarország csatlakozása az Európai Unióhoz", *Közgazdasági Szemle*, 41 (10).

Kolodko, G., 1997, Euro 2006 - Poland on the Path to European Union Currency, mimeo.

Pearce, J., 1995, "Comments to "Association Agreements and Central Europe's Trade with the European Union", in: Mizsei, Kálmán and Rudka, Andrzej, From Association to Accession: The Impact of the Association Agreements on Central Europe's Trade and Integration with the European Union, Institute for East West Studies, The Windsor Group.

Radzyner, O., and Riesinger, S., 1996, "Exchange Rate Policy in Transition - Developments and Challenges in Central and Eastern Europe", *Focus on Transition*, 1(1).

Radzyner, O., and Riesinger, S., 1997, "Central Bank Independence in Transition: Legislation and Reality in Central and Eastern Europe", *Focus on Transition*, 2 (1).

Rosati, D., 1996, "Exchange rate policies during transition from plan to market", *Economics of Transition*, 4 (1).

Surányi, Gy., 1997, *Lecture at Euromoney Conference* in Vienna on January 21-22 on the implications of EMU for Hungary.

Chapter 8

Echoing the European Monetary Integration in the Czech Republic

OLDRICH DEDEK

1. EASTERN AND WESTERN TRANSITIONS

The end of the 1980s was a milestone in the history of the Czech Republic and other Central European countries (CE countries), which shrugged off bureaucratic planning systems and soon afterwards worked out their blueprints of economic reform. These newly born CE transition economies embarked on a painful transformation from a command to a market oriented system. One could observe a great variety of approaches in handling macroeconomic stabilisation, privatisation or restructuring of state-owned enterprises. The speed in fulfilling reform objectives also differed with a couple of setbacks scattered around transition paths. The diversity in both approaches and outcomes shared, however, a common denominator which was the establishment of permanent political and economic links with developed market democracies. Among them, prospective membership in the European Union was declared a top-level priority for the sake of securing the long-term interests of CE nationals.

In fact, the European Union is a moving target, which is undergoing far-reaching economic and institutional reforms as well. The break-up of the Soviet bloc occurred just about the time of intensive political negotiations leading to the Maastricht Treaty (agreed in December 1991). This Treaty was another milestone in European history. It provided the legal basis for the consummation of European Monetary Union, which would deliver participating states a common currency, managed from one monetary centre. By agreeing upon specific convergence criteria, the Treaty also outlined the transition towards it. By all standards, the transition requirements in terms of the Maastricht criteria, as well as those reinforced in the Stabilisation Pact (reached in the Dublin summit in December 1996) have been and still are hard to comply with for many EU economies. No wonder, therefore, that the project of a single currency has been permanently surrounded by large controversies. Seen from this perspective, the term 'transition economy' might be thus given a much broader geographic background.

The group of CE economies appear to live rather far away from the heated disputes over the costs and benefits of a single currency. Many economists would agree that this fact reflects the natural sequence of events. After all, CE countries are just standing in the queue for EU membership and in the meantime are expected to address some more elementary issues related to their 'Eastern transition': complete the institutional framework for a liberal market economy, keep up the momentum in privatisation, strengthen parliamentary democracies, harmonise legislation with EU standards and many other tasks.[1] The spell of their waiting time for EU accession will also largely depend on how the EU itself handles the trade-off between deepening and widening.[2] Any serious setback in getting the single currency off the ground may cause even more waiting.

So even in the case of an optimistic scenario of joining the EU at an early stage in the next century, CE countries are highly unlikely to participate in the take-off stage of EMU. This outlook seems to give some support to the view that disputes related to the 'Western transition' are too forward-looking for policymaking in CE countries. Therefore, one might be inclined to conclude that the best thing for them to do is to assume, for the time being, the role of a careful observer.[3]

The above conclusion, however, seems to be unduly inflicted with the administrative line of reasoning. Is it really the case that CE countries can simply divide the time axis into a 'before period' confined to problems specific to the 'Eastern transition' and an 'after period' in which the issues of the 'Western transition' will have matured for a serious debate? This paper will argue that there are a number of overlaps between the two transitions. Inspired by the experience of the Czech economy, it elaborates on the point that a sustainable growth in a small and open CE economy must be backed by a high degree of macroeconomic discipline, in many respects not so much unlike that embedded in the Maastricht convergence criteria.

2. DO CENTRAL EUROPEAN COUNTRIES FORM A PART OF AN OPTIMUM CURRENCY AREA?

From the theoretical point of view, the accession into a monetary union means a deliberate selection between two options: either a country relinquishes the national currency, which results in the loss of a sovereign exchange rate and monetary policies or it retains the national currency keeping thus the discretion in setting the above policies. The theory of an optimum currency area gives some clues about the costs and benefits of the two alternatives. To this aim, it recommends running a set of standardised tests - openness to trade, diversity of production, mobility of labour, wage and price flexibility, frequency of asymmetric shocks - which should make it clear whether the economic welfare of a country is improved by joining a monetary union or whether a country will suffer from losing important policy tools.[4]

Table 1. The Quantitative Size Structure of NAFTA and EU

NAFTA		USA (100.0); Canada (10.1); Mexico (4.7)
EU	Present members	Germany (100.0); France (70.2); Italy (64.7); UK (55.1); Spain (29.3); Netherlands (16.7); Sweden (12.7); Belgium (11.5); Austria (9.5); Denmark (7.7); Finland (7.1); Greece (4.0); Portugal (3.6); Ireland (2.8)
	Prospective CE members	Poland (3.4); Hungary (1.6); Czech Republic (1.5); Slovenia (0.8); Slovakia (0.7)

Note: The number in parenthesis after the country's name shows the percentage size of the country's GDP vis-à-vis the GDP of the leading country in the region (year 1992 in constant 1990 US dollars).
Source: United Nations Yearbook, Fortieth issue, 1995.

Following the hints of the theory of an optimum currency area, there are robust pieces of empirical evidence, which make CE countries an objective candidate for the EMU membership. Table 1 shows that in terms of their economic strength CE countries are small economies. Approximately, Poland is less than 4 percent, the Czech Republic and Hungary less than 2 percent, Slovakia and Slovenia less than 1 percent of the German GDP. The economic potential of every single CE country is definitely insufficient to influence the power structure within the EU. This feature remains still valid even if these countries are viewed as one bloc, not saying that a temptation to speak in one official voice would be opposed by a widespread aversion to resurrect any appearance of the former Council of Mutual Economic Aid.[5]

Table 2. Indicators of Export-Import Openness for Selected Countries

Country	Exports	Imports
Czech Republic	51	56
Hungary	35	37
Poland	25	25
Slovakia	63	59
Slovenia	59	60
Austria	38	37
Belgium	71	65
Greece	18	27
Portugal	28	35
Sweden	40	35

Note: The table shows the export-import of goods and services as a proportion of GDP (as of 1995 in purchasing prices).
Source: Nachtigal (1997).

Table 2 supplies another piece of important evidence. It shows that CE countries are small as well as very open economies. The highest share of both exports and imports on GDP was reached by Slovenia and Slovakia, amounting to about 60 percent of their GDP. The Czech Republic's ratio of about 50 percent is slightly less but still surpassing that of comparable countries like Austria, Sweden, Portugal or Greece. The Hungarian and Polish ratios are matching those of the comparable West European countries.

Moreover, the collapse of the CMEA spurred a massive reorientation of trade flows from the East to Western markets. According to Hrncir (1997), in 1995 almost two thirds of Central and East European exports went to the Western economies, compared with 43 percent in 1989. The most important and the most dramatic part of this shift has been the trade with the EU. Compared to only about one third of Central and East European exports in 1989, the EU accounted for more than 60 percent in 1995.

Spectacular progress has been achieved in the area of capital flows. Within the span of several years, the CE economies succeeded in opening up their economies to a degree of capital mobility that took most industrial countries several decades to realise.[6] This rapid opening reflected however, not only the rapid pace of economic reforms, but also the radically different conditions in today's world financial markets that make capital controls far more difficult and costly to maintain. The EU is the main country of origin for the inflow of foreign capital that takes a very active part in privatisation, joint ventures and restructuring processes which are going on, on a large scale, in CE economies.

The concepts of synchronisation of business cycles and frequency of asymmetric shocks are considered another important determinant of the costs of entering a monetary union. In this respect, transition CE economies lack a sufficient track record that could be used to illustrate the relevance of the point. As a matter of fact, these economies have not yet gone through a typical business cycle, all of them rather experienced a kind of unique 'transformation recession' caused by deep systemic changes. Similarly, the majority of asymmetric shocks had their origin in the collapse of the communist rule, including the most serious ones as the break-up of the Soviet Union, German reunification, war in Yugoslavia and, particularly important in the context of the Czech economy, the dissolution of former Czechoslovakia. There is, however, a growing consensus that both peaks and troughs of the business cycles in major EU countries do have an increasing influence on growth rates in the CE region.

Strong empirical evidence thus points to the conclusion that although the CE region was for a long time insulated from the West European economic integration, within a relatively short period of time it succeeded in establishing firm links with the EU common market. From this perspective, CE countries do not lack strong incentives to participate in all undertakings that EU countries have designed and are promoting for the sake of removing barriers to mutual trade and fostering economic co-operation. In other words, however sceptical one might be about the current readiness of CE countries to become members of EMU, the intrinsic potential to do so is definitely there.[7]

3. EXCHANGE RATE STABILITY IS BENEFICIAL FOR SMALL AND OPEN CENTRAL EUROPEAN ECONOMIES

Now, the issue of EMU membership can be approached from two directions. The 'band-wagon' argument would continue stressing the point that the economic region composed of CE countries never ceased to be a natural part of the European economic area even though for a long time it was deprived of assistance in integrating processes occurring there. So as a corollary, if Western Europe has opted, for whatever reasons, for a deep monetary co-operation maturing in the idea of a single currency and if this should become the backbone of further European integration then there is no other choice for CE economies than to 'climb on the band-wagon' and take an active part in the undertaking. By the same token, if all perspective EMU members are expected to comply with a set of convergence criteria, there is no other way for CE economies than to strive for the same degree of monetary and fiscal discipline.

A practical consequence of the band-wagon view of EMU membership is the feeling that it is an external authority that is pressing for submission to the given policy constraints. This flavour of foreign involvement then may give legitimacy to the question why the externally imposed notion of low inflation, sound governmental finances and exchange rate stability fits in the framework of policy objectives convenient for a CE transition economy? And if so then why now? Is it genuine economic reasoning or rather unwarranted political ambitions? After all, the Maastricht criteria are not the EU accession criteria. By and large, the band-wagon view is likely to stimulate an impression that the EMU qualifying requirements should be understood as a longer-term objective whose fulfilment can wait until a CE country sees the EMU membership a hot issue for political debate.[8]

The alternative 'self-imposition' argument sees the problem from the inside of CE economies. The bottom line is the fundamental feature of being small and open that then invokes numerous benefits of keeping the exchange rate stable. The policy of a stable exchange rate, however, is not a free lunch. Its credibility depends on whether it is backed by a proper degree of macroeconomic discipline: inflation has to be kept under control, government must not run excessive budget deficits, a country should avoid larger internal or external imbalances.

The implication is that in order to reap the benefits of a stable currency the country ends up with a need to observe a sort of self-imposed 'Maastricht homework'. Understandably, the more disciplined the anchor country, the more demanding the underlying requirements. Seen from this perspective, the geographic location of CE countries makes them a natural member of the D-mark zone. It means that an anchor economy is one of the best anti-inflationary performers with an excellent track record in observing sound rules of macroeconomic stability. The German voice will be strongly echoed in the concept of a strong euro. Therefore, one cannot count on deducting much from the arduousness of maintaining a stable currency if practised against EMU.[9] In this sense, the degree of macroeconomic discipline and the resulting loss in autonomous decisionmaking under the self-imposition argument may be almost as strict and narrow as under the band-wagon one.

Now, why should a small and open economy strive for exchange rate stability? The list of potential benefits may look as follows:

a) For a country with a large proportion of foreign trade, exchange rate stability, to a great deal, influences internal price stability. The exchange rate directly determines many prices in the domestic economy, some being key inputs into the production sector. A decline in the domestic currency tends to translate itself into an inflationary thrust that may provoke inflationary expectations in the course of induced wage and price increases. The less flexible is the supply side of the economy in responding to demand changes the faster works the transmission link between currency weakening and inflation.

b) Restoring external competitiveness by realigning the exchange rate often misses the point if the exports of a small open economy have large import loadings. This sort of exports on imports dependency usually has a technological origin. It is a reflection of the fact that to make tradable products competitive abroad they have to be equipped with high-technology components obtained in the framework of international specialisation and co-operation. Under such circumstances, a devaluation paradoxically may impair external competitiveness if higher prices for imported intermediate goods make them too expensive to consume. By the same token, a devaluation discourages imports of investment goods that usually conflicts with the restructuring objectives of CE transition economies.
c) If a weakening of the currency triggers higher inflation then it also exerts upward pressure on interest rates. As a result, the business sector has to cope with more expensive access to credit. Another structural drawback ensues because the tradable sector is not usually able to increase prices so fast as the non-tradable one. It will be then exposed to higher real interest rates, which undo a substantial part of the competitive edge created by the previous exchange rate weakening.
d) Relying on the exchange rate may delay or protract necessary structural changes to the detriment of the long-term competitive position of the country because the protective exchange rate cushion tends to relax financial discipline and disrupts non-price forms of competition.[10] It gives some additional edge to low value-added exports but it is still questionable whether CE countries can successfully compete in these articles with Third World countries. Moreover, the bottom line of some frequent shocks asking for an exchange rate accommodation should be understood as an appeasement of fundamental imbalances. In the environment of unsettled ownership rights this may be an excess growth of real wages over and above labour productivity. Large budget deficits are another typical example. Under such lax macroeconomic behaviour, any exchange rate manipulation has a short-lived impact fuelling in the end only domestic inflation.
e) While major benefits of a stable exchange rate for a small and open economy are derived from the point of view of current account transactions, the capital account view is no less important. Exchange rate stability removes a large part of the uncertainty for long-term investment decisions, encouraging thus the inflow of foreign direct and portfolio investment. A stable exchange rate also reduces the risk of capital flight and protects the economy from the vagaries of short-term speculative capital.

f) If the business sector is a net holder of foreign liabilities, its exposure to exchange rate risk may turn, in the case of a larger devaluation, into a financial distress hitting not only indebted firms but also domestic banks.[11]

To the discomfort of practical policymaking, the question about whether a given exchange rate is overvalued or undervalued is one of the most tricky to answer. Paradoxically, the exchange rate sometimes owes its stability to the fact that opinions about a 'right' or 'equilibrium' exchange rate level differ across the market participants. Frankly speaking, economic theory is barely helpful in this respect. The very concept of equilibrium on the foreign exchange market lacks a broader consensus, analytical procedures tend to suffer from oversimplification or low operational workability.

Last but not least, the issue of exchange rate stability spills over into the field of political economy. One can often observe a sort of systemic unwillingness of government to accept the political costs of a devaluation. The act seen by an economist as a pure price correction may be perceived by politicians as the ultimate evidence of previous mistakes. While a strong currency is a reason for national pride, a weak one may be looked on as a concise expression of weaknesses plaguing the economy.

Whatever are the prevailing reasons for the aversion to deliberate manipulation of the exchange rate - let it be sound economic arguments, rational or irrational political views or a weak theoretical support - they all point in the same direction. The exchange rate should not be thought of as an ordinary instrument available for usage on a day-to-day basis. It rather resembles an insurance policy: it may bring some comfort as the last resort measure but many would want to avoid the emergency circumstances, which would warrant its employment.

To draw an interim conclusion, if a country gives priority to the objective of exchange rate stability then many complaints about the high costs of giving away an autonomous exchange rate and monetary policies in a monetary union are on shaky ground. The underlying demands to support the exchange rate may squeeze the autonomy of home-made policies to such a degree that when a country relinquishes its own currency it loses not a true independence but rather the facade of independence.

In fact, being a member of a monetary union looks like a natural enhancement of the previous strategy oriented on a stable exchange rate. While preserving and strengthening the hitherto benefits, one can add a couple of new ones:

a) A credible exchange rate stability requires that the domestic fundamentals be realigned with those in the anchor country without any chance of taking part in the formulation of the anchor country's policies. Being a member of a monetary union gives the opportunity to have some say, strictly limited but some. The presence in a collective decisionmaking body opens the way to the expression of opinions about the impact of monetary decisions on the home economy. If nothing else, the direct contact with the highest rank insiders in the area has substantial intrinsic value.

b) A distinguishing currency leaves open all the time the contingency that exchange rates vis-à-vis other currencies will change in the future. Therefore, the room for bets of speculative capital movements is still there. The more liberal and smaller the economy, the more vulnerable to speculative behaviour. Besides, even slight profit opportunities may lure speculators in current globalised and low transaction costs financial markets. By entering a monetary union a small country becomes a part of a much larger unit which is incomparably better shielded form disruptive exchange rate speculation.

c) The emergence of euro which will bundle a larger part of Western Europe in a single currency trade area will also enlarge dramatically the anchor economy against which the exchange rate stability will be worthwhile maintaining.

To sum up, heading to a monetary union entails both costs and benefits. But the crucial point is that many of those costs associated with the loss of the national currency would have to be incurred anyway if a country wants to reap the benefits of a stable currency. To put it differently, the policymaking should not be trapped by the kind of schizophrenia which, on the one hand, worries about the high costs of giving away an independent exchange rate and monetary policy in a monetary union, while, on the other hand, acknowledges the advantages of a stable currency for a small open economy. It should be understood that the latter also implies substantial constraints on autonomy in decisionmaking. Both policy objectives, i.e. heading to a monetary union or to a credible exchange rate stability, thus point in the same direction and need not substantially differentiate themselves in terms of disabling some policy tools.

4. SELECTED TRANSITIONAL ISSUES

The Maastricht convergence criteria are giving formal expression to the general point that before a country irrevocably locks the exchange rate in the EMU it must reach certain standards of macroeconomic consolidation. The economic literature abounds with critical reviews which comment on topics such as the choice of numerical values for these criteria, their stronger or weaker interpretation, their integrity which is one time blamed for an incomplete structure, another time for redundancies. But whatever disputes may surround this set of prescriptions, one can scarcely deny that they became a respectable source of reference and that they do suggest directions in which CE economies need to further upgrade their fundamentals.

Table 3 summarises the key data about economic development in the Czech Republic and thus offers a concise picture about the progress of macroeconomic stabilisation. Up to 1996, the Czech economy was strengthening the image of a country, which successfully manages the transition from a command to a market oriented system. At the inception of economic reform, the country experienced a relatively deep recession, which was, by all means, inevitable due to vast structural distortions and inefficiencies inherited from the planning era.[12] The decline of output was also partly the price paid for a tough programme of macroeconomic adjustment whose realisation, on the other hand, gained the country the reputation of the best disinflation achievements and the healthiest government finances in the group of transition economies. The recovery was delayed by the break-up of Czechoslovakia at the end of 1992. At the beginning of 1994, however, satisfactory growth rates resumed. Prevailing political stability as well as the ambitious programme of external sector deregulation was conducive to the massive inflow of foreign capital. The optimism about the ability of the Czech Republic to assume soon the obligations of EU membership and about a fast progress towards the Maastricht standards was barely limited.

The events in May 1997 revealed, however, that the picture was not so bright as previously conceived. The Czech currency fell under speculative pressure. In the wake of it, the general public saw the breathtaking jump of interest rates and a series of painful budgetary cuts. Growth was seriously affected. The government sought vote of confidence in the Parliament. A slim majority of the government coalition parties became a hotbed of recurring waves of political instability.

Quite naturally, the currency crisis sparked off controversies about the causes of such destructive development and intensified preoccupations about how the optimal policy mix should look. Some aspects of the ensuing debate are highly relevant for the transitional issues related to the speed with which the Maastricht norms of macroeconomic discipline should be taken on. The following section addresses some of the most challenging.

Table 3. Indicators of Economic Development, 1990-1997

	1990	1991	1992	1993	1994	1995	1996	1997
Real GDP (% change)	1.2	-11.5	-3.3	-0.6	2.7	5.9	4.1	1.0
Inflation (CPI)	9.7	56.6	11.1	20.8	10.0	9.1	8.8	8.5
Unemployment[1]	0.8	4.1	2.6	3.5	3.2	2.9	3.5	5.2
Government budget balance	9.3	-4.5	-1.7	1.1	10.4	7.2	-1.6	-15.7
(1. CZK bn, 2. % GDP)	1.6	-0.6	-0.2	0.1	0.9	0.5	-0.1	-0.9
Central government debt				158.8	157.3	150.0	155.2	178.7
(1. CZK bn, 2. % GDP)				15.8	13.8	11.2	10.2	10.7
Current account balance		0.95	-0.31	-0.05	-0.74	-1.36	-4.29	-3.21
(1. USD bn, 2. % GDP)		2.9	-1.02	-0.16	-1.88	-2.7	-7.64	-6.03
Gross external debt	9.2	10.9	7.1	8.5	10.7	16.5	20.8	21.0
(1. USD bn, 2. % GDP)	31.8	30.9	23.7	24.7	26.9	32.8	37.1	39.8
External reserves[1] (USD bn)		1.4	0.8	3.9	6.2	14.0	12.4	10.2
(1. official, 2. banking sector)		1.9	2.8	2.3	2.7	3.4	5.1	4.8
Exchange rate[2]		29.49	28.29	29.16	28.78	26.55	27.14	31.63
(1. CZK/USD, 2. CZK/DEM)		17.79	18.12	17.64	17.75	18.52	18.06	18.29
Non-state sector (% GDP)	12.3	17.3	27.7	45.1	56.3	66.5	74.7	80.1

Note: 1) End of period, 2) Yearly average. Until 1992 aggregate data for Czechoslovakia, since 1993 for the Czech Republic.
Source: Publications of the Czech National Bank and the Czech Statistical Office.

4.1 Real versus Monetary Convergence

It is a well-known fact that the Maastricht criteria do not explicitly address, as a precondition for a sustainable monetary union, the so-called real convergence. They pay attention to the monetary and fiscal issues, but the real side of mutual convergence, measured conventionally by the level of real GDP per capita, has been left aside.

The debate among western economists took the route of whether the omission of real convergence in the list of the EMU accession requirements will hamper or not the smooth functioning of a single currency. Some commentators are worried about wages behaviour between higher and lower productivity countries and the negative consequences of an ensuing wage drift for the rates of unemployment and thus the social coherence of the union once limited labour mobility and scanty fiscal redistributions on the Community level are taken for granted.

The issue of real vs. monetary convergence has its exponents among Czech economists and policymakers as well. The debate is closely related to the twin goals faced by every transition economy: the desire to catch up with EU productivity and welfare levels on the one hand and to continue with disinflation and overall economic stabilisation on the other. A sort of trade-off has been advocated between the two convergences: if policymaking is ambitious in getting ahead with disinflation and other Maastricht requirements it can achieve it only to the detriment of the growth rates affordable in the catching-up process.

The above view resembles the saying that some inflation is good because it greases the wheels of the economy. Indeed, CE countries are viewed as a place pregnant with a deep conflict between the needs of structural adjustments and pervasive market rigidities. While the former ask for the winding up of many inefficient enterprises and transferring the released labour force to new jobs, the latter stands up as a serious hurdle to labour mobility and flexibility of relative prices. Too fast disinflation under such circumstances may then allegedly lead to high sacrifice ratios and thus to a much longer catching-up period.

Table 4. Catching-Up Periods for Selected Combinations of Growth Rate and Economic Level Differentials (numbers of years)

Economic level differentials	Growth rate differentials 2.0	3.0	4.0
60.00	9.4	6.3	4.7
70.00	17.3	12.0	8.7
80.00	24.2	16.0	12.0
90.00	30.0	20.0	15.0

Note: The formula $T = \ln(2D(G)) / \ln D(L)$ was used for calculating cell numbers, where T is the spell of the catching-up period, $D(G)$ is the expected growth rate differential and $D(L)$ is the targeted economic level differential. It is assumed that the initial economic level of the catching-up country starts at 50 percent of the level of the anchor country which itself is growing by 2 percent a year.

As Table 4 indicates, the catching-up process is all but a short-term episode. Of course, different underlying assumptions lead to different results. But under any reasonable circumstances the time needed to achieve, for example, 70-80 percentage level of the anchoring EU countries may span over one or two decades. Against this backdrop, the idea about the trade-off between real and monetary convergences or the desirability of the greasing effect of inflation does not square well with the textbook propositions. It seems to be a variant of the long-run Phillips curve whose existence is doubted by the contemporary macroeconomics.

Up to the currency crisis in May 1997, the Phillips curve argument would sound too academic to influence the debate. And above all, an inverse relationship between inflation and long-term growth can be clearly documented for high rates of inflation while for low or moderate ones the empirical evidence is rather inconclusive.[13] But the currency turmoil gave a new ammunition to the dispute as the public had still in living memory the skirmish between the central bank and government about a very related topic.

The quarrel was about what reasons led to the growth deceleration and the subsequent shortfall of tax revenues in the first quarter of 1997. The government blamed the monetary tightening made a half year ago. In contrast, the central bank pointed to several unhealthy trends in the economy such as widening current account deficits, an excessive real wage growth outstripping the increase of labour productivity, a weaker fiscal discipline. A combined effect of these unfavourable trends threatened to revive inflationary pressures that gave the mandate for monetary tightening.

It should be noted that the Czech National Bank followed no cold-turkey disinflation strategy. Instead, a consensus prevailed that a drop of inflation by about 1 percentage point a year has been enough owing to many structural frictions in the Czech economy.[14] But the position of the government was a typical example of the reasoning that there exists a Phillips curve trade-off. A mundane counterpart of the rhetoric about the high costs of a too fast disinflation thus boiled down to the inclination to play down the signs of overheating. It resulted in an unwillingness to correct imbalances, on a pre-emptive basis, whenever the salutary measures might interfere with economic growth. The currency crisis, hopefully, delivered the lesson that the growth rates, if not underpinned by a healthy macroeconomic background, are short-lived and bring only lags into the catching-up process.[15]

4.2 The Frontiers of Fiscal Consolidations

In the Czech Republic, fiscal policy has always formed an integral part of the overall pattern of prudent macroeconomic behaviour. Year by year, two axioms were strongly adhered to in preparing the government budget: first, budgetary revenues and expenditures shall be projected as balanced and second, the size of government, measured by the ratio of government expenditures on GDP, shall be subject to a gradual decline.[16]

Of course, a projection might differ from the actual outcome and close scrutiny might detect some disguised forms of deficit financing.[17] But lapses of this kind can hardly cast doubt upon the value of fiscal policy in supporting macroeconomic stability during economic transition. Indeed, a glance at Table 3 shows that government finances operated with a substantial slack if measured against of the Maastricht fiscal criteria.[18]

The above conduct of fiscal policy may serve as an example of the self-imposition discipline as opposed to the band-wagon one. No reference to any external commitments but strong conservative arguments about crowding out private investment or shifting costs of extravagant spending to our children were upholding the prudent fiscal philosophy of the Czech government. If Maastricht rules were occasionally mentioned, it was rather with the aim to criticise an allegedly too restrictive stance of state finances. The three-percentage limit has been understood as a sort of entitlement to run a budgetary deficit. By not 'drawing the quota' the government was accused of grudging money for activities like export promotion, housing construction, education or health care. This tune was whistled particularly by the opposition Social Democratic Party.[19]

Despite quite impressive results in fiscal performance, one should bear in mind some still unsettled problems that may become a potential drain on governmental finances. These are the most outstanding:

a) In the Czech Republic, the reform of the pension and health care systems has not been completed yet, the latter was even trapped in serious disarray. The foundations of current arrangements are still rooted in the paternalistic view of the government and lack efficient feedbacks against wasteful outlays and overconsumption of publicly provided goods. International evidence shows that the transition period in which a new system takes off or a previous failed reform is winding up tends to be costly in terms of government budget assistance.
b) The initial fast growth of the Czech financial sector was followed by a consolidation period that witnessed a couple of banking failures, some spectacular frauds in the mutual fund industry or battered confidence in the largest insurance company. Despite a noticeable involvement of the government and central bank assistance in sharing the costs of consolidation, financial institutions are still in many respects fragile and prone to distress, particularly after being fully exposed to the pressure of international competition. Therefore, a bill for building-up the financial infrastructure may have not been presented to the government in full.[20]
c) Last but not least, there is a blend of miscellaneous items which are unfolding with the run-up to the EU accession. For example, substantial government expenditure will have to be incurred to achieve the EU environmental standards, modernise the transportation network or build up required reserves of crude oil. And not surprisingly, the government budget will have to accommodate commitments for NATO membership.[21]

Despite a host of pressures on the state budget, the government was quite successful in handling them in the framework of the hitherto philosophy of a balanced budget and its declining redistribution function. The government was confident about continuing with this philosophy even in the future and believed that fiscal policy could hardly do more for the benefit of macroeconomic stability. But the currency turbulences in May 1997 shattered this view. The reason was quite simple. To achieve a fast and visible improvement in net exports, domestic absorption had to go down.

And because the private sector could not be counted on to rapidly change its investment and saving habits, then the brunt of adjustment had to be born by the government sector.

Of course, this straightforward reasoning implied a politically unpalatable decision to move the budget into a surplus. The government would strongly resist this option under normal circumstances. Therefore, it was only the imminent threat of a speculative attack that forced the government, as part of the stabilisation package No. 1, to orchestrate the first batch of expenditure cuts. The speculative attack itself then gave birth to the stabilisation package No. 2[22] and the second batch of cuts.[23]

The currency crisis surely exaggerates the need of fiscal adjustment but it does not miss the general point that a more active role for fiscal restrictions seems inevitable. The main problem with monetary tightening is that higher interest rates tend to provoke exchange rate appreciation to the detriment of external competitiveness. At the same time, a higher interest rate sensitivity of investment means that monetary tightening tends to impair capital formation while only marginally discourages consumer imports. For this reason and in order to forestall recurrent currency crises, the restrictive fiscal policy has to assume a prominent place in the policy mix targeted at finding an effective solution to large current account deficits. This role of fiscal policy goes beyond traditional perceptions about fiscal prudence in a transition economy and creates quite unfathomable frontiers of fiscal restriction depending on how resilient the external imbalance will prove to be.[24]

4.3 A Roundabout Route to the Irrevocably Fixed Exchange Rate

Earlier in the paper an emphasis was put on the beneficial effects of a stable exchange rate for a small and open economy. Seen from this standpoint, the Czech road towards lasting exchange rate stability seems to be far from resembling a straight line.[25] Up till now, one could observe four distinct segments of the trajectory.

Policies of the early transition starting at the beginning of 1991 were designed in line with conventional wisdom about the exchange rate fulfilling the role of a nominal anchor in a transforming economy. At about the middle of 1994, the economy merged smoothly into the second stage in which the previous fixed exchange rate regime was confronted with the accelerated process of external liberalisation and deregulation. This period witnessed mounting policy dilemmas as a result of excessive capital inflows. The inevitable change in the exchange rate regime came in February 1996 when the Czech National Bank widened the band from the hitherto 1 to 15 percent. This move marked the beginning of the third period, which can be described as an unmanaged floating within a wide band. Finally, the speculative attack which burst in May 1997 led to the retreat from declared exchange rate commitments and started off the period of a managed floating.

A short history of the exchange rate arrangements in the Czech Republic is thus relatively rich and may give an impression that it moves the economy away from the proclaimed advantages of exchange rate stability. There is, however, a logic behind the above sequencing, which is better understood if evaluated in a wider framework of the Czech disinflation strategy.

Now, what are the main lessons to be learnt from the experience with different exchange rate regimes? And what are the chances to take on the obligations from a more fixed arrangement, defined, for example, by the rules of an ERM II? These are some tentative answers.

The anchor of macroeconomic stabilisation. Exchange rate policy for the early stage of economic transition was designed in line with the paradigm of an anchor whose stability would be the most conducive to the stabilisation of the rest of the economy. Several arguments supported the view about a nominal exchange rate well suited to assume this role: beneficial impact on price stability, a notorious instability of the money demand function in a transition economy, advantages for building up the central bank's credibility.[26]

With the benefit of hindsight, the exchange rate anchor proved highly effective in maintaining a stable macroeconomic environment. Within a half year following sweeping price liberalisation, monthly inflation settled down to average levels not far above single digit yearly figures and kept at these levels, disregarding one-off non-monetary spikes (e.g. the adjustments of regulated prices or the introduction of the VAT tax reform at the beginning of 1993). But one should be cautious about the disciplinary role of the exchange rate anchor alone. A fuller description of the peg must pay a proper regard to a series of large opening devaluations (totalling almost 90 percent against USD)[27] as well as to the corset of both intentional and unintentional tight macroeconomic policies.[28] While the large undervaluation functioned as a cushion, which increased chances for a longer-term sustainability of the chosen parity, the corset minimised the speed with which the cushion was exposed to a continual flattening due to the real exchange rate appreciation.

To sum up, the fixed exchange rate which existed in the early period of economic transition owed its successful performance primarily to the unique features of an economy shrugging off only gradually the remains of a command system. The prevailing frictions, particularly with respect to capital movements, granted monetary authorities a high degree of autonomous decisionmaking, which was exploited for a fast disinflation. However, the approach was not fast enough to completely wipe out a noticeable inflation differential vis-à-vis industrial countries. Therefore, a slow but steady real exchange rate appreciation continued that might have eventually led to currency overvaluation, loss of external competitiveness and consequently to a potential confidence crisis over the pegged exchange rate parity. The main attack on the fixed exchange rate, however, came from another direction constituted by progressive capital account deregulation and a rapid heading towards full convertibility of the Czech currency.[29]

Withering benefits of the fixed exchange rate. The period of the decline and subsequent fall of the fixed exchange rate had no definite beginning but broadly coincided with a wave of easing capital controls and integrating the Czech financial sector into the family of industrial countries.[30] In principle, these new trends gestated the clash known as a violation of uncovered interest rate parity: the joint effect of interest rate differential (having its origin predominantly in the inflation differential) and the absence of any exchange rate risk (due to keeping the exchange rate fixed) encouraged one-way capital movement with the aim to reap excess and safe returns.[31]

The amazing thing was how strongly capital flows responded in the Czech Republic.[32] To give an illustration, in 1994 the share of net capital inflow in GDP reached 8.5 percent, peaking at a record level of 16.6 percent in 1995.[33] During this episode of massive capital inflow, the official external reserves witnessed an increase from almost zero at the beginning of 1993 to USD 14 bn at the end of 1995.[34] The share of net foreign assets as a component of the change in the money supply doubled from 45 percent in 1993 to 80 percent in the last quarter of 1995. Major rating agencies were upgrading their evaluation of the country risk further strengthening the confidence of foreign capital.[35]

There was no doubt that sterilised interventions conducted with the mandate to defend the fixed exchange rate posed policy dilemmas.[36] The massive sterilisation prevented interest rate differentials from diminishing and so enticed even larger amounts of foreign borrowing and speculative capital. At the same time, these operations only transferred the problem of excess liquidity into the future because banks accumulated an inflating pool of standby liquidity available for credit expansion once they started to deplete the pool by selling the paper back to the central bank. The leading monetary aggregate M2 overshot the corridor that the monetary programme saw as compatible with intended disinflation objectives. The best clients took advantage of lower interest rates abroad so domestic commercial banks ended up with a riskier borrower profile. For those producers who lacked projected export earnings, the fixed exchange rate operated as an ambush encouraging foreign borrowing without taking proper account of hedging against exchange rate risks. Last but not least, sterilised interventions proved costly for the central bank itself.[37]

A delicate policy issue is to recognise the change in climate when the hitherto benefits from maintaining the nominal exchange rate anchor were already outweighed by costs attributable to the functioning of the anchor. The anticipated change was made on 28 February 1996 when the 5 years old regime of the fixed exchange rate was modified by adopting a wider horizontal band: 7.5 percent above and below from the unchanged central parity. For some policymakers it was a difficult decision to shelve one of the most prominent features of the Czech transition but events were pressing. The Czech macroeconomic policies entered a new era of a more volatile exchange rate.

The exchange rate behaviour in a wider band. The salient feature of the new exchange rate regime consisted in an increased role of market volatility. As Figure 1 shows the exchange rate did exhibit a substantial amount of volatility. But the issue is to what extent the observed fluctuations, which were delivered by market forces, corresponded to proclaimed objectives.

In the first place, the underlying atmosphere of excessive capital inflows wanted the exchange rate volatility to play an active role in repelling the hot money component of incoming capital. To this end, an amount of USD 660 mil (representing approx. 5 percent of the central bank's foreign exchange reserves) left the country within three days as an immediate reaction on widening the band. However, this outflow should be attributed to the surprise effect of the given policy change rather than to normal functioning of the new exchange rate regime.

The assessment of the repelling quality of the band can hardly end up with a high score. In fact, to offset the interest rate differential by an increased exchange rate risk, the exchange rate has to display, on average, a depreciation trend. But that situation cannot happen, on a sustainable basis, in a horizontal band. On the contrary, by triggering an appreciation trend, not so difficult on a shallow emerging market, the speculator can earn, in addition to the gains from the interest rate differential, a gain from any favourable exchange rate movement. To provide some quantitative evidence, Figure 2 depicts such yields of notional speculation. As can be seen, it was rewarding for most of the time during the observed period.[38]

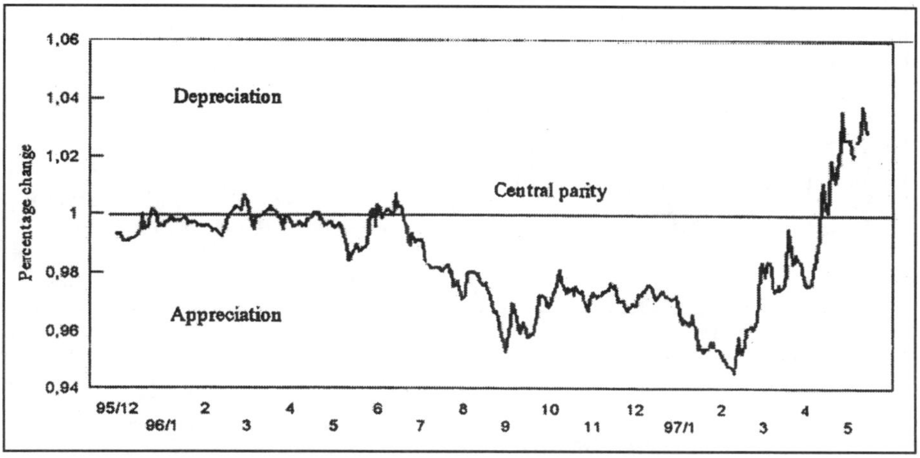

Figure 1. Market exchange rate in a wider band

Note: Figure 1 shows the index of the market exchange rate in the structure of the currency basket as quoted about 5 p.m. (so called closing exchange rate).

The objective of discouraging the hot money component of capital inflows taken separately would indicate that the band should be widened from the hitherto 1 to approx. 4-7 percent.[39] But there was also a troublesome trend towards growing current account deficits that demanded some respect for the contingency that a realignment might become unavoidable at some future point in time in order to prop up external competitiveness. Therefore, a considerable margin was added to the width of the band derived solely for the purpose of the hot money repelling function. It was expected that the vast potential for nominal depreciation within a wide band would accomplish the same job without reneging on the exchange rate commitments. Endowed with such discretion, market forces were thought to identify a fundamentally more correct exchange rate level, which had been kept unchanged for more than five years.

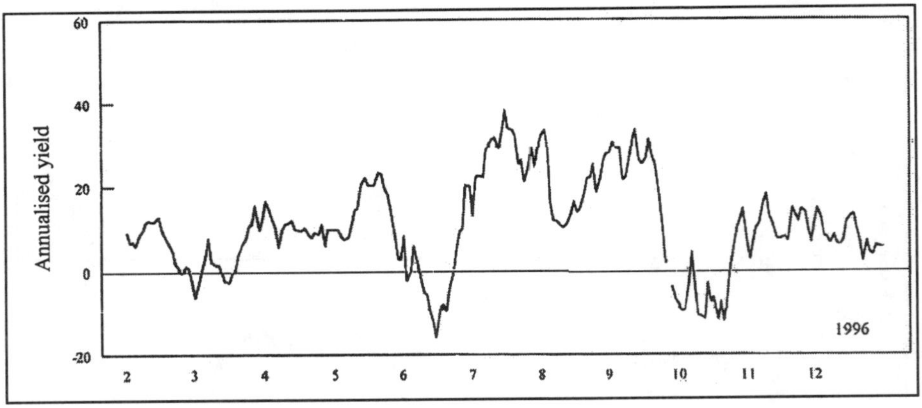

Figure 2. Notional yields of short-term speculation

Note: Figure 2 portrays the hypothetical profit and loss profile of 1-month speculation measured by the sum of the annualised 1-month interest rate differential and the annualised exchange rate change for 1-month holding period. Both variables are reflected in the structure of the currency basket.

The above hopes were barely met, particularly if the concept of a fundamental exchange rate equilibrium should be understood from the current account point of view. Instead, a strange but logical pattern seemed to perpetuate. Permanent and large interest rate differentials dragged the exchange rate towards the lower, i.e. appreciated, edge of the band, just to the contrary of what was seen as desirable for an improvement in the current account. In order to counteract this tendency, a broader spectrum of bad news had to move expectations of market agents in the other direction. For example, the regular monthly data plunged the yearly forecast of the current account deficit into a still bleaker perspective, foreign direct investment slowed down while foreign portfolio investors increased their voice in accusing the domestic capital market of a lack of transparency and unfair practices against minority shareholders. Parliamentary elections in June 1996 installed a slim minority right-wing government and the political scene became more unpredictable. Inflation proved more stubborn to control, the growth of output lagged behind projections, and the sector of small private banks was hit by a confidence crisis. But even this higher frequency of currency weakening announcements was not enough to relocate the exchange rate into the depreciation half of the band. It only brought the market oscillations nearer to the central parity.[40]

To sum up, the exchange rate flexibility relieved monetary authorities from some policy dilemmas, but the ensuing comfort or gain in autonomy was not terribly high. After all, the later occurrence of the speculative attack made it clear that all kinds of repelling or protective safeguards lose their strength once the economy already establishes firm links with the world financial markets but neglects the disciplinary implications for domestic policies.

Managed floating. Unlike the previous change in the exchange rate regime, the switch to a managed floating on 26 May 1997 occurred under the pressure of massive exchange rate speculation. To the great bad luck, the currency turmoil in the distant Thai market spilled over to the Czech currency which was debilitated by deteriorating current account deficits and growing political instability.[41] The monetary authorities tried to ward it off for a while. They resorted to direct interventions and squeezing liquidity on the money market. But when the household sector became also inflicted with the craze of speculation, monetary authorities retreated from defending the band and let the exchange rate float.[42] There is no doubt that the currency crisis was a kind of a penalty paid for neglecting fundamental imbalances. It was the failure of the government to recognise the fact that the Czech Republic had already become a part of the globalised financial markets, which tend to punish reckless policymaking.

Despite this unhappy take-off, managed floating is a legitimate exchange rate mechanism, which may have some competitive edge over other arrangements under given circumstances.[43] First, there is no internal conflict between a managed floating and the objective of exchange rate stability. It all depends on how the adjective 'managed' has been interpreted in day-to-day operating procedures. In this regard, not only direct interventions but also interest rate policy plays a key role in determining exchange rate behaviour. At the same time, the floating better demonstrates that exchange rate stability does not arise from any official rules of the adopted exchange rate regime but is a sort of by-product of a concerted effort of all economic policies. And to the extent that the consequences of domestic policies on the exchange rate cannot be ignored, it becomes illusive to pretend that under a floating the Czech authorities can enjoy an increased amount of autonomy in decisionmaking.

By and large, the system of managed floating may not pose any hurdle for monetary authorities that are pursuing a disinflation strategy. It gives enough room for correcting perceived misalignments or overshooting while it does not entice speculators who like to test declared commitments. So both legs are equally important: the exchange rate is floating as well as managed.[44] One can thus easily conceive the scenario in which the managed floating will become the final exchange rate arrangement that guides the Czech economy on its road towards the Maastricht standards.[45]

4.4 Continuing with a Resolute Disinflation

The Czech Republic succeeded in reducing the rate of inflation to single digits within a relatively short period of time. Thanks to a concerted mix of restrictive policies, Czech inflation has not been stuck in persistent moderate levels that can be observed in some other transition economies.[46] This track record was considered a remarkable achievement in comparison to other post-communist countries. But it still looks too rough if judged from the perspective of the Maastricht inflation criterion.[47]

Now, the point to the debate is whether the Maastricht concept of a desirable level of inflation should already flash as a benchmark for monetary authorities in the Czech Republic or, alternatively, whether such orientation is premature considering a wider choice of policy objectives.

The issue of a desirable inflation should be approached from the understanding that the current single-digit but still relatively high levels do pose a problem for maintaining macroeconomic stability:

a) In the longer-run, a still marked inflation differential causes a permanent real exchange rate appreciation over and above an increase of labour productivity. This disparity leads to an erosion of external competitiveness and makes the exchange rate prone to continual weakening that encourages inflation.
b) In the shorter-run, the inflation differential gives rise to interest rate differentials whose existence puts into motion the forces of interest rate arbitrage. Ensuing capital inflows tend to strengthen the nominal exchange rate while paying only a little regard to the development of the current account. A boom-bust pattern thus may evolve: worsening trade imbalance threatens to provoke a currency crisis, the avoidance of which asks for consolidation that recovers the confidence of foreign capital and starts a new wave of currency appreciation. The chain of events before and after the speculative attack tracked this scenario quite closely.
c) The inflation rate acts as a ratchet for the decrease of nominal interest rates, because negative or low real interest rates would impair savings formation. That outcome would be at variance with the restructuring needs of a transition economy as well as with the endeavours to contain external imbalance. It also creates an unlevel playing field among producers who differ in their ability to pass over higher prices of inputs to buyers. The tradable sector seems to be more exposed to this distortionary effect.
d) Continuing inflation is a major stumbling block in attempts to suppress indexation practices in wage bargaining. It also triggers automatic adjustments in various benefit entitlements.[48] The longer an economy

lives with a given inflation, the more entrenched will become the inflation inertia.

The self-imposition argument thus demands continuing with resolute disinflation up to the point at which the above troublesome effects lose the strength to jeopardise macroeconomic stability. It is of minor importance whether this point lies nearer to or further from the Maastricht inflation requirement. What really matters is the fact that current low inflation is still high if seen from the objective of undisturbed economic development. Any other approach, which flirts with the idea of the greasing effects of inflation, would give misleading signals for policymaking.[49]

By stressing the importance of further disinflation, a set of issues deserves attention. These seem the most challenging:

Faster or slower deregulations. A sweeping price liberalisation at the beginning of economic reform increased the share of goods and services with a market price setting from almost zero to approximately 80 percent of GDP. Nevertheless, the prices of some sensitive commodities like housing, energy, telecommunications, water supply or public transport remained under central control and were subject to piece-meal deregulation. At the same time, cautious attempts were made to convert free public goods like health care and education to mixed ones whose cost burden would have to be shared by private individuals as well. A matter of concern was the high weight of deregulated items in the consumption basket (see Table 5).[50] Of course, deregulations represented a 'compulsory' part of inflation because without it the structure of relative prices would suffer from permanent distortions. But the permanence itself is dangerous as it entrenches inflation inertia that then plagues price and wage setting policies.

The mixed experience with the slow pace of deregulations shifted some interest to the alternative option that called for an acceleration of the whole process. A few radical price jumps should get rid of this part of inflation. This option, however, was not free from perils, leaving aside the political consequences of such unpopular steps. This manoeuvre might come to nothing if too generous social transfers would be paid off in compensations for price increases or claims for wage adjustments were not firmly opposed. An essential part of the problem was the fact that a majority of regulated prices fall to the domain of natural monopolies, which lacked a proper regulatory framework.

Table 5. The Composition of Czech Inflation

	1995	1996	8/1997	1995	1996	8/1997
	Inflation rate			Share in total inflation		
Total inflation	7.9	8.6	9.9	100.0	100.0	100.0
Regulated prices	9.7	11.2	19.6	30.0	31.4	42.4
Food prices	5.4	7.9	5.6	22.5	30.2	19.2
Core inflation	8.8	7.6	8.3	47.5	38.4	38.4

Source: The Czech National Bank

Interestingly enough, it was the currency crisis, which gave impetus to a more radical approach. A cool economic reasoning would suggest that the income effect from higher prices of necessity goods would be conducive to limiting aggregate demand and thus to improving external imbalance. Similarly, the co-ordinated restriction in the wake of stabilisation packages should lead to higher unemployment that might effectively counteract the wage-push inflation. But no less important was the regained political backing for faster deregulations. The government accepted the right-wing critique that policies of self-complacency and loss of courage to go on with necessary transformation changes need not guarantee the votes of the electorate. The currency crisis thus quite unexpectedly helped to create the determination to find an early solution to one of the thorniest issues of economic transition.

Using the exchange rate for reducing inflation. On many occasions, the Czech authorities declared that a stable and strong currency is one of the best vehicles of transformation changes and a key device for preserving macroeconomic stability. Indeed, the promoted policy of a fixed exchange rate kept in check price increases of exporters who then shifted the price discipline to domestic suppliers. Competitive prices of imports proved a powerful weapon against the monopolistic structure of the domestic business sector. By cutting down on chances to inflate prices, non-price forms of competition were encouraged that led to the improvement of the export structure. All of these disciplinary effects were further enhanced when the exchange rate set off on the appreciation trend within a wide band.

Of course, the currency crisis resurrected the dispute whether the monetary authorities did not go too far in fostering a hard currency option. After all, the data showed a permanent real exchange rate appreciation that was held responsible for deteriorating export performance and widening current account deficits.[51] The opponents pointed to a direct link between these unfavourable outcomes and tight monetary policies arguing that higher interest rates primarily provoke more capital inflows and currency strengthening rather than limiting aggregate demand. The centrepiece of their recommendation has been a relaxation of the exchange rate in one way or another.[52]

Indisputably, the exchange rate is a delicate tool for combating inflation, which may easily turn into an overkill. One can also admit that a sort of trade-off between deteriorating external balance on the one hand and improving inflation on the other was taking place for a while. To put it differently, if aggregate demand increasingly chases imported goods, it is automatically diverted from chasing domestic goods and services. This switch is beneficial for measured inflation but at the cost of a wider external imbalance. The monetarist view may add that a current account deficit, other things equal, is tantamount to the outflow of money or to lower growth rates of the money supply.[53]

However logical sounds the above reasoning, it does not imply that the Czech monetary authorities were happy about depressing inflation in this myopic way which only entices a balance of payment crisis and takes the toll of higher inflation in the future. At the same time, however, they disagreed with viewing an isolated currency weakening as a way out of accumulated difficulties among which the large external imbalance was the most pressing.

To defend this standpoint, it is noteworthy that excessive current account deficits vex a majority of countries from the former Eastern bloc. Besides, exchange rate policies differ in these countries, some of them are quite accommodating in offsetting inflation differentials but still incapable of solving the problem. These observed similarities suggest the existence of common underlying determinants of current account deficits such as a robust investment wave, delayed consumption boom or a closer dependence on growth in developed market economies. Under such circumstances, the choice of the exchange rate regime seems to be of minor importance.[54]

But more importantly, an isolated exchange rate weakening would only bring temporary relief to a debit of central bank credibility. It was more than likely that a larger currency depreciation would be transmitted both to cost-push inflation (due to higher prices of imports and ensuing wage demands under existing weaknesses of corporate governance and labour market rigidities) as well as to demand-pull inflation (a higher domestic demand released from a current account improvement would be met by a low responsiveness of the supply side). An effective solution to unsustainable external imbalance would command expenditure reducing policies with a fiscal tightening having a pivotal role.[55] Unfortunately, the government was ready to contemplate such an unattractive but badly needed remedy only under the imminent threat of a currency crisis.

As far as the future role of the exchange rate is concerned, the Czech economy can hardly avoid walking on a thin dividing line which separates a positive disciplinary pressure of the exchange rate in reducing inflation from the destructive consequences of an overvalued currency. It is widely understood that any return to the policy of creating transformation cushions would jeopardise many achievements of the economic reform: low inflation, financial discipline, structural improvements or confidence in domestic currency. Moreover, the very existence of the above elusive line comes from the existence of the inflation differential, so a reasonable policy mix must concentrate on closing and not widening the gap.[56] On the other hand, the overdosing of the disciplinary role of the exchange rate is no less damaging for the inflationary record. The message from the currency crisis should be read in the way that safe limits of using the exchange rate for disinflation objectives are shaped in conjunction with other government policies, which should closely co-operate with those of the central bank.

Convergence of long-term interest rates. The rationale behind this requirement is seen in the assurance that not only current economic performance is monitored on a regular basis but a convergence of long-term inflationary expectations of whatever generating reason is also under way.[57] The previous text paid attention predominantly to the economic side of the convergence. In this respect, the interest rate criterion should signal whether there are no hidden risks that might spark off some problems in the future. It is argued that if markets are not confident about containing those risks they will demand interest rate premiums to the discomfort of achieving the reference value of the criterion.

But equally important is the technical side of the problem that would assure that the interest rate criterion has the same meaning in CE transition economies as in developed ones. To this end, financial markets have to achieve enough depth, liquidity and mutual consistency. Without these qualities the interest rate criterion would falter in fulfilling its signalling role. Now, these are some issues which are closely related to the improvements in the above mentioned direction:

a) It is fair to say that the Czech Republic has made dramatic progress in integrating domestic financial markets into the world economy.[58] Remaining capital controls are barely binding and there is a timetable to phase them out completely.[59] Not surprisingly, currency turbulences in May and June 1997 opened the debate whether capital controls were not lifted too fast and whether to reconsider the timing of abolishing residual regulations. These views, however, did not gain a larger support, so the programme of external sector deregulation did not suffer from any noticeable backsliding.[60] This is a crucial achievement because with strict regulation of capital movement a country fails to demonstrate its ability to withstand the pressures of a fully-fledged market economy.

Table 6. Central government debt

	1. 1. 1995	1. 1. 1996	1. 1. 1997
Total	157.3	154.4	161.6
Domestic debt	90.3	101.2	117.3
T-bonds	28.8	41.7	43.9
T-bills	23.8	42.0	69.1
Direct CB credit	32.4	12.5	0.0
Other	5.8	5.1	4.3
Foreign debt	67.1	53.1	44.3

Source: Ministry of Finance.

b) The capital market is both a close substitute and complement of investing in the bond market. So, without orderly functioning of the former, one can hardly speak about unbiased functioning of the latter. The sad fact is that the Czech authorities for a long time neglected the regulatory framework of capital market institutions. They were driven by the philosophy that a minimum regulation serves best the reshuffling of ownership rights in the wake of their opening distribution via privatisation. The criticism of unfair practices was frequently rejected as an outcry of those who failed in bidding for ownership. But this attitude crippled the capital market in its function of mobilising domestic saving and revealing investment opportunities through correct asset prices. It was only some flagrant cases of abusing minority investors that persuaded the government about an urgent need to restore battered confidence in this segment of the Czech financial markets. Reform initiatives are aimed at enforcing legal contracts, protecting minority shareholders, improving disclosure practices, clamping down on insider trading, eliminating the fragmentation of trading places, increasing the signalling role of asset prices and some other tasks.

c) As Table 6 shows, the item Direct credit from the central bank now assumes zero value. The Czech Republic thus has already fulfilled one of the preconditions of EU membership which demands that a country renounces any direct central bank financing and any existing government debt held by the central bank has been replaced by tradable securities. Despite this progress, the government debt still suffers from a structural deficiency in the sense that long-dated Treasury bonds do not exist. The yield curve constructed from outstanding T-bonds does not stretch beyond 5 years, the commonest maturity has been 2 years. But the Maastricht interest rate criterion takes for reference purposes the yield of 10-year bonds. In fact, this maturity gap means more than a pure technical omission in the available structure of government bonds. It reveals still buoyant inflationary expectations because longer-term bonds would by accepted only at lower prices for buyers, that is at higher costs for the government budget.

5. CONCLUSIONS

A general pitfall of the summary section is that its condensed statements often end up with no more than abstract theses with only limited hints for practical policymaking. Now, the chances of being trapped by this nuisance are pretty high for such an elusive issue, as is the outlook for the inclusion of the Czech Republic into the process of European monetary integration. This is particularly true if this undertaking takes place well ahead of the practical steps of administrative bodies. Against this background, this paper intended to deliver a couple of ideas whose skeleton structure may look as follows:

a) The goal of exchange rate stability is not a relic of the transition period. Some domestic commentators seem to think otherwise judging from their parallels between the Czech floating and exchange rate volatility of major world currencies. But the project 'One market - one money' says just the opposite. It aims to secure permanent exchange rate stability for the benefit of all participants. The Czech Republic, being a small, open and trade dependent economy, is a genuine prospective candidate for joining this project.

b) Worries over the loss of autonomous exchange rate and monetary policies in a monetary union are increasingly irrelevant for a small and open economy, which has been integrated into the globalised financial markets. In a world which frowns upon any barriers to capital mobility, this economy cannot afford larger misalignments against the neighbouring environment. Currency turbulences in May 1997 should be understood as a penalty for the failure to recognise this fact. If the country has submitted voluntarily to the pressure of the external discipline, it is mainly the facade of autonomy that will be lost at a time of entering a monetary union.

c) Maastricht criteria are not EU accession criteria. In this sense, they need not yet bother decisionmakers in the Czech Republic. But they point to the right directions in which fundamentals of the Czech economy have to be improved. The adherence to the disinflation strategy is a key issue because current single-digit but high levels of inflation are unsustainable from the point of view of macroeconomic stability. Therefore, although no 'Brussels bureaucrats' are pressing to comply with the discipline embedded in the Maastricht convergence criteria, the Czech economy should work hard on its 'Maastricht homework' for the sake of withstanding competitive pressures as well as reaping benefits of capital mobility. By progressing in that direction, the Czech economy will put its money where its mouth is.

d) Do believe that in mainstream economics there is nothing like a long-run Phillips curve. Chivalry against inflation will not make the catching-up process faster. The rhetoric about the high cost of disinflation, when no one actually pushes through a cold-turkey treatment, just fosters the inclination to underestimate widening imbalances and thus, in the end, brings only time lags into the catching-up process. This is the way, how we should read the message delivered by the currency turmoil. Fortunately enough, the recent lesson proved less damaging than initially expected. So, if a small crisis helps to avert a bigger one, it was good because it increases chances that the catching-up process will not become repeatedly stuck by enforced market corrections resulting from the forbearance towards fundamental misalignments.

NOTES

1 The Copenhagen summit held in June 1993 laid down these prerequisites in the following way. A candidate country shall achieve: i) stability of institutions guaranteeing democracy, the rule of law, human rights and respect for and protection of minorities; ii) the existence of a functioning market economy as well as the capacity to cope with competitive pressures and market forces within the Union; iii) the ability to take on the obligations of membership, including adherence to the aims of political, economic and monetary union. Within this framework, the European Commission published in July 1997 an expert account Agenda 2000 in which the Czech Republic was given, in spite of some rebukes, a benign evaluation both from the political and economic criteria.

2 It is widely recognised that so called Eastern enlargement puts forward demands for deep institutional reforms of some EU arrangements as well. One of them is the overly generous West European welfare model. This model is held responsible for labour market rigidities resulting in high levels of EU structural unemployment. The fears about low labour cost competition then give rise to a restrictive access for CE agricultural and other sensitive products to EU markets. At the same time, the potential temptation to imitate the costly social schemes would be a trap with detrimental effects on macroeconomic stability of CE economies. Along the same line, given the existing income gap of associated CE countries, the costs of some EU programmes, namely CAP and regional policies, would be prohibitively high to be borne by member states. The other group of obstacles to the enlargement is related to decision-making processes. Their rules were designed for a limited number of founding members. They would become cumbersome and entirely non-productive after admitting additional members form Central and Eastern Europe. Without appropriate reforms, the Eastern enlargement may appear a burden that would be too difficult to accommodate.

3 A passive observing position is meant here as a mode of behaviour related to the prospective EMU membership. But on the assumption that EMU will go ahead, the very emergence of this gigantic body will force a couple of adjustments on the part of all those 'outs', including CE economies, that will be exposed to new competitive pressures. One

can foresee, for example, manifold responses to the widening and deepening of financial markets including mergers in the banking sector, changing proportions of world reserve currencies and others. This line of reasoning is not followed in this paper.

4 Among many authoritative evaluations of both costs and benefits of EMU see, for example, Gros and Thygesen (1992), De Grauwe (1994), Kenen (1995), Taylor (1995).

5 Table 1 reminds of the complex structure of the EU trade area comprised of several big members and a rich fringe of medium and small ones. For comparison, the structure of NAFTA is outstandingly simpler both in terms of the numbers and the relative strength of the participants. Therefore, the EU trade area is extremely vulnerable to all kinds of 'beggar-my-neighbour' behaviour, particularly reflected in competitive devaluations. The theory of an optimum currency area with its stylised picture of a country performing the prescribed cost-benefit analysis does not seem to pay a proper regard to the notion of the exchange rate as a pervasive externality. Therefore, against winners there are always losers from a given exchange rate movement. So, even if a country might have benefited from exploiting exchange rate and monetary policies for solving domestic problems, it may refrain from the selfish option if wider trade interests are at stake. From this point of view one can easily comprehend long-term efforts for very close policy co-ordination among West European countries which value the concept of fully-fledged common market and other joint activities.

6 The World Bank calculates a summary measure of liberalisation (ranging between 0 and 1) for developing countries based on internal, external and private sector criteria. For CE economies this liberalisation measure rose from extremely low levels (0.16-0.34) in 1990 to quite high levels (0.86-0.90) only four years later. See Abramson (1997).

7 A similar point was raised by Hochreiter and Winckler (1995). They claim that Austria opted for the hard currency strategy at a time when the prerequisites for an optimum currency area were not yet met, but triggered-off adjustment processes ultimately made Austria part of the optimum currency area with Germany.

8 In a best-case scenario, the first Eastern enlargement is expected not before 2002, more conservative estimates postpone this event to the year 2005. For the time being, none of these dates became an official benchmark influencing macroeconomic policies in the Czech Republic.

9 Good examples exist. There are other small open economies in the D-mark zone such as Austria or the Netherlands that have based their exchange rate policy on tying hands with the German mark. They have demonstrated that this approach may be rewarding in terms of a stable economic development. See Hochreiter and Winckler (1995) for the discussion of the Austrian example.

10 A related point was raised by Bean (1992). He argues that no amount of manipulation with the Westmark - Ostmark exchange rate could avoid the crisis of East German industry. He reasons that the core of the problem consisted of the demands of East German workers for the West German standard of living. In other words, while much of East German industry might have been viable at some Westmark - Ostmark exchange rate, this would only be so as long as East German workers were willing to accept correspondingly low real wages. And because there could surely have been wage inflation in the East, the initial low exchange rate would only postpone the day of reckoning.

11 It became a common practice of Czech commercial banks to extend domestic firms so called foreign exchange credits or even to reclassify standard credits into this category. The product has been designed in such a way that a domestic firm borrows domestic currency while the principal of the loan is linked to a given amount of foreign currency. Therefore, the owing amount denominated in domestic currency changes in line with the prevailing exchange rate. A business firm may be interested in a foreign exchange loan by

paying a lower interest rate while the bank may find it attractive as a tool for hedging foreign exchange exposure. In reality, however, the bank may have only swapped the foreign exchange risk for the credit risk, depending on whether the firm hit by the exchange rate losses defaults on the loan.

12 In summer 1997, the Czech Statistical Office (CSO) released updated figures about the growth performance in the years 1990-96. The new time series took account of some methodological refinements inspired by OECD and EU statistical practices (a modified treatment of taxes and subsidies, inclusion of imputed rents, estimation of the output produced in the hidden economy, and some others). According to the new data, the transformation recession was less severe than formerly reported. For example, the cumulative decline of real GDP in 1991-93 was adjusted from 20.4 to 13.9 percent. The CSO also published an updated GDP per capita estimate. While the old number was USD 10,626 (in terms of purchasing power parity) that represented 54.8 percent of the EU average, the fresh one is USD 11,221 meaning 57.9 percent of the EU average.

13 This point is mentioned, for example, by Fisher (1996).

14 In fact, the IMF criticised Czech policy for not being ambitious enough in reducing inflation.

15 Differences in opinion between the government and the central bank also surrounded the pre-crisis package No. 1, which was launched in April 1997. While the government was stressing the growth objective behind the stabilisation programme, the central bank supported it primarily as a more balanced mix of restrictive policies that better served disinflation objectives on the background of a large external imbalance. Many commentators would agree that the growth rhetoric of the government was one of the reasons why the package failed in averting the speculative attack because markets suspected the government of not being honest about fulfilling austerity measures while pressing on the central bank for interest rate cuts.

16 In conformity with the second principle, the share of the state budget expenditures on GDP dropped from 35.2 percent in 1993 to 31.8 percent in 1996, for the public sector (consolidated state and local government budgets) the decline was more moderate from 41.5 percent to 39.1 percent during the same period.

17 For example, the state budget was never waterproof from privatisation receipts (administered by the Fund of National Property) which were used for repaying the interest on government debt. Another debate arose about using the surplus collected in the pension system for financing current expenditures. A sort of fiscal relaxation also occurs if the government decreases the size of budgetary surplus between two consecutive years.

18 The sustainability of the fiscal position is to be assessed in terms of the budget deficit of general government (i.e. net borrowing of central, regional or local government and security funds) which should not exceed 3 percent of GDP at market prices, and the gross debt of general government which should not exceed 60 percent of GDP at market prices.

19 The entitlement interpretation of Maastricht seems to ignore the strengthening of fiscal rules under the Stabilisation Pact. According to this agreement, a country should strive, in principle, for a balanced budget while the occurrence of deficits is to be tolerated as exceptional episodes justified, for example, by a severe economic decline or a natural disaster. A system of penalties has been devised for those who fail to observe the limit. Within this scheme, the entitlement approach might disable the stabilising function of budgetary policy. That is to say, if a country tolerates, on a regular basis, budgetary deficits 'up to the stop' then it might be fined or criticised for excessive deficit financing just when going into the red might alleviate the country's bad times.

20 In the banking sector, for example, the total amount of expenses incurred in relation to rescuing operations such as the recapitalisation of banks, deposit insurance, supporting take-overs of a problem bank by a sound one or reimbursements for part of bankruptcy costs has been estimated at about USD 3 bn.

21 In this respect, the share of military spending is expected to increase gradually by up to 2 percent of GDP around the year 2000 in comparison with a current 1.2 percent.

22 To give a brief description, the pre-attack package No. 1 contained both short-term measures meant to prevent without delay any further deterioration of the external and internal imbalances, as well as measures influencing the economy in the longer-term perspective. As far as the short-end of the package is concerned, budgetary cuts of CZK 25.5 bn (4.6 percent of projected expenditures) were agreed upon, the wage increase in the government sector was reduced from 11.9 to 7.3 percent and so called import deposits were imposed (depositing 20 percent of the value of selected imports on an interest-free account for 6 months). The long end of the package embraced, for example, the creation of an independent Securities and Exchange Commission, the establishment of a special team responsible for investigating serious financial crimes, acceleration of privatisation, regulation of municipal debt, stricter performance of ownership rights in state-owned enterprises. The post-attack package No. 2 reacted to a 'too little, too late' impression of the previous package. The government publicly confessed its fault for underestimating imbalances in the economy and approved additional budgetary cuts of CZK 16.9 bn. The total burden of budgetary cuts thus reached 2.7 percent of GDP. The promise was given to draw up the 1998 budget with a surplus. Meanwhile, the Czech Republic witnessed in the summer of 1997 catastrophic floods. This natural disaster put one third of the Czech territory under water and inflicted damages of approx. USD 2 bn. The outlook for a surplus 1998 budget thus became quite uncertain.

23 The following story is typical for the disorder during a currency crisis. Dramatic cuts did not prevent the budget from getting into serious troubles. On the expenditure side, the anecdotal evidence pointed to accelerated spending induced by the announced freezes while on the revenue side firms were rumoured to default on timely tax payment because post-crisis interest rates went above the penalty rates. To overcome the expenditure-revenue gap the law said that the budget was entitled to issue Treasury bills up to CZK 16 bn and that the central bank could buy Treasury bills up to 5 percent of the previous year revenues. However, when the 16 bn limit was reached, the lawyers discovered that the government could borrow short-term only by issuing Treasury bills and this rule was incompatible with the reference to the looser 5-percentage limit. The budget then practised the lagging of outlays but it stopped it after the outcry from civil servants whose salaries were lagged by a couple of days. The government had to initiate an emergency amendment in which the maximum for Treasury bill borrowing was increased to CZK 33 bn.

24 The alternative view, strictly opposed by the government as well as by the IMF, has been advocated by the opposition Social Democratic Party. Instead of budgetary restriction, the competing 'anti-package' of Social Democrats recommended some fiscal loosening to cure the problem by injecting economic growth. The main source of additional funds for the growth promoting activities was to be secured by an import surcharge, which was also seen pivotal for the improvement of current account.

25 To comply with the Maastricht exchange rate criterion the member state has to respect the normal fluctuations margins without severe tensions for at least two years before the examination. In particular, the member state should not have devalued its currency's bilateral central rate against any other member state's currency on its own initiative for the same period.

26 For a more detailed discussion of the exchange rate regimes for transition economies see, for example, Dornbush (1994) or Sachs (1996).

27 The series of exchange rate realignments started on 8 January 1990 by unifying 15 CSK/USD commercial rate (used for trade related transactions) and 10 CSK/USD non-commercial rate (used for selected unilateral transfers) on the official level of 17 CSK/USD. A new tourist rate of 38 CSK/USD was established, revalued to 23 CSK/USD in the middle of the year. On 15 October 1990 the official rate was further devalued to 24 CSK/USD and the tourist rate to 30 CSK/USD. At the same time, a set of rules regulating payment conditions from and to abroad came into effect. On 28 December 1990, just before getting the economic reform off the ground, the official rate was devalued to 28 CSK/USD, the tourist rate was abolished and consumer imports were subject to a 20 percent import surcharge. It should be noted that a substantial part of such a radical decline of the external purchasing power was a pre-reform move towards a more reasonable price of foreign currencies rather than devaluations in the true sense, bearing in mind that in the former planning system the exchange rate belonged to the most distorted prices and convertible currencies were subject to very strict rationing schemes.

28 At this point, monetary authorities resorted to a tight control of credit and money. The embryonic stage of financial markets, typical for the initial period of economic transition, allowed deployment of some administrative measures like credit and interest rate ceilings. Moral suasion was also practised against a couple of large commercial banks that had emerged from the previous monobank system. The economy remained still closed on the capital account, thereby being insulated from monetary effects of capital inflows. Two additional features complete a fuller description of the corset. Firstly, an unexpectedly high initial price jump brought about a sharp drop of real wages (by 26 percent during the first year of economic reform) that came as a surprise and was only gradually, for the benefit of price stability and credibility of the exchange rate peg, reversed by subsequent wage demands. Incomes policy was also put in place penalising wage increases above legally approved regulatory limits. Secondly, the fiscal position was tight or neutral but never expansionary and it fitted closely with the orientation of central bank anti-inflationary policies.

29 At the inception of the economic reform on 1 January 1991 the Czech koruna was pegged against a basket of currencies whose composition was periodically updated. From 28 December 1990 through 1 January 1992 the structure of the basket was as follows: DEM 45.52 percent, USD 31.34 percent, ATS 12.35 percent, CHF 6.55 percent, GBP 4.24 percent. From 2 January 1992 through 2 May 1993 the structure was selected as follows: USD 49.07 percent, DEM 36.15 percent, ATS 8.07 percent, CHF 3.79 percent, FRF 2.92 percent. Since 3 May 1993 until the demise of the basket currency on 26 May 1997 the structure was simplified into two currencies only: DEM 65 percent, USD 35 percent. In the early period of the fixed exchange rate, the former State Bank of Czechoslovakia had no discretion in influencing the price of traded currencies while dealing with commercial banks. The exchange rates were fully determined by the arithmetic of the basket. Since 28 September 1992, the Bank was authorised to manage the exchange rate within a narrow band of 0.5 percent above and bellow central parity. In April 1995 the band was effectively increased from hitherto 1 to 1.5 percent when the CNB started to charge 1/4 percentage bid-ask spread in dealing with commercial banks. The trading technique was guided by the rules of the so-called fixing. This procedure required a commercial bank to submit by 11.00 a.m. the volume of currencies (denominated in USD, DEM or ECU) to be bought or sold. At 11.30 a.m. the CNB trading desk fixed the rates, taking into account actual cross-rates of the basket currencies (momentarily quoted by the Reuters screen

service) as well as a disposition for managing the exchange rate within the band. In December 1995, the fixing procedure switched to the American-style auction. So, along with volumes of currencies (reduced by the time to only DEM and USD denominations) commercial banks had to announce the price at which they would be willing to make the deal. The CNB then aggregated submitted orders, applied the confidential algorithm for determining the so-called cut-off exchange rate and executed all orders whose conditions were no worse than the cut-off rate.

30 Serious commitments to rapid external liberalisation found their expression in the amended Foreign Exchange Act (enacted in September 1995) in which the Czech Republic accepted the obligation of the so-called Article VIII of the IMF. The Act thus removed all restrictions for current account transactions and above that it preserved only a handful of the most sensitive capital controls. An important driving force for external liberalisation was the prestigious primacy of becoming the first OECD member among post-communist countries. This undeclared but serious-minded objective came true in 21 December 1995. For a more detailed discussion of the external sector deregulation in the Czech Republic see Dedek (1995).

31 It should be noted that the fixed exchange rate in terms of a currency basket entails some volatility vis-à-vis the separate basket currencies. For example, yearly volatility of the Czech currency vis-à-vis USD or DEM was 2.37 percent or 0.81 percent respectively. However, the correlation coefficient between CZK/USD and CZK/DEM time series was nearly -1, that is a direct consequence of the construction of the peg.

32 Naturally, not all forms of incoming capital took part in the classical interest rate arbitrage. For example, the prevailing motives behind the inflow of foreign direct investment lay in the platitude of profitable opportunities that were accessible by taking part in the extensive privatisation and restructuring of the domestic business sector. Similarly, foreign portfolio investors seemed to pay primary attention to the growing variety of promising securities traded on the emerging Czech capital market. On the part of domestic firms, a substantial portion of foreign borrowing resulted from the unwillingness of domestic commercial banks to extend longer-term credits on a larger scale.

33 For comparison, some other countries which also experienced a surge of capital inflow displayed the following percentage shares in GDP: Chile (1990) 10.6, 3.5, 8.1; Mexico (1989) 2.4, 4.6, 7.4, 7.6; Spain (1979) 3.8, 2.7, 3.8, 3.1. The year in parenthesis after a country's name refers to the first year of the capital inflow episode. See Schadler et al. (1993).

34 The successor states of former Czechoslovakia, the Czech Republic and the Slovak Republic, formed on 1 January 1993 a monetary union which abruptly terminated after 38 days, experiencing a short period of massive speculation that questioned the viability of the union. During the speculation attack the central banks of the two Republics lost almost all their foreign exchange reserves. For more details see Dedek et al. (1996).

35 In January 1992, Moody's extended the former State Bank of Czechoslovakia the best speculative grade Ba1. In March 1993, the agency upgraded the rating to Baa3 so the Czech Republic became the first among post-communist countries that was awarded an (lowest) investment grade. In May 1994, the rating was increased to Baa2 and in September 1995 to Baa1. The co-operation with Standard and Poor's began in July 1993 by granting the investment grade BBB. In June 1994 the agency improved the rating to BBB+. In 1995 S&P's even skipped one rung in the ladder by awarding investment grade A. See Opravilova (1995) for more details.

36 The first reaction was to close the window for refinancing facilities and shift government owned deposits from commercial banks to the central bank. Reserve requirements were increased and a sort of 'throwing sand into the wheels' measure in the form of limiting the

non-resident short-term open positions of commercial banks was also tried. The key role, however, was given to the open market operations. The shortage of government securities that resulted from the balanced budget policy compelled the CNB to issue its own bills.

37 Even sterilised interventions can make a profit for the central bank if only a part of excess liquidity resulting from purchases of foreign reserves is mopped up by issuing the central bank debt. Under these circumstances, the central bank still pays higher interest rates on issued liabilities and earns lower interest rates on acquired foreign assets but the principal on the earning side is larger than that on the paying side. In assessing the total cost of sterilisation, one should bear in mind the high opportunity cost due to the need to offset an increasing share of foreign assets by reducing the share of domestic credit that entails a loss of market interest. On the other hand, the central bank's balance sheet profits from an increase of non-remunerated reserve requirements.

38 In fact, while the average interest rate differential in the indicated period was equal to 7.99 percent, the average yield from the exchange rate movement added additional 2.65 percentage points.

39 The back-of-the-envelope calculations might look as follows. Provided a major part of the speculation is conducted with six months instruments, then for the 6 percent annualised interest rate differential the band must be no less than 3 percent if the exchange rate is expected to fluctuate across the whole width of the band, or no less than 6 percent if only one half of the band is to create the same amount of the exchange rate risk.

40 In the first quarter of 1997, the Czech economy was even exposed to a new wave of capital inflow in the form of Eurobond issues denominated in Czech currency. During this short period there were 35 new issues in the outstanding value of approx. USD 1.7 bn (for the whole of 1996 it was 26 issues and USD 1.2 bn). The exchange rate reacted with a sharp appreciation reaching its high of 5.5 percent from the central parity. The main reason behind the surge of Eurobond issues was definitely a high interest rate yield, although many observers might question the efficient market hypothesis in the light of increased exchange rate risks because the Czech current account deficit was already one of the largest among emerging markets at that time. Indeed, many retail investors suffered substantial losses when the later depreciation of the Czech currency was taken into account. On the technical side, the issuing of Eurobonds was frequently accompanied by cross-currency swaps whose aim was to secure a cheaper access to US dollars or D marks for the issuers among whom one could find, for example, the Austrian government, the European Council or large European banks.

41 There were plenty of signals that the external imbalance attacked some prudential limits. The share of current account deficit in GDP exceeded in 1996 the 8 percentage level and was one of the worst ratios among emerging economies without any indication of an early improvement. Foreign exchange reserves in terms of monthly imports dropped from 6.2 as of the end of 1995 to 4.3 in 1996 and rapidly approached the 3-month precautionary standard. The switch from domestic to foreign exchange denominated deposits gained momentum, and mushrooming comments of foreign analysts pointed to an overvaluation of the Czech currency. On the political side, the general elections in June 1996 resulted in a minority right-wing government and brought more rifting into the political scene. The Czech Republic lost the hitherto image of a post-communist country which is free from political stalemates and maintains continuity in the reform programme.

42 In a sense, the currency crisis is a unique and exciting event in which some key monetary variables take on unbelievable values. For example, one week PRIBOR which is the money market interest rate targeted by the CNB was 12.5 percent just before the speculative attack but climbed to 85.6 percent within two weeks. The one-week bid-ask

spread jumped from pre-crisis 0.27 up to 27.83 percentage points. The difference between the short-end and the long-end of the money market yield curve (one week - one year spread) widened from 0.65 to 42.18 percentage points. The overnight rate reached its high of 197.5 percent. A massive squeeze of liquidity in order to cool down speculative profits compelled commercial banks to dispose of the CNB bills whose holdings in commercial bank portfolios dropped from CZK 65.9 bn to CZK 24.6 bn within a short period of time. The volume of foreign exchange reserves spent in direct interventions amounted to USD 2.3 bn (approx. 20 percent of the pre-attack value).

43 The switch to a managed floating led to the demise of the currency basket (65 percent DEM, 35 percent USD) by means of which the band was defined and the actual position of the exchange rate was measured. Nevertheless, it became customary to continue expressing the exchange rate fluctuations in the old fashion for the convenience of visualising the degree of exchange rate changes under new circumstances. In the new system, however, the pivotal role in measuring exchange rate volatility has been assigned to the price of the German mark in terms of domestic currency. The flotation avoids any official commitment to defend a particular level or a band vis-à-vis the reference currency, but it does not preclude the central bank from forming its own view about smoothing out 'fundamentally unsustainable' deviations. As far as the technical side of interventions is concerned, the procedure of exchange rate fixing proved quite clumsy owing to the acquired understanding that an effective intervention has a lot to do with such things as optimal timing, surprising the markets, minimising publicity and other psychological tricks that are unfeasible within the rigid scheme of fixing.

44 Interestingly enough, soon after the currency crisis the foreign capital regained confidence and started to return in large quantities. If the CNB did not occasionally intervene, a resulting exchange rate appreciation would smash a fragile recovery from the attack and initiated a new wave of currency turbulences.

45 The factual exchange rate stability may not be sufficient to fulfil the Maastricht exchange rate criterion because it requires not only the observation of normal fluctuation margins without a devaluation but also a country's participation for a period of two years in the Exchange Rate Mechanism of the European Monetary System. The latter provision then would force to taking on of commitments of the so-called ERM II designed for those EU members who do not participate in a single currency. But such institutional constraint seems to raise no serious obstacle if the ERM II will take over the 30-percentage band used in the current ERM. In fact, with such permissible fluctuations the Czech economy would still qualify even after the currency crisis.

46 See Krzak (1996) for a detailed description of the Polish and Hungarian experience with moderate inflation.

47 According to the Maastricht Treaty, a high degree of price stability is interpreted as an average rate of inflation observed over a period of one year before the examination that does not exceed by more than 1.5 percentage points that of the three best performing member states in terms of price stability. Inflation shall be measured by means of the consumer price index on a comparable basis.

48 In the Czech Republic, the inflation indexation has been used in the procedures of calculating pensions and subsistence income. According to current rules, pensions command an adjustment whenever the CPI index is higher by more than 5 percent from the last adjustment. The law stipulates the compensation equal to the inflation plus at least 1/3 of the average real wage increase during the previous two years. Subsistence income is a notional income on the base of which a system of multiples determine various social benefits. The law instructs, but does not command, the government to make a change in

subsistence income whenever the CPI index grows by more than 5 percent from the last change.

49 Let us recall some arguments that were meant as a theoretical underpinning of the view about the alleged ineptitude of tight anti-inflationary policies. The so-called catching-up principle maintained that it is counter-productive to put brakes on inflation in the face of a large gap between domestic and world prices. The magnitude of the gap was measured by the deviation of the market exchange rate from that based on purchasing power parity. The hands-off implication was that a tight monetary policy cannot remove the gap, it only artificially stretches the time period domestic prices need to catch up with the world level. And by reaching this end-point, inflation will supposedly evaporate by itself. The catching-up argument became increasingly odd when growing current account deficits suggested overvaluation rather than undervaluation. It also left aside the possibility of an inflationary spiral in which price increases feed exchange rate weakening which feeds price increases, and so on. Some attention was also paid to a Balassa-type theory based on the interplay between the tradable and non-tradable sectors. This approach gives support to the conclusion that higher inflation does not hurt if it is generated by the productivity gap between the two sectors (see Balassa (1964) for a formal treatment). However, this kind of analysis which represents a more sophisticated version of purchasing power theory puts the gravity of the exchange rate determination on the current account of the balance of payments and thus misses the core of the problem. Interestingly enough, internal CNB calculations of the 'optimal' inflation based on the Balassa-type reasoning led to the range of 5-6 percent implying a rather strong disinflation input of the Czech monetary authorities.

50 Table 5 shows another conspicuous feature of Czech inflation. This is a high weight of agricultural products whose prices are mostly driven by non-monetary factors such as weather conditions. As a consequence, so called core inflation, understood as that part of the CPI index which has been adjusted for 'non-monetary' price increases, has a quite narrow base. Indeed, only less than one half of the consumption basket is left after deregulations and agricultural price have been put aside. This low representation of core inflation may complicate the adoption of inflation targeting.

51 It should be noted that real exchange rate appreciation only evidences a worsening of price competitiveness, not the loss of price competitiveness. The latter has been frequently measured by the so-called ERDI (Exchange Rate Deviation Index) defined as a ratio between the market and the PPP based exchange rates. In this respect, the data suggest a still noteworthy competitive edge of the Czech economy. For example, a UN sponsored Program ECP 93 identified for the Czech currency as high as 2.81 undervaluation against USD and 3.57 undervaluation against DEM. Using turnovers with 31 major trade partners, Capek (1997) estimates the ERDI for years 1993, 1994 and 1995 as high as 2.58, 2.45 and 2.09 respectively. A straightforward interpretation would thus indicate that the Czech currency was undervalued by as much as 100 percent in 1995. The same author also experiments with different measures of real exchange rate appreciation and concludes that between the first quarter of 1993 and the third quarter of 1996 the Czech currency strengthened in real terms by 15-25 percent, depending on the method of calculation. Putting the two pieces of information together, the real exchange rate appreciation could hardly be the main cause of unsustainable current account deficits because it seemed to cut away only a slim slice from the underlying undervaluation. A similar conflicting evidence between the level of price competitiveness and the rate of its erosion can be obtained from using labour cost indicators. As claimed by Vintrova (1997), the average wage in the Czech Republic reached in 1996 only 17.8 percent of that of the EU-15. For unit labour

cost it was 42 percent. Notwithstanding a large margin of error in the above pieces of evidence, they seem quite robust to throw some doubts on the allegation that deplorable currency turbulences were the consequence of the loss of price and wage competitiveness brought about by excessive real exchange rate appreciation. The problem with this diagnosis is the logical suggestion that not a comprehensive stabilisation package but just offsetting exchange rate weakening would comprise the sufficient remedy against widening external imbalance.

52 The criticism of the CNB's exchange rate policies was also marked by some confusion or barely acceptable arguments. For example, some critics urged on a devaluation even after the wide band had already replaced the fixed exchange rate regime. Others advocated the flotation in order to give market forces the freedom in determining the exchange rate level but failed to notice that the wide band had not been constraining market fluctuations for more than one year. The CNB was also criticised for not intervening when the exchange rate experienced a sharp appreciation within the band. But it should be noted that the current account deficit was rapidly approaching prudential limits at that time, so an official intervention was likely to precipitate a collapse of currency. The Mexican experience with an attempt at a corrective devaluation just on the eve of the currency crisis in December 1994 may provide a warning parallel (see Griffith-Jones (1996)). Finally, one should dismiss accusations that the CNB wasted external reserves and stifled business activity by high interest rates in the course of warding off the speculative attack. The point is that without defensive steps the exchange rate might be afflicted by an unforeseeable fall. A likely overshooting would provoke massive inflationary pressures, which would have to be fended off by a prohibitive increase of interest rates. So, the economy would not be spared a distress that might be even more painful than that actually perceived.

53 An easy exercise with T-accounts may explain the following paradox: even if a current account deficit is matched by the capital inflow of the same magnitude, the money supply may yet drop by up to the given amount of current account deficit. A key to the answer lies in the treatment of residents' and non-residents' banking deposits for the purpose of measuring money supply. While the former is a regular part of money (irrespective of currency denomination of deposits), the latter is not.

54 Hungary, known for frequent irregular devaluations, launched a stabilisation programme in March 1995. According to Kornai (1996), an important factor that educated the socialist Hungarian government about the necessity of austerity measures was a fear not to repeat the dreadful Mexican scenario. At the time of finalising this paper, Slovakia was trapped by more than 10 percent share of current account deficit in GDP, deploying the import surcharge and stricter administrative controls to back up the exchange rate as well as promising a kind of stabilisation package. Also Poland whose crawling peg was to prevent real exchange rate appreciation in producer prices became a target of accentuated discussion whether a growing external imbalance will not get out of control.

55 See Patria Finance (1997) for a graphical exposition of this argument.

56 This is probably the main reason why a crawling peg or band did not attract serious support in the Czech Republic. At the time the fixed exchange rate started to falter, it seemed a too radical departure from predominantly positive experience with the nominal exchange rate anchor and a step back from achieved consolidation of the economy. A predetermined rate of mini-devaluations was feared to find its way into wage bargaining, so many doubted whether it was worthwhile to give fresh jolts to inflationary expectations once the economy already enjoyed single digit inflation. The impact on export performance was thought minuscule, particularly if the pace of the crawl would be based on the PPI index whose increase was roughly half of that based on using consumer prices.

57 The interest rate criterion demands that over a period of one year before the examination a member state has an average nominal long-term interest rate that does not exceed by more than 2 percentage points that of the three best performing member states in terms of price stability.

58 An important indicator of financial openness is the foreign exchange turnover in respective currencies. According to BIS data, the Czech Republic is a plain forerunner among East European economies. While the total turnover for the whole region was estimated at USD 8.1 bn in April 1997, the Czech koruna accounted for 5.1 bn. For the Hungarian forint it was 0.4 bn, Polish zloty 0.4 bn, Russian rouble 1.4 bn and Slovak koruna 0.4 bn.

59 When the Czech Republic entered the group of OECD countries it signed a document in which it pledged to complete liberalisation in line with the following timetable. By 1997, the authorisation of government to impose interest-free deposit requirements should be waived from the Foreign Exchange Act. By 1998, no restrictions should constrain the extension of credits and financial guarantees by a resident to a non-resident. By 1999, foreign securities should have free access to domestic primary and secondary markets. By 2001, non-residents should be allowed to purchase domestic real estates and residents could keep deposits abroad.

60 In fact, currency turbulences revealed a dubious protective value of legal controls in the achieved degree of capital mobility. On the one hand, the Foreign Exchange Act authorises the government to suspend many features of currency convertibility in case of balance-of-payment emergency situations. But when the economy was really hit by the currency crisis and some politicians publicly spoke about triggering the suspension article, the CNB felt that the impact of such suggestions on the depth of the crisis would be devastating. Therefore, the Bank was fast and resolute in denouncing any idea of re-regulating capital outflows.

REFERENCES

Abramson, D., 1997, The Euro and Central European Currencies; in Central Europe and the Euro; BCA Publications; Montreal 1997, forthcoming.

Backé, P., 1997, "Integrating Central and Eastern Europe into the European Union: The Monetary Dimension", *Conference paper in Reforming the European Union and Prospects for Enlargements,* Warsaw, May 1997.

Backé, P., and Linder, I., 1996, "European Monetary Union: Prospects for EU Member States and Selected Candidate Countries from Central and Eastern Europe, *Focus on Transition,* 2/1996, Österreichische Nationalbank.

Balassa, B., 1964, "The Purchasing-Power Parity Doctrine: A Reappraisal, *Journal of Political Economy,* No. 72, 1964.

Bean, Ch.R., 1992, "Economic and Monetary Union in Europe", CEPR, *Discussion Paper* No. 772, CEPR, October 1992.

Buch, C. M., and Heinrich, R. P., 1997, "The End of the Czech Miracle?" *Kiel discussion paper 301,* Institute für Weltwirtschaft, June 1997.

Capek, A., 1997, "Real Effective Exchange Rate: Problems of Measuring (in Czech)", *Working paper No. 73,* Institute of Economics of the Czech National Bank.

Commission of the European Communities, 1990, "One Market, One Money", *European Economy,* 44, October 1990.

Cottarelli, C., 1993, "Limiting Central Bank Credit to the Government", *Occasional Paper No. 110*, International Monetary Fund, December 1993.

Dedek, O., 1995, "Currency Convertibility and Exchange Rate Policies in the Czech Republic", *Eastern European Economics*, November-December 1995.

Dedek, O., et.al.. 1996, The Break-up of Czechoslovakia: An In-depth Economic Analysis, Avebury, England.

Dedek, O., and Derviz, A., 1995, "Exchange Rate Policies in a Wider Band (in Czech)", *Politicka ekonomie*, 1996/5.

De Grauwe, P., 1994, The Economics of Monetary Integration; Oxford University Press.

Dornbush, R., 1994, Exchange Rate Policies in Economies in Transition; in: Barth, R.C., and Wong, Ch.-H., Approaches to Exchange Rate Policy, IMF Institute, Washington.

Dornbush, R., and Fisher, S., 1993, "Moderate Inflation", *World Bank Economic Review*, Vol. 7, No. 1.

Eichengreen, B., 1990, "Currency union", *Economic Policy*, April 1990.

El-Agraa, A.M., 1990, The Economics of the European Community; 3 ed., Philip Allan.

European Commission, 1997, Agenda 2000: For a Stronger and Wider Union, Strasbourg, July 1997.

European Monetary Institute, 1995, The Changeover to the Single Currency, November 1995.

European Monetary Institute, 1997, The Single Monetary Policy in Stage Three, January 1997.

Fisher S., 1996, "Why are Central Banks Pursuing Long-Run Price Stability?", in: Achieving Price Stability, Federal Reserve Bank of Kansas City, August 1996.

Garber, P.M., and Lall, S., 1996, "Derivative Products in Exchange Rate Crisis", *Conference Paper,* Managing Capital Flows and Exchange Rates: Lesson from the Pacific Basin, Federal Reserve Bank of San Francisco, September 1996.

Goldstein, M., 1996, "Presumptive Indicators/Early Warning Signals of Vulnerability to Financial Crises in Emerging-Market Economies", *Preliminary Paper*, Institute for International Economics, January 1996.

Goodhart, C.A.E., 1995, The Political Economy of Monetary Union, in: Kenen, P. (ed.), Understanding Interdependence: The Macroeconomics of the Open Economy, Princeton University Press.

Griffith-Jones, S., 1996, "The Mexican Peso Crisis"; *ECLAC Review*; December 1996.

Gros, D., and Thygesen, N., 1992, European Monetary Integration, Longman, London.

Helpman, E., Leiderman, L., and Bufman, G., 1994, "A new brand of exchange rate bands: Chile, Israel and Mexico", *Economic Policy*, October 1994.

Hochreiter, E., 1995, "Necessary Conditions for a Successful Pursuit of a Hard Currency Strategy in an Economy in Transition", *Annual Meeting of the Western Economic Association*, San Diego, July 1995.

Hochreiter, E., and Winckler, G., 1995, "The advantages of tying Austria's hand: The success of the hard currency strategy", *European Journal of Political Economy*, Vol. 11.

Hrncir, M., 1993, "Foreign Exchange Rate Regime and Economic Recovery", *Prague Economic Papers*, 1993/1.

Hrncir, M., 1997, "The Global and Regional Outlook in Central Europe", *Conference Paper, Regionalism and Economic Integration and Global Economic Cooperation*, Prague, January 1997.

Hrncir, M., and Klacek, J., 1991, "Stabilization Policies and Currency Convertibility in Czechoslovakia", *European Economy*, Special Edition, 2/1991.

Icard, A., 1994, "The Transmission of Monetary Policy in an Environment of Deregulation and Exchange Rate Stability", *Journal of Monetary Economics, 33.*

Ilzkovitz, F., 1996, Challenges to the Monetary and Exchange Rate Policies of Central and East European Acceding Countries: An EU Perspective, in: Radzyner, O., and Havlik, P. (ed.), Monetary Policy in Central and Eastern Europe: Challenges of EU Integration, Österreichische Nationalbank and the Vienna Institute for Comparative Economic Studies, Vienna.

Institute of International Finance, Country Reports, various issues, Washington.

Janackova, S., 1997, "European Union Accession: Selected Topics for Czech Monetary Policy", *Working Paper, No. 72*, Institute of Economics of the Czech National Bank.

Jilek, J., 1996, "Foreign Capital Inflow and Foreign Exchange Positions of the Banks" (in Czech), *Politicka ekonomie*, 1996/1.

Kenen, P.B., 1988, Managing Exchange Rates, Routledge, London and New York.

Kenen, P.B., 1995, Economic and Monetary Union in Europe: Moving Beyond Maastricht, Cambridge University Press.

Kim, S.B., 1997, Thailand: Challenges After the Float, Goldman Sachs, Economic Research, July 1997.

Kornai, J., 1996, "Adjustment Without Recession: A Case Study of the Hungarian Stabilization", Collegium Budapest, *Discussion Paper No. 33*, August 1996.

Krzak, M., 1996, "Persistent Moderate Inflation in Poland and Hungary", *Focus on Transition*, 2/1996, Österreichische Nationalbank.

Masson, P.R., and Taylor, M. P., 1992, "Common Currency Areas and Currency Unions: An Analysis of the Issues", CEPR, *Discussion Paper No. 617*, February 1992.

Mathieson, D.J., and Rojas-Suarez, L., 1992, Liberalization of the Capital Account: Experiences and Issues, IMF Working Paper, June 1992.

Nachtigal, V., 1997, "The Czech Economy in the First Half of 1990s: Comparison with Similar European Economies" (in Czech), *Working Paper, No. 66*, Institute of Economics of the Czech National Bank.

Opravilova, R., 1995, "Development of the Czech Republic's Rating" (in Czech), *Bankovnictvi*, 20/1995.

Patria Research, 1997, Macroeconomic Survey - July (in Czech), Patria Finance, Prague.

Sachs, J. D., 1966, "Economic Transition and the Exchange-Rate Regime", *AEA Papers and Proceedings*, May 1966.

Schadler, S., Carkovic, M., Bennett, A., and Kahn, R., 1993, Recent Experiences with Surges in Capital Inflows, IMF Occasional Paper 108, Washington DC, December 1993.

Schuitemaker, E., 1996, EMU & Euro: The Consequences, ABN-AMRO Bank, Economic Department, November 1996.

Taylor, Ch., 1995, EMU 2000?, The Royal Institute of International Affairs.

Tosovsky, J., 1996, Disinflation in the Czech Republic: Looking Both Backward and Forward, in: Achieving Price Stability, Federal Reserve Bank of Kansas City.

Tosovsky, J., 1997, "European Monetary Integration from the Perspective of Central European Countries", *an address given at the London School of Economics*, March 1997.

Vintrova, R., International Position and Competitiveness: Comparison of Macroeconomic Indicators with European Union (in Czech), Finance a uver; forthcoming.

Williamson, J., 1993, "Exchange Rate Management", *Economic Journal*, January 1993.

Wyplosz, Ch., 1997, Monetary Options for the "Outs", in: Monetary Policy in Transition in East and West: Strategies, Instruments and Transmission Mechanisms, Österreichische Nationalbank, Vienna .

Chapter 9

Monetary Arrangements and Exchange Rate Regime in a Small Transitional Economy (Slovenia)

IVAN RIBNIKAR

1. INTRODUCTION

The monetary arrangements, monetary policy, exchange rate regime and exchange rate policy that have been in existence in Slovenia since October 1991, when Slovenia became independent, had not been introduced in an empty space. There were very important left-overs, especially in the financial sector, of the market-planned economic system, that had to be replaced by the market economic system (or capitalism), and there were quite a few experiences with a kind of monetary integration. The replacement of the market-planned economic system means in the first place abolishment of the social ownership of business enterprises. As this has been done in the first place according to the wishes and whims of politicians, and contrary to the logic of economics and efficiency, the chosen method of the abolishment of the social ownership of business enterprises must figure at the same level as left-overs of the past and experiences with previous monetary arrangements, when monetary arrangements, monetary policy, exchange rate regime and exchange rate policy are analysed.

In the second part of the paper the impact of the past and/or endogenous changes that triggered off the beginning of transition already at the end of 1988 are analysed. In the third part »privatisation«, i.e. the chosen method of abolishment of the social ownership of business enterprises, is explained and/or analysed as to how it should be understood. In the fourth part the impact of the chosen method of »privatisation« on macroeconomic saving and capital markets is explained. So in the first four parts of this paper a kind of background to the topic of the paper is presented and analysed.

In the fifth part of the paper, the experiences with a former monetary integration within the Yugoslav Dinar »currency area« are analysed. The lesson is: never again join the monetary integration. But something must be added: at least, if good money cannot be achieved and sustained. In the sixth part of the paper, an analysis is given of all available monetary arrangements in combination with exchange rate regimes at the beginning of transition or monetary independence. In the seventh part, an answer is given to the question of why one should have one's own money.

In the eighth part of the paper, the problems and peculiarities of the monetary system and monetary policy are to be found. In the ninth part, the problems and mechanisms of exchange rate policy, i.e. of sterilisation, are presented and analysed.

In the final, tenth part a kind of summing up is given. For the monetary arrangements, monetary policy, exchange rate regime and exchange rate policy in the future, the question is put: should a transitional economy like Slovenia strive to join the European single currency area?

2. THE IMPACT OF THE PAST AND/OR ENDOGENOUS CHANGES THAT TRIGGERED OFF THE BEGINNING OF TRANSITION

If we want to understand how the changes that can be designated as the changes due to transition - the name that came into use later (in Yugoslavia those changes began at the end of 1988) - occurred in Slovenia, we must at first understand the past. As will be seen, it is not just understanding the (economic) past, but should have been much more: it should have been taking into account its peculiar economic past in designing transition, but this was not the case. We have, of course, in mind a peculiar economic system, the so-called market-planned economic system and the consequences or left-overs of that economic system. External shocks, the collapse of communism in Eastern Europe and the Soviet Union and the disintegration of Yugoslavia, came later and they did not trigger off the changes in Slovenia or, at that time, in Yugoslavia. They might have had important influences on the path of transition, and we may say something about that later in our text, but they did not start the changes - the transition process. We will, of course, be interested not so much in what was happening in politics but mostly in what way the economic changes were initiated endogenously and, to some extent, what the impact was of external shocks on the speed and trajectory of transition.

The case of Slovenia (and/or Yugoslavia until its disintegration) may be of interest because it is in a way an empirical proof that a third way or third economic system - the economic system that is neither market or capitalist nor centrally-planned - is not possible, at least not in the long run. It may now seem unimportant since capitalism has become dominant, but, as people in so-called transitional economies are not very enthusiastic about "real" capitalism[1] (as they were not satisfied with "real" socialism), some alternative or a third way may come to their mind.[2] The functioning of that third economic system, we will call it a market-planned economic system (we may call it the economic system with social ownership of business enterprises or with workers' self-management), made finally, for instance in the second half of the eighties, such radical changes necessary to undermine the very essence of the system. We shall try to explain the logic of the system, its functioning, in what way the system deteriorated and how it came to its end. What was happening outside the economy before the end of 1988 was very noisy, but fundamental changes were taking place in the economy. And it was these changes that started the transition and have influenced it so far, although external shocks were added later. In some respects they might have played even the major role.

* * *

In Slovenia the past is a market-planned economic system, introduced at the beginning of the fifties. We are not interested in why it was introduced. Maybe we can provide the shortest answer by saying that it was the only way of not having a centrally-planned economy (Yugoslavia was, for instance, a federation with fairly diverse component parts but without a leading nation), but at the same time not having either a market economy or capitalism. It should have been a socialist country with the "leading role" of the Party, even if the Party should have been decentralised. And we can say, so decentralised that the country finally fell apart, the credit for which should go primarily to the communists who in the meantime turned into nationalists under fancy names like liberals, democrats, etc.

If we go back to our subject, we must say that at the basis of the economic system there was social ownership of business enterprises. Social ownership means that business enterprises are owned neither by private persons nor by the state. They are owned by nobody in particular but by everybody in general. And social ownership should mean this ownership by everybody (in Yugoslavia) in general. In all other respects business enterprises are the same as or, at least, very similar to business enterprises in a market economy. They are legal entities and they own all their assets (real and financial). They can buy and sell assets. On the liabilities side of their balance sheet they have debts, in the first place to banks and to other business enterprises on the basis of trade credits. They have also nondebt capital, something similar to equity, but it was not equity. We can call it quasi equity because it was on the one side the same as equity. It was not repayable as long as the business enterprise was a going concern (and business enterprises were never, or at least very seldom gone concerns - probably because there were no proper provisions for new business enterprises to appear) and no contractual payments were to be paid for this capital. But on the other side it was quite different because behind it one could not find owners if, of course, one is not satisfied with society as a whole as the owner. That part of capital was called "business fund" and later, when the transition had started, it was wrongly renamed as "social capital".[3]

At the first sight one may think that it might be quite an ingenious idea for abolishing state ownership and/or a centrally planned economy without introducing private ownership and/or market economy or capitalism. By keeping what should have been ownership of individuals or the state in limbo by not declaring to whom it belongs, one does not come to equity, which does not belong to the state, but one comes at least to quasi equity not belonging to the state. If one is not very particular about the fact that there is quasi equity instead of equity, one may be satisfied that there are business enterprises very similar, some might have said even equal, to business enterprises in a market economy. And economists were not very particular about that - not only in Yugoslavia.[4] They usually stressed workers' self-management and some were even overwhelmed by it.[5]

It was probably good that such "subtle differences" - i.e. that there was quasi equity and not equity - were neglected at the beginning, when there was the question of whether the new economic system would be sold to (i.e. taking into account its ideological content), and/or accepted by ideological watchdogs. We may say that the negligence and/or ignorance, as concerns what social ownership really means economically or financially, helped to replace the centrally-planned economic system and state ownership of business enterprises. However, it took too long before it became clear and was accepted by those with power in what way the ownership that replaced the state ownership was peculiar, how it was undermining the financial system and through it the very basis of the economy, how useless or counterproductive some quite logical measures and endeavours were, for instance endeavours for interest rates to be positive in real terms, for the system to function.[6] Throughout its lifetime there were more or less permanent reforms, but none of them touched upon the essence of the system: the impact of social ownership of business enterprises on finance and through it on its economic performance and viability.

But social ownership or quasi equity (capital) of business enterprises in social ownership is not just an ingenious escape from state ownership and capitalism at the same time, but something much more. It not only allows, but also requires somebody with power, i.e. the Party, to interfere in the affairs of business enterprises. In some cases, for instance when a new business enterprise is to be created or when big investments are to be made, they were required to intervene directly. Business enterprises needed money and those with power provided it like a "deus ex-machina". Therefore we must show what legal and financial framework was required for business enterprises to operate: to appear or be born at all at first, and to invest and/or expand afterwards once they existed. As will be seen quite a peculiar framework was required because of the social ownership of business enterprises.

* * *

Quasi equity may be looked upon as something ingenious only until one comes to two very simple questions and finds out that there is no answer within the legal framework of social ownership and within a normal financial system.[7] The first question is how a new business enterprise begins. Who provides the money for a business enterprise to start? As we know, at the very beginning in the first place nondebt capital is required. This means that equity is required in the sense that somebody must be prepared permanently to put its money into a newly created business enterprise. At that moment, society or everybody in general and nobody in particular, it means quasi equity, does not suffice. Anonymous cannot invest money. We come to the first major flaw of the system.

A similar question is how the already existing business enterprises expand, i. e. increase their (real) assets. Where are funds coming from? They should, actually, not be able to increase their (real) assets on the basis of externally increased nondebt capital, because in this case somebody in particular is required as well. However, we may say that nondebt capital should be increased in the existing business enterprises only internally, and this may be taken as a minor problem? But this brings us immediately to the second major problem of the system and/or to the second question.

It turns out namely that business enterprises in social ownership should be highly leveraged. They should be such from the moment they appeared and/or after big investments as there were no provisions for their nondebt capital to increase externally. But that is not the end of the story. Debt capital was treated as something transitional, contrary to the very essence of the business enterprises with workers' self-management. They were supposed to exercise their self-management rights on the basis of "business funds" or social ownership and not on the basis of debt capital belonging to others, their lenders. According to this it was required of business enterprises to start repaying their debts very soon and to repay them in a short period of time.

And so we come to the second question: i.e. how the highly leveraged business enterprises (it was not unusual for ninety percent or even more of all capital to be debt capital), were able to service their debts, if the amount of repayments of loans and payments of interests exceeded their (free) cash flow. This might mean exceeded by several times, which was quite normal for new business enterprises or business enterprises after big investments. Since workers' self-management was based on nondebt capital - the "business fund" or quasi equity - the quick repayment of debts, for quasi equity to replace debt capital, formed the second pillar of the system, if we take social ownership or quasi equity as the first pillar.

Let us look for the answers to the two questions. As concerns the first question, nobody (in particular) was prepared to put his money into a business enterprise for quasi equity to appear or be increased externally, the answer may be that altruists would be prepared to do this. This is true, but as soon as we come to altruists whom we should rely on in economics, we are living in a utopia. Nevertheless, funds were coming externally to business enterprises, usually in small proportions of all external funds flowing into business enterprises, but from or through the interventions of realists and not from altruist. We have already said that those in power outside business enterprises were required to intervene for the system to function, and this is the one case when they must intervene. Usually they made somebody put his money permanently into a newly created business enterprise. It was usually a small proportion of all money. In this way, among other things, it was in fact easier to make the major flaw of the system invisible (it was a question of small or negligible amounts of funds flowing into business enterprises for which a proper solution had not yet been found – this might have been the answer if somebody had put embarrassing question), because all other capital came easily as debt capital via bank loans. As those in power had the banks under their control they were playing the role of the "deus ex-machina" via the banks. The problem of funds flowing into business enterprises was being solved. They made the functioning of the economic system possible with the first big flaw: quasi equity or ownership of business enterprises by all in general instead of equity and ownership of business enterprises by individuals and/or entities in particular.

But there is then the problem of how to repay debts in an amount bigger than the (free) cash flow, and these repayments were required because otherwise there would not be the basis for workers' self-management – i.e. nondebt capital. The only escape for a particular business enterprise was to increase its prices and through higher prices increase its cash flow to be able to service its debt. And it was a usual phenomenon that business enterprises after big investments increased the prices of their products because of the debt-servicing burden. Other business enterprises followed, and through the partly known mechanism of price and wage increases and inflation, that had other causes as well, made debt burden easier because nominal interest rates in general, until mid-eighties at least, did not increase on account of inflation.

Interest rates were negative in real terms and made business enterprises able to service their debts, to replace debt capital by quasi equity (capital) in a relatively short period of time.

The solution of the problem for the business enterprises - how to repay their debts and pay interests in amounts greater than their (free) cash flows - was found in inflation that changed nominal positive interest rates into negative real interest rates and/or loans into grants. So we can talk about inflation as a natural habitat for business enterprises in social ownership.

Thus we have a logical and interesting phenomenon. Because business enterprises were not allowed to increase their nondebt capital externally in the normal way, i.e. on the basis of interests of those who had money and wanted to invest it permanently into some business, once they came somehow into existence (for newly created business enterprises those in power took care that the seed of nondebt capital should be provided without being forced to rely on altruists), peculiar or abnormal methods for the increase of their nondebt capital externally had been found. External funds were flowing into business enterprises as debt capital, but because of the negative real interest rates the important part of these inflows of funds were grants that were increasing the nondebt capital of business enterprises. We can see some consistency:[8] inflation as something abnormal becomes a natural habitat or something normal for business enterprises that are prevented from doing something quite normal, namely, externally increasing their nondebt capital.

So there are two major financial peculiarities for business enterprises in social ownership. The first is the required interference of those in power in the affairs of the business enterprises. This interference meant providing for inflow of funds into business enterprises. It was never institutionalised and those in power did not mean a central authority or in the first place a central authority, for instance the government, but those in power at lower or at various levels. Power means decentralised power. The second peculiarity was inflation and through it the required negative real interest rates. This requirement had a devastating effect on banks (they were relied upon to see to it that enough funds came into business enterprises through their loans that must have been to a great enough degree grants), saving (voluntary saving existed only if households and business enterprises were for instance able to keep savings in foreign currency deposits with banks - but this undermined banks and later the government because of increasing bank losses due to their short foreign currency position), the balance of payments and foreign indebtedness, investment and growth.

As time passed it became ever more difficult to finance investments, provide growth and prevent a further increase in inflation. Once indexation had been introduced for loans, the logic of the market-planned economic system disappeared. Inflation exploded but, nevertheless, it was not possible any more, because of the indexation of loans, to ensure the accumulation of quasi equity capital of business enterprises. They became unable to repay their debts so that the investments of business enterprises decreased.

We may say that indexation of loans was introduced too soon or that the authorities, those in power or the Party, recognised or acknowledged too late - at the end of 1988 - the logic of the system. It was of course not a question of changing the system or economic policy, but rather of abolishing social ownership of business enterprises and/or workers' self-management. This may be looked upon as an arrangement based on a utopian idea or as an arrangement of enabling the Party to stay in power, even though the centrally-planned economy or state ownership had been abolished, by making it indispensable not only in politics; this necessity may be eroded after some time, but in the economy and through it in politics. The Law on business enterprises at the end of 1988 should be taken as a breakthrough. The legal framework for the abolishment of social ownership (and/or workers' self-management) was erected. That was the beginning of transition.

* * *

If, at the end of this section, we take a market-planned economic system as an alternative to the centrally planned economic system, then we must take it as something very positive or good. Its performance was much better than that of any centrally planned economic system. It was in essence a decentralised economic system, business enterprises were autonomous, and the market played an important role. Its utopian character or the necessity for somebody outside business enterprises or outside economics to interfere in the affairs of business enterprises as "deus ex-machina" should be taken as a necessary price that had to be paid for this much better performance (and much softer dictatorship). As the system was utopian, if looked upon through laws, pragmatism or the so-called "creative interpretation of laws" had been the very essence of the system.

But as has been seen, its utopian character, because of the social ownership of business enterprises, made finance peculiar. One of the main requirements of finance had been to enable business enterprises to increase their nondebt capital through bank loans. We know how these strange requirements were achieved and that finance was the main victim of the functioning of the system. And it was finance that required changes, i.e. a turnaround, or a new framework for the transition.

The market-planned economic system came to its end, or approached it, as a financial collapse. The new framework for transition at the end of 1988 appeared in some way endogenously. But later external shocks, for instance the disintegration of Yugoslavia, became important in shaping the transition. If we say in shaping the transition, not so much in shaping the abolishment of social ownership of business enterprises (as will be seen, all mimicked what had been wrongly suggested by experts coming from abroad), as in shaping the monetary stability, liberalisation of foreign trade and international flow of capital, the exchange-rate regime and openness of the economy.

3. PRIVATISATION AND "PRIVATISATION", I.E. ABOLISHMENT OF SOCIAL OWNERSHIP OF BUSINESS ENTERPRISES

We can talk about privatisation in market economies if state ownership of business enterprises changes into private ownership through free distribution or sale of shares of state owned business enterprises. We can talk about privatisation in centrally planned economies with state ownership as well. But in a market-planned economy with social and not state ownership of business enterprises we cannot talk about privatisation but rather about abolishment of social ownership of business enterprises. If we are to stay with privatisation, we should talk about so-called privatisation or "privatisation".[9]

If we talk about "privatisation" in the case of Slovenia, it is not just an unnecessary formal distinction. Formally the state had not much more say in socially owned business enterprises than it had in privately owned business enterprises in market economies. The function of the "deus ex-machina" was not provided by the state but informally by those who had power in various institutions. Among them were usually members of the Party, not grass roots, but those who had higher positions in the hierarchy. But, contrary to the market economies, in which power is in the hands of those who are rich, in a market-planned economic system the power was in the hands of those who were politically strong. So we cannot talk about privatisation because there was no state ownership and it was not the state that had power in business enterprises. It was social ownership, and the power in business enterprises was not concentrated in the hands of one but dispersed among the powerful. The problem was to abolish social ownership and the power in business enterprises that was associated with it. The power was not in the hands of those who had permanent ownership stakes in business enterprises because, as we know, nobody was allowed, not even the Government, to have such a permanent stake.

Additionally, the economic system was decentralised and business enterprises were autonomous. The market, more or less only the commodity market, was crucial for them. We cannot otherwise explain the permanent struggle of business enterprises for prices either to be increased, if they were administrative, or to be liberalised, if business enterprises felt strong enough to compete with others. Wages and other benefits of workers depended to a great extent on the performance of business enterprises, although performance was not ascertained in the same way as in market economies. The cost of capital and/or return on it was somewhat peculiar, so that the ability to pay wages and other benefits was crucial and was, if we simplify a bit, a measure or an indicator of economic performance of the business enterprises. So it was not social ownership per se that was accountable for the much better performance of business enterprises than the performance of business enterprises in centrally-planned economies, but the decentralised nature of the economic system, the autonomy of business enterprises and the role the (commodity) market was allowed to play. Financial markets were much less developed. We cannot talk about a market for bank loans and their deposits. As we have said, the banks played a very important and peculiar role. Through them the funds were flowing into business enterprises. Some forms of financial markets were non-existent, as was the case of the (capital) market for equity securities.

If we take the example of Slovenia, "privatisation", although the door was opened for the transition at the end of 1988, came to a standstill once it became evident to those involved, i.e. politicians, that it was crucial for the future distribution of power in a society who would become rich.[10] "Privatisation" is to be the quickest and simplest way for the concentration of wealth and through it the power in the right (i.e. their) hands. And it took quite some time before all concerned agreed how to abolish social ownership, i.e. how to ensure that they would get what they thought they were entitled to. The law was passed at the end of 1993 with provisions that by the middle of 1995 all social ownership would disappear, which has been in the meantime several times prolonged and now at the end of 1997 social ownership has, at last, disappeared.

* * *

"Privatisation" was to take place in the economy with the following characteristics. Business enterprises have in general a lot of nondebt capital, renamed, as was said, as "social capital". There are, of course, heavily indebted business enterprises or business enterprises with negative "social capital", but they are not a majority.[11] The process of permanent redistribution of wealth from banks (or the process of permanent primitive accumulation of "social" capital, if we refer to A. Smith and K. Marx), and through them only partly from their depositors (because households were allowed to have foreign currency deposits) to business enterprises, was the only way for business enterprises to change their financial structure (to decrease debts and to increase nondebt capital), but it left losses and bad loans (banks were obliged to expose themselves tremendously to business enterprises by disregarding all prudential criteria, exceeding the amount they should have given in loans even ten or more than ten times) on the assets side of banks' balance-sheets. Both items were counterparts, together with what depositors cumulatively lost as bank depositors on deposits that were not protected by being foreign currency deposits, of that part of nondebt capital of business enterprises that was not created properly, i.e. on the basis of retained genuine and not inflationary earnings.[12]

Banks and business enterprises should be taken together if one wants to understand how business enterprises were able to have so much nondebt capital, when there were no provisions for its appearance, and why banks had so many losses and bad loans. Slovenia was one of the countries where rehabilitation of the banks could have been combined with "privatisation" of business enterprises - because of formal and not only substantive reasons.

Until some time ago (in 1990), when banks were allowed to transform themselves over night into joint stock companies, banks were owned by business enterprises who were owners with unlimited liability. Because of this, all bank losses and bad loans could have very simply disappeared and been replaced by claims to business enterprises as good debtors. Business enterprises as banks' owners should have been required to rehabilitate their banks by replacing on the liabilities side of their balance sheets "social capital" with debts to their banks. If that had been the case, "privatisation" would have started with cleaned up banks and much less "social capital" to be distributed freely or sold (these two common sense solutions were finally accepted), and there would have been far fewer problems, as will be seen.

But this was not the case. Banks were rehabilitated by government bonds to the burden of all taxpayers, the amount of "social capital" remained inflated and will probably come, as will be seen, into the ownership of a small group for very little money. This is in accordance with what "privatisation" should be politically. It should be the moment when the distribution of power through the distribution of wealth should be decided. Because of this priority, it was important that there was as much wealth, "social capital", as possible to be distributed freely or sold. Following rehabilitation of the banks separately by government bonds or taxpayers' money, there is quite a great amount of "social capital" waiting for "privatisation". All political parties or fractions agreed on such a solution. All claim credit for the collapse of the system that collapsed by itself - and want to be paid for it.

We can say that the system came to its end after - if we neglect the last ten years or so - it had completed its role as the only viable alternative to the centrally planned economic system. A market economy or capitalism was not a viable alternative until the end of 1988. Although nobody can claim to be credited for something that happened by itself, like the collapse of the economic system, which collapsed also legally by law at the end of 1988, nevertheless, there appeared substantial wealth, greater than should have been, waiting for its owners. In such an environment the main question appeared and remained, until the end of 1993 when blueprints were established, who the owners would be and how to distribute free and/or sell shares of business enterprises to be "privatised".

There is, as was said, a combination of free distribution and sale of shares of business enterprises to be "privatised" - with much more emphasis on free distribution. About 40 percent (citizens got certificates whose value was expressed in monetary units) have been or should be distributed through certificates or vouchers. They are to be exchanged, the majority of them have already been exchanged, for shares in business enterprises or investment funds ("authorised" - established just for this purpose - closed end investment companies). Those who are employed in business enterprises to be "privatised" opted mostly for shares of their business enterprises. Others that could not find shares of business enterprises decided for investment funds. Because there is a combination of two principles for distribution of shares, absolute or nominal value for citizens and percentages for three public funds, it emerged that there were not enough shares for citizens to exchange or spend their certificates. Such a combination of two principles would have been possible only if the value of capital of business enterprises to be "privatised" had been by some magic known in advance. It is just an indicator of how seriously the question of "privatisation" has been approached.[13]

Sixty percent of shares should go to three public funds. The Pension Fund and Compensation Fund (of those whose property had been nationalised but are unable to get it back "in natura") should get ten percent each. The remaining 40 percent should stay, at least for some time, in the ownership of the Development Fund, if business enterprises have not decided to sell those remaining shares through public sale and/or to their employees.

In the framework set up by law on "privatisation", besides normal economic activity - at least, desired normal economic activity - there are activities provoked by the way shares of business enterprises had been distributed and/or are to be distributed. Almost all transactors or sectors are involved: citizens or households, "authorised" closed end investment companies, business enterprises, banks, capital markets, the central bank. The way "privatisation" had been done has importantly influenced and will influence in the near future monetary arrangements and exchange rate regime. And it is not only its impact on macroeconomic savings that is our next topic.

4. MACROECONOMIC SAVING AND CAPITAL MARKETS

The role which the capital markets, namely secondary capital markets, should play once the "privatisation" is over is supposed to be very important. It should enable establishment of the equilibrium of the ownership structure of business enterprises. Instead of formal or notional (primary or "original") owners, business enterprises should come via secondary capital markets to genuine, proper, "serious" owners.[14] Before the law on "privatisation" had been passed, if we go for a moment back into history, all efforts went into the discussions about the advantages and drawbacks of two common-sense solutions: free distribution, direct or indirect through investment funds, against the sale of shares in the open market - to the highest bidder, of course. The first solution was supposed to be equitable or socially conscientious. Everyone should get their part of the cake. The second should be purely market oriented. Shares should be offered on the open market and sold to the highest bidders. All wealth should be distributed through the market and, since the market price should be paid for it, it should be at the same time the just solution to the problem of to whom the ownership should go.

Before we explain why such simplified or common-sense solutions are wrong, and why the supposed differences between them - one equitable and the other market oriented - are not that important, we wish to make evident the problems the countries in transition are facing. Western advisers suggested that those countries should do what they probably would never suggest their governments should do, unless their economies were terminally ill, and it did not matter what was done. One should just think about the following task. All business enterprises in Western countries are nationalised or changed into social ownership - by decree. The next day those responsible for the revolution change their minds and want to reintroduce private ownership. But in the meantime, overnight, all records are lost and all records in the memory of people as well. Nobody knows to whom something belonged before the revolution. What to do? If the advice of Western experts and/or academics is to be followed (and this is at the same time in complete accordance with the opinion and interests of those powerful and important - to give them chances to become rich quickly), the solution is very simple. There are only two options: either free distribution - for instance to everybody the same part - or the market? We can be quite sure that something quite different would have been suggested.

What we are interested in is not, of course, whether the first solution is equitable - because it is very simple to make it such, for some time - or that the second solution is an economically correct one - ex-ante or in principal. We are interested in what will be happening economically and socially before an equilibrium ownership structure comes out, and what this ownership structure will look like. If we say an equilibrium ownership structure, we mean until firm holders of shares appear. We are not interested in what happens at the beginning, whether it is equitable and/or market "oriented". We are interested in what follows before a kind of a new equilibrium is restored and/or what will be happening during transition to the new equilibrium ownership structure. Let us now look at what will be happening with saving when the process of the changing ownership of shares begins and proceeds.

Before we do that only one remark is necessary. Private ownership of socially owned business enterprises can be also achieved by the sale of shares at the very beginning, i.e. without any free distribution of shares at all. Nevertheless, almost all would be the same as concerns equity and economic efficiency. In that case, the first phase - free distribution of shares - is omitted, which does not mean really very much as concerns equity, although it may mean something or even very much notionally. The government would probably have many problems politically selling privatisation and/or "privatisation" without free distribution of shares, or without the first phase. This may be the reason why most of the governments started with the first phase and why advisers advised them to do so. In the first place, it is something that may be easily sold to the public because it costs nothing. Ultimately, the same result would be achieved. The ownership of business enterprises would come into those hands into which it should come. For instance into the hands of those who did most to cause the economic system that collapsed, to collapse by itself, if we have in mind Slovenia. We need not analyse the second method of "privatisation" because it is the same as the first. Only the first phase, free distribution of shares, is missing.

What has been happening in transitional economies like Slovenia to their financial markets is just the opposite to the development in the economies with a normal economic history - if we go back to our theme. Shares and government bonds, which came into the possession of banks during their rehabilitation, did not have a normal birth. They did not come into possession of their primary owners via a primary capital market. They were simply given to them. As the primary owners did not come into their possession because they wanted to have them, we may presume that those financial assets, let us stay with shares, are in the majority of cases not wanted or desired. It is the secondary capital market that will resolve the problem by moving them into the possession of those who do want them. The secondary capital market will, for instance, enable workers to sell their shares and thus enable business enterprises to come to dominant external owners, and through external owners to turn the enterprises into open business enterprises - open to the inflow of external funds. Let us explore what consequences are to be expected if great trading on the secondary capital market were to take place.

It is known that the net worth of an individual may increase only by his savings, if we do not take into account capital gains or losses. If we want shares of business enterprises to come into the possession of those who wish to have them from those who do not want them, via secondary capital market, we should take into account how somebody's wealth increases. We come to savings that are the basis for the increase of somebody's wealth. Transactions via the secondary capital market will enable the sale of shares from the part of those who wish, through the sale of shares, to decrease their wealth, they want to go into the current consumption with the proceeds from the sale of their shares, if there are others who will be increasing their wealth by their savings and will want to have additional wealth in the form of shares.

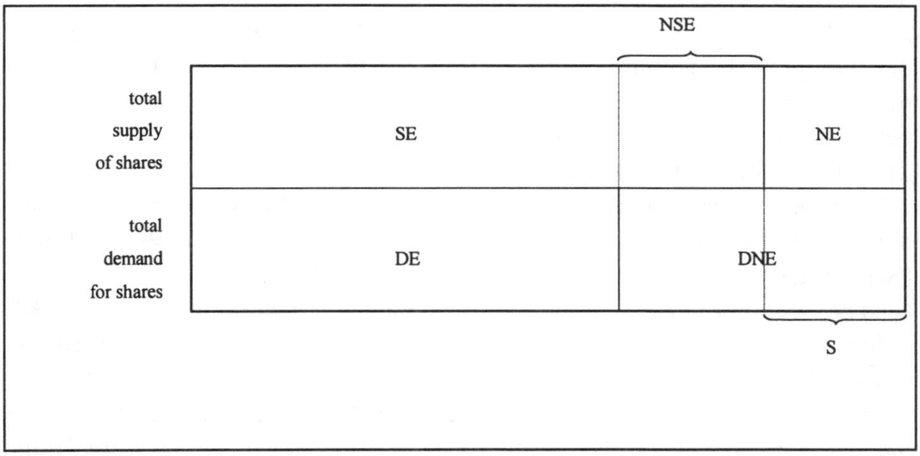

Figure 1. The supply of shares on the primary (NE) and secondary capital market (SE), net supply of shares (NSE) and the demand for them on the part of those who change one form of shares into another (DE) and others who want to increase their portfolio of shares (DNE)

The macroeconomic problems that may follow can be presented by Figure 1. The space designated by SE represents the sales of shares on the secondary capital market and the space designated by NE is newly issued shares. Purchases should be equal to sales. Purchases result from the part of those that have sold other shares, and just want to change their portfolio of shares, and that part of purchases is represented by space DE, and from others who wish to increase their wealth. They are represented by space DNE. Let us suppose, to make things simple, that all macroeconomic savings go into new shares. It this case NE is equal to macroeconomic savings. From Figure 1 it is obvious what the consequences are if SE is higher than DE - macroeconomic saving decreases.

If there is a perfect balance, then SE and DE are equal. Investors change the composition of the portfolios of shares through the secondary capital market. However, there are no serious problems if SE is a bit higher (smaller) than DE. In that case, macroeconomic savings are somewhat smaller (higher) than they should have been, but this is accounted for by the usual small changes in the propensity to save and/or to invest.

If the social (or state) ownership of business enterprises is to be abolished through the free distribution of shares to individuals and institutions, created for that purpose, followed by the creation of a secondary capital market to transfer shares which come from those who do not want them into the hands of those who do want them, then it is obvious that a very great difference will appear between SE and DE. Net sales of shares (NSE) might be so great that savings (S) become very small, zero, or even negative.

In Figure 2, the NSE curves show what will happen to savings (S) depending on the volume of the net sales of shares on the secondary capital market. The volume of net sales of shares is the volume of net sales in the period for which we have the volume of savings (S) on the horizontal line. The same volume of net sales of shares means twice as much, relative to S, if it is made in a period that is only half as long. In the diagram we always have the same time period and the same volume of (hypothetical) savings (S_h), which is the volume of saving if SE is equal to DE.

The NSE_0 curve is drawn under the unrealistic assumption that the market value of shares remains unchanged at various possible levels of their net sales. Other curves, to the right, are drawn under the more realistic assumption that the market value of shares is changing. The more their price decreases the more they shift to the right, or the more convex they are. In the extreme situation, when shares are sold at zero price, we have an NSE_2 curve, which is a vertical line. In that case, savings (S) are equal to the hypothetical savings (S_h). Even if all shares are sold on the secondary capital market as net sales (NSE) there will be no decrease in the savings (S).

From Figure 2 we can see that if the decrease in savings is small, then the decrease in the market price of shares is relatively large. There are two unrealistic extremes, represented by the NSE_0 and NSE_2 curves, and a realistic possibility, represented by curve NSE_1, where prices of shares are decreasing at an increasingly higher rate, while net sales of shares are increasing. We would expect the market price of shares to decrease if there are net sales of shares. But just how much their price will decrease depends on the price elasticity of supply and demand. In Figure 2 we have all the time the same volume A of the net sales of shares. So it is clear that the consequences of the net sales of shares are a decrease in savings (S) and domestic investment, decrease in the price of shares, and an increase in the market rate of interest. But there are social consequences as well. The greater is the decrease in the market price of shares, the greater the consequences are. A minority is becoming rich on the basis of redistribution of wealth through the capital market.

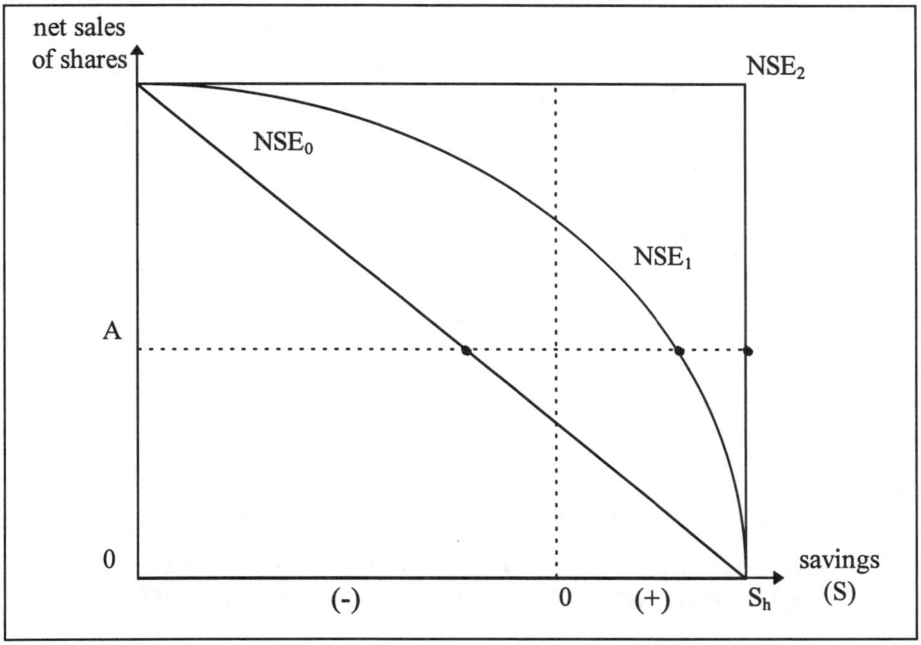

Figure 2. The impact of the net sale of shares (NSE) on the macroeconomic savings

As a precipitous sale of shares by workers (and others) is one of the solutions that we face if we want to prevent the euthanasia of the old business enterprises because they would be financially closed, we should have in mind what consequences are to be expected. We have seen how important is its impact on the savings or, if we put it differently, how important it is that the rate of savings stays as high as possible. If, for instance, by some magic the rate of savings were to adapt to the volume of the net sales of shares, (NSE), there would be no decrease in savings, investment, and prices of shares and therefore no increase in interest rates would be expected. How unpleasant is to be the process of changes in share ownership of business enterprises, through which business enterprises would become financially open, would depend on the behaviour of households and others as concerns their propensity to save. In the amount of the net sales of shares (NSE) savings of others are lost, if everything else remains unchanged, because these net sales would enable the increase in consumption of those who are net sellers of shares so that, consequently, macroeconomic savings (S) would decrease by that amount.

So we have, of course, no basis for expectations that the precipitous sale of shares, which may resolve the ownership problem of business enterprises, will not cause even a financial crash. There is therefore a dilemma: dominant internal ownership of business enterprises, which may mean euthanasia for quite some of them (funds will be flowing into new business enterprises; but this replacement of old business enterprises with new ones will be a costly endeavour), or a quick enough change of the ownership structure of those business enterprises via a financial crash. C. Diaz-Alejandro (1985) has, for instance, explained it for countries undergoing financial liberalisation and deepening. The dilemma should, surely, be attributed to the chosen method of abolishment of social ownership of business enterprises or to the fear of not making transition in the same way as others, and as has been advised by foreign advisers. On both accounts it meant primarily to make the transition to favour the interests of the emerging "nouveaux riches".

5. EXPERIENCES WITH PREVIOUS MONETARY ARRANGEMENTS OR MONETARY INTEGRATION AS A LESSON FOR THE ARRANGEMENTS EXISTING UNTIL NOW, AND FOR THE FUTURE

With political independence, and the separation of Slovenia from Yugoslavia, there necessarily come monetary separation as well. So there is nothing to be said about why this - monetary separation - happened, nor will anything be said about that. But what may be of some interest, following the title of this paper, is what are the experiences, lessons, advice, dangers to be remembered and avoided in the future from the functioning of the former Yugoslav monetary system - a form of monetary integration. This was a decentralised central banking system, in some respects similar to the emerging European central banking system (with, for instance, the European Central Bank and the European System of Central Banks). Here, a few more words might be added.

Yugoslavia had a problem with money - with its stability - for two reasons. The first and the basic one was social ownership of the business enterprises. Such business enterprises could function only if real interest rates were negative and sufficiently high, so that funds coming into business enterprises as bank loans had been *de facto* grants. This is probably now well known in Slovenia, since it has already been explained in texts from 1973 (Ribnikar, 1988) and 1984 (Ribnikar, 1984), and later in many other texts. This inflow of funds into business enterprises as grants - although they were nominally bank loans - could be achieved by positive nominal interest rates only if the inflation rate were higher than the nominal interest rates. Inflation was a "natural habitat" for business enterprises under social ownership. Therefore it was not possible to have good money together with social ownership of business enterprises. This truth was accepted even by the old establishment at the end of 1988, when the law on business enterprises was passed, thus allowing funds to enter business enterprises as equity capital. The end of social ownership had been announced, and had begun.

However, the abolishment of the social ownership of business enterprises or - since this process lasted many years - the emergence of business enterprises with ownership without an adjective (not necessarily in direct private ownership) was only the necessary condition for good money. Yet, throughout the whole period of the social ownership of business enterprises there were other reasons for bad money. These were in a way more technical: how the monetary system had been conceived, what were the channels for base money creation, and what was the central bank position vis-à-vis the government and/or politics.

If we start with the last reason, the central bank was not independent at all, and the most important channels for base money creation were rediscounts of commercial banks' loans. These rediscounts were allocated among banks according to the purposes for which their loans were given. The so-called priorities (for instance export, some imports, agricultural production, etc.) were established by the parliament, and the central bank was obliged to follow and allow an increase in base money according to these priorities. There was no short-term government paper - or no "generalised claims", as had been emphasised (Ribnikar, 1988) - and no basis for grading banks and their customers according to their credit and other risks; therefore, there was no basis for rediscount or open market operations by the central bank. The only proper channel for base money creation would have been purchases of foreign exchange. But this could not have been realised since the central bank retained, more or less permanently, its international monetary reserves at the minimum level.

The obligation of the central bank to keep increasing its base money by financing priorities established by the parliament - in kind and in value terms - could not mean anything other than a permanently expansive or inflationary monetary policy. This was in accordance with the requirement for the inflationary milieu (inflation was a "natural habitat" for business enterprises in social ownership) but at the same time it meant that the abolishment of the social ownership of business enterprises was not sufficient for good money, without fundamental restructuring of the monetary system.

So the third point - how the monetary system had been conceived - could not be of great importance. The central banking system was decentralised. Each of the republics and autonomous provinces had its central bank; consequently there was a system of eight central banks. Within each of the eight areas, all claims and debts to the central banking system - with the exception of currency as a claim and as a debt - were claims and debts to the central bank of that area. The governing body was composed of the governors of all central banks. It was very close to the European System of Central Banks (ESCB) in preparation.

Because of the two characteristics already described - no independence of the central bank from politics, and the channels of base money creation - it was clear that even a decentralised central banking system resembling the later European central banking system could not bring us to a noninflationary monetary policy and to good money. Hence, there were proposals for parallel currency in 1989 (Ribnikar, 1989b) and later, in 1991 (Ribnikar, 1991), various possible solutions for the Yugoslav monetary system were analysed and proposed. Among them were the independent central banks – this meant monetary disintegration within Yugoslavia. So the political independence (of Slovenia) should not be taken as the reason (or the only reason) why the country created its own currency area, although monetary independence logically followed political independence. Might this have happened – i.e. the creation of a separate currency area - even if Yugoslavia had not disintegrated politically? Yes, if the right economic and/or monetary solution had been chosen; but this, of course, was impossible.

The point is not whether this - i.e. monetary disintegration within the former Yugoslavia - might have happened, but that monetary integration and/or abandonment of monetary sovereignty may be too great a sacrifice, even within the economic area such as Yugoslavia was, if within this area good money could not have been achieved, and afterwards sustained. This is a point that has perhaps no relevance for the possible future monetary integration of Slovenia, although it may be of importance for European countries with strong currencies. For Slovenia, mainly other considerations will come to the fore, as will be seen later.

Slovenia, however, succeeded in achieving its political independence, and therefore there was no question of whether necessary changes in the monetary sphere would be made, but what new monetary arrangements should be introduced.

6. AVAILABLE MONETARY ARRANGEMENTS AND EXCHANGE RATE FOR SLOVENIA AS A NEWLY EMERGENT COUNTRY AND A COUNTRY IN TRANSITION

To the question what monetary system should have been introduced, the answer could not have been simply different from the one that existed in Yugoslavia, nor could it have been the opposite. There were many possibilities. But we are not interested in these possibilities for their own sake. We have in mind the possible future monetary integration of Slovenia. And if we want to evaluate what the chances are for a transitional economy, like that of Slovenia, to join the European single currency, i.e. the only conceivable monetary integration in the near future, and what problems it will be facing on its path to single currency, we must take into account its present monetary situation. Since this choice is predominantly the result of Slovenia's recent history - of the last six to eight years - the monetary arrangements introduced at the beginning of transition should be taken into account. We will deal with this in what follows in this section.

Especially if we take into account what has been suggested by foreign experts, and even if we just take into account what arrangements have been introduced elsewhere, we can say that almost all available monetary arrangements had been potentially possible, or at least the good or the best ones. If we say monetary arrangements, we have in mind those in connection with the exchange-rate regime and/or exchange rate policy. As will be seen later in the paper, monetary systems from the point of view of base money creation and the arrangements between the central bank and banks had much less space for diversity and/or very special arrangements.

The case of Slovenia is not, actually, a general one. The country, in fact, had separated itself from the previous federation and at the same time had been dedicated to pursuing and accelerating its process of transition, which started (in Yugoslavia) already at the end of 1988. Separation and political independence required monetary independence as well. Monetary independence had meant the creation of a new currency area, and the creation of something new (new currency, new central bank, new monetary arrangements in general) usually provides a greater variety of choices. And even if we take into account only the case of Slovenia - although many of the transitional economies had meant newly emergent countries like Slovenia - we can say that all possible monetary arrangements were deemed possible and had been advocated by experts, although *de facto* only one arrangement had been possible - the one adopted in 1991.

In Figure 3, all available arrangements are presented. Slovenia had correctly started with an almost pure floating exchange rate system, but back in 1990 and 1991 there were serious proposals for a currency board system, although Slovenia as a newly emergent country had no international monetary reserves, and therefore we can say that all possibilities were open. The system adopted in Slovenia is the one on the far left side of Figure 3, and the system advocated by foreign experts (although, we can say, just the result of fancy imaginings) is on the far right of Figure 3, if, of course, we neglect the cosmetic differences between the currency board and not having one's own or national money at all.

If we put ourselves in the position of the newly established central bank of Slovenia, it is quite obvious that its main goal had been to fight inflation (the monthly rate had been 21.5 percent) via monetary restrictions. Therefore its control over monetary aggregates had been indispensable. Monetary arrangements were required to give it unhindered control over monetary aggregates. Not only was the right side of Figure 3 irrelevant, but so too was the left side, with the exception of arrangements that gave the central bank unhindered control over money. There had been a pure floating or almost pure floating exchange rate regime, because from the very beginning the central bank had been buying foreign exchanges in an amount that was consistent with its restrictive monetary policy. But such arrangements were at the same time the only ones possible, because at that time the central bank had no international monetary reserves.

If we are interested in the possibilities for a transitional economy like Slovenia joining the system of the European single currency, then we are interested in the conditions under which this economy would be able to move to the right side of Figure 3, across the line that separates regimes where a country has monetary sovereignty from regimes where the country cannot be monetarily sovereign, and how fast it will be able to move. It must arrive at the system where its exchange rate is irrevocably fixed, i.e. pegged to the euro . At that moment it would be *de facto* within the European single currency area, although *de iure* it may happen much later, or maybe never. If we have in mind monetary policy it should move from the present situation, where it can pursue an independent monetary policy, to a situation where it will lose monetary independence completely. This, of course, cannot happen overnight. It may not happen at all, or it may not be advisable that it should happen. During transition, if it is to be moving across in Figure 3, it will be losing its monetary independence step by step. Finally monetary independence will be gone if, of course, it abandons its money and accepts the single European currency.

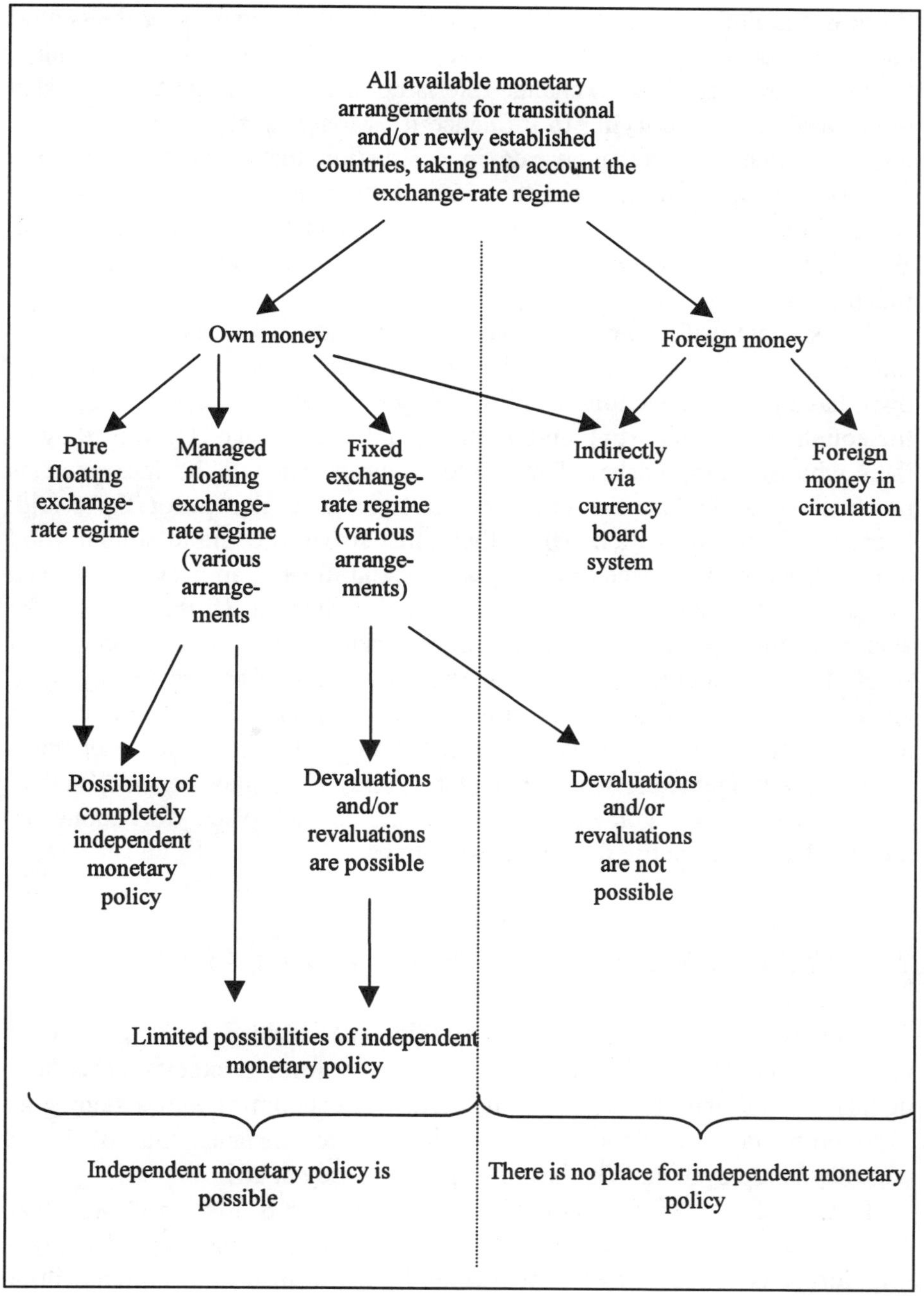

Figure 3. All available monetary and/or exchange rate arrangements for transitional and/or newly established countries

But being able to pursue a completely independent monetary policy, up till now and in the near future, does not mean that the country or the central bank is not concerned about the exchange rate. As will be seen in part nine, for the central banks the exchange rate is not only very important, but also the central banks are trying to influence it. Monetary aggregates are more important than the exchange rate in a situation that does not allow the countries or their central banks to achieve both goals at the same time. It is worthwhile for them to sacrifice the exchange rate for monetary control. When the exchange rate is more important, monetary policy cannot be so independent.

But it is not just a question of what is more and what is less important for the country. It is true if the countries are pursuing a monetary policy of their own, having no connections with monetary policies in other countries, or if the countries are supporting and/or changing the exchange rate according to their whims and/or wishes. But if the countries want to be integrated as much as possible into the broader economic area, Europe or the world, because of the economic benefits, they must strive to come to similar good money as exists in Europe or in the world. And, finally, an irrevocably fixed exchange rate regime is to be introduced, when or if the benefits of abandonment of monetary control, i.e. replacement of national money by a single European currency, are greater than the costs of an irrevocably fixed exchange rate, i.e. of the impossibility of devaluation and/or revaluation. So a transitional economy must cross the line in Figure 3 that separates monetary arrangements, where monetary policy is or may be independent, and monetary arrangements, where there is no place for monetary independence or, finally, for one's own money.

7. WHY HAVE ONE'S OWN MONEY AT ALL?

Only few more words about why Slovenia decided to have its own money, although there had been suggestions by foreign experts - to whom domestic politicians without any knowledge of economics were listening as if to prophets - to adopt foreign money by, for instance, introducing a currency board system. Why have one's own money at all?

It is usually so - for instance, it may be found in S. Fischer (1982), that even for a very small country the benefits of having one's own money - seigniorage is collected by national central bank instead of a foreign central bank whose money is in circulation or in the vaults of the currency board – outweigh the costs, in the first place additional transaction costs. But there are more hidden benefits and costs as well. As concerns benefits, the country may pursue its own monetary policy and exchange rate policy. But this freedom to pursue an independent monetary and exchange rate policy may be a cost at the same time. The central bank may pursue the wrong monetary policy and stay with it permanently if the exchange rate is adapting to it. Or the central bank may provoke a balance of payments crisis, if it does not allow the exchange rate to adapt to domestic monetary policy

Every country, especially a small one, may in principle introduce a currency board system or irrevocably fix its exchange rate and force everything (prices, wages, interest rates) to adapt to an irrevocably fixed exchange rate as an anchor. The question is only: what would be the costs of such therapy compared with the costs of gradual monetary stabilisation?

Slovenia decided rightly for gradualism (its economy was not in bad shape at all compared with other transitional economies, the process of the abolishment of social ownership of business enterprises ended only recently, and it came to a fairly independent central bank) and it can be put into life only if the country has its own money. The politicians opted for our own money for another reason, although quite a few of them wanted shock therapy. They wanted our own money, like a flag, as the symbol of national independence, fulfilment of dreams, etc. But in addition to its own money the central bank must have the power to control monetary aggregates, which means that the exchange rate should be in second place among central bank priorities. And only one's own money and the floating exchange rate system, which Slovenia has had since October 1991, has allowed its central bank to keep gradually decreasing the inflation rate. The problems of pressure on the domestic currency to appreciate were tackled and attempts were made to alleviate them separately, as will be seen, and in such a way that the central bank was able to remain in a position to control monetary aggregates.

In the case of Slovenia, its own money has been a kind of a vehicle, transferring from bad money within the Yugoslav monetary integration to much better money so far, but it is not the end of the road. Will it be in the future a vehicle for travelling further down the road to good money and, as will be discussed later, eventually to new monetary integration?

8. MONETARY SYSTEM AND MONETARY POLICY

The exchange rate regimes, examined earlier in the paper, determine in a very important way the monetary system and monetary policy, but there remain still several additional elements. We are interested in them: what have been their characteristics so far, in what directions are they changing and how must they change, if a country like Slovenia is to join the single European currency?

The monetary system and monetary policy, instruments and procedures used, depend upon the chosen exchange rate regime on banks and financial markets, in first place the money market. At the beginning of transition the banks were in most cases insolvent. Their rehabilitation had started with delay. During their rehabilitation, they had been rehabilitated at first only from the stock point of view - i.e. their net assets became positive because their bad loans had been swapped by government bonds - the central bank took care of their liquidity. To be able to do that, the central bank was obliged to adapt its instruments of monetary policy to this goal. If the rehabilitation of the banks is maybe over, their restructuring has not yet started, or is at its beginning. Therefore the behaviour of banks has been changing, and is still not quite the same as in other economies.

The financial markets are very shallow. The same is true for the money market. The central banks in transitional economies are not able to rely on them in a way similar to the central banks in nontransitional economies.

For both reasons, the monetary system and monetary policy have acquired some specific characteristics. There are even more of them in the case of a very small currency area, such as we have in Slovenia.

It is known that the structure of central bank assets, domestic assets (DA) - mostly Treasury Bills and short-term loans to banks - versus foreign assets (FA), foreign exchange reserves, depends in the first place on the dimension of the currency area. In such a small country as Slovenia (and in other somewhat larger countries) there is in general no place for Treasury Bills among the central bank assets. There is hardly enough space for foreign exchange reserves, even if we do not take into account the problems of an overvalued domestic currency, inflow of capital and sterilisation, which will be discussed later. So the base money creation is mostly on the basis of purchases of foreign exchanges (Figure 4 shows the structure of the assets, DA vs. FA, in the BoS balance sheet) and short-term loans to banks and on the basis of some other transactions with them that enables the central bank to keep banks liquid and to have, at the same time, control over base money.

The experience of other central banks and the theory, which is predominantly a generalisation of the experiences of developed and great economies, can be used only “cum grano salis”. It became clear very soon that, because of the behaviour of the banks and the shallowness of foreign exchange and financial markets, the central bank cannot decrease the amount of base money simply by selling foreign exchanges, bills, bonds, or securities, without disrupting the markets, i.e. without provoking unnecessary and undesirable volatility on those markets.

The central bank was obliged to take this into account. Most purchases of foreign exchanges and securities, if there are transactions in them (as will be seen later, these are predominantly its short-term bills), are REPO transactions. Most loans are very short-term loans. On the basis of both these transactions that result in an increase in base money, the opposite transactions follow automatically without disruptive influence on markets. The central bank must have in mind how its money will be withdrawn when it is increasing its base money. Through REPOs and very short-term loans to banks the central bank ensures automatic opposite transactions - reflux of funds.

It is quite logical that in such circumstances the volume of transactions through which the BoS has been changing - increasing and decreasing - the quantity of base money (B), in comparison with the average quantity of base money, has been (relatively) very high. And, in addition to this, net increases or decreases in the quantity of base money have been very small, so that in most cases gross increases (or decreases) in base money have been neutralised by reverse transactions from the part of the BoS. The yearly turnover of the average quantity of base money was as much as 3.5 in 1994 (for previous years the data are not available). Since then the turnover has been decreasing. In 1997 it was between 1 and 1.5, which was probably still high.

What matters most is, of course, the final result: how stable - as concerns its purchasing power - the money is, due to monetary policy and/or how the inflation rate is decreasing. The problems the central banks are facing as concerns monetary policy during transition to a fixed exchange rate regime - or, if we have in mind a more distant and maybe unachievable goal, irrevocably pegging their currencies to the euro - are irrelevant if, or once, the central banks finally achieve their goal. They are, nevertheless, relevant because they will affect the way the country will be approaching the European single currency area, and determine how quickly this will be happening.

How, and how fast, it will be happening depends on other things as well: on the chosen method of privatisation or abolishment of the social ownership of business enterprises, as is the case of Slovenia: what owners of business enterprises emerge; how badly macroeconomic saving is being affected because of free distribution of shares to those who would rather quickly sell them and spend the proceeds on consumption; how effectively pressure on the domestic currency to appreciate is being alleviated through cautious step-by-step liberalisation of international capital flows and sterilisation policy.

The role of the central bank cannot be seen only through its instruments of monetary control in the proper sense. The central bank has actually been obliged to take care of the exchange rate as well, or else it could not leave the exchange rate completely to the market or to the market, where distress exporters have been dominant and where funds have been flowing from abroad (Ribnikar, 1994a). As is known, both goals - quantity of money in circulation and exchange rate - cannot be generally achieved at the same time. If we want to understand the problems the central bank has been facing, and will be facing in the near future, we must look at its activities in connection with the exchange rate.

9. EXCHANGE RATE POLICY

A central bank without international monetary reserves, like the Bank of Slovenia (BoS), which was present at the beginning, cannot support and keep at a higher level the external value of its money, but it can keep buying foreign money on the foreign exchange market and via those transaction put at least some pressure on foreign exchanges. It very soon became clear to the BoS that the amount of foreign exchanges it could take from the market was negligible for two reasons. First, as the BoS had been committed to a restrictive monetary policy, the permissible increase in the quantity of base money had been strictly limited - only so much as had been necessary for a desired or necessary increase in M1. And, additionally, part of the free space the central bank had for increase in base money through purchases of adequate assets had to be used for short term loans to banks so that they - in the first place those undergoing individual rehabilitation - should stay liquid. Secondly, the surpluses, at unappreciated domestic currency, on the foreign exchange market originated from current account, repatriation of capital (at first mostly on the basis of foreign currencies taken from 'mattresses' and brought to banks) and small amounts of the inflow of capital.

As it was obvious that this was not something normal that might last forever, surpluses in the current account were due mostly to the peculiar behaviour of business enterprises, waiting for those who would become their owner (they behaved like distress borrowers and exporters and did not want to invest, because that might increase their value), and repatriation of capital would have to end in the near future, the central bank felt responsible for doing as much as it could to prevent the appreciation of the domestic currency, and through it to prevent still further the deterioration of the competitive position of the tradable sector. From the very beginning the central bank interventions on the foreign exchange market, and various obstacles to import of capital that began to be introduced later, had been intended as something transitory until the behaviour of business enterprises, due to the establishment of proper corporate governance, became normal. Nobody thought that this would have been still necessary after almost six years, i.e. at the end of 1997.

What problems the central bank has had with the exchange rate, and how it has tried to alleviate if not to solve them, can be deduced from its balance sheet where its relations with other sectors, especially banks, can be seen. A simplified balance sheet of the BoS (at the end of February 1997) in Figure 4 may help us.

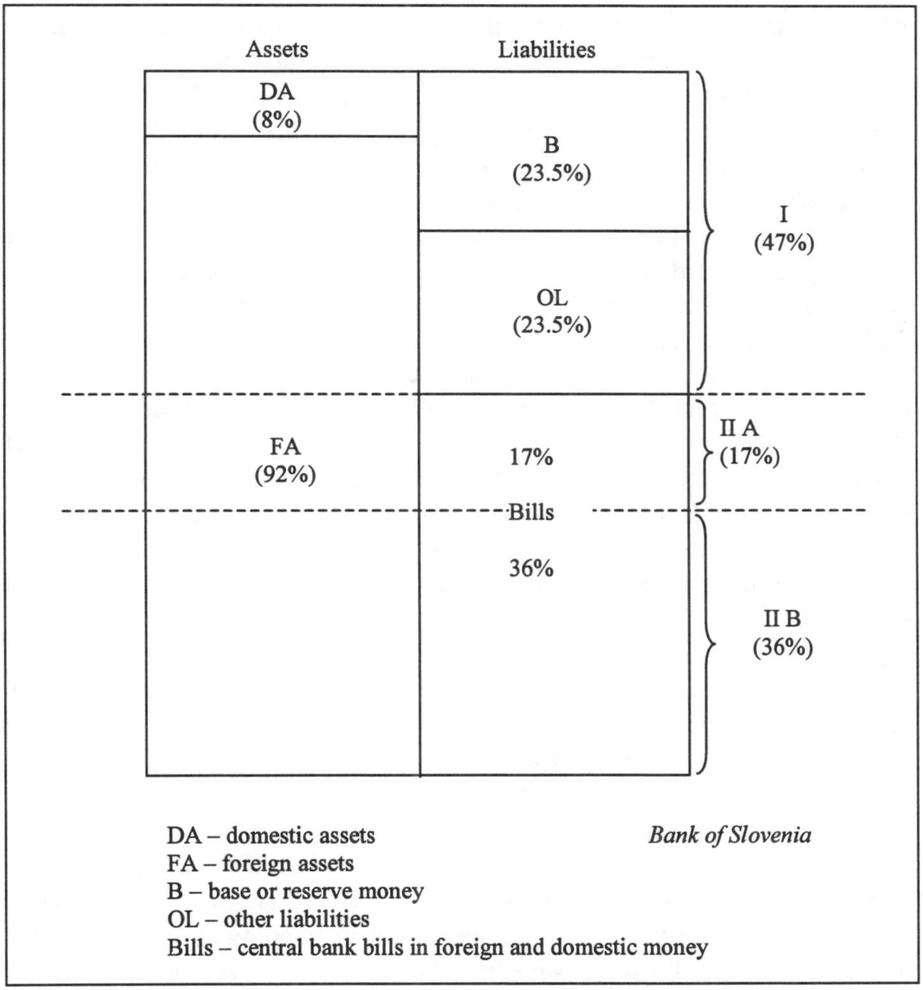

Figure 4. Three parts (I, II A and II B) of the simplified balance sheet of the Bank of Slovenia (at the end of February 1997) delineating its three functions

Taking the balance sheet as a whole, there are 92 percent of foreign assets (FA), i.e. mostly foreign exchanges, and only 8 percent of domestic assets (DA), i.e. various short-term loans to banks. On the liabilities side there are 53 percent of short-term bonds or bills outstanding, which is something not quite usual for the liabilities side of the central banks. That part of its balance sheet, which has on the liabilities side its bills outstanding and on the assets side foreign assets (foreign exchanges), should probably not be counted as an integral part of the balance sheet of the central bank as the institution responsible for money, i.e. as the monetary authority. So the balance sheet of the BoS as a monetary institution is only 47 percent of its whole balance sheet. On the liabilities side it has base money (B) in the amount of 23.5 percent of its balance sheet, and some other liabilities which are not its bills outstanding. These other liabilities by coincidence amount to the same percentage of its whole balance sheet. On the asset side are various loans to banks and some other items, in the amount of 8 percent of its whole balance sheet, while all remaining assets are foreign assets.

The other part of the balance sheet is to be explained by the efforts of the BoS to put pressure on the exchange rate to be higher. Usually sterilisation takes place in such a way that the central bank is on the one hand buying foreign exchanges and on the other hand in the same amount - the same amount in terms of domestic currency - selling Government bonds (Krugman, Obstfeld, 1996; Obstfeld, 1982; Calvo, 1991). The BoS could not sterilise in that manner because it had no Government bonds or any other assets to sell. So the BoS was obliged to sell something that it did not have - and that was its short-term bonds or bills. Its bills started to appear on the liabilities side of its balance sheet. At the end of February 1997 they amounted already to 264 billion Slovene tolars, or 53 percent of its balance sheet.

That part of the BoS balance sheet has nothing to do with monetary policy. Besides, sterilisation could have been done by some other institution or by the Government directly, or through the central bank as its agent. It simply happened that the central bank has been sterilising surpluses on the foreign exchange market through sale of its bills.

Most of the bills in foreign or domestic money issued by the central bank have been bought and kept by banks, although central bank bills may be found at other financial institutions, business enterprises and households as well. But we cannot treat all central bank bills outstanding as equal. We must distinguish among those that have been bought and kept voluntarily, because of their expected earnings, risk and liquidity attractiveness for investors, and those that have been bought and kept because that was what investors were required to do. The banks have, in fact, been required to keep at least 60 percent of their required foreign assets, as a counterpart to their foreign currency deposits and some other foreign currency liabilities and the volume of international payments, in central bank foreign currency bills ("minimum foreign exchange balances"). The banks themselves have been required to help the central bank with sterilisation or, better, to take care of their foreign currency exposure.

The second part of the central bank balance sheet, relating to the exchange rate policy, must be subdivided into two parts. The major part (II B), about 36 percent of the central bank balance sheet at the end of February 1997, is due to the sterilisation that the banks themselves are required to do. It is just that, the central bank, instead of them is keeping balances with foreign banks, and therefore the banks have central bank bills in foreign money instead of balances with foreign banks among their (foreign) assets. That part of the central bank balance sheet cannot be attributed to its sterilisation. It is the result of the sterilisation done by banks, if we can call sterilisation also what the banks have been required to do to diminish their short position in foreign currencies.

The smaller part of the second part of the central bank balance sheet (II A) is the result of its sterilisation efforts. At the end of February 1997 it amounted to about 17 percent of the balance sheet. On the liabilities side of that part of the balance sheet are its bills sold to banks and others. Only for that part of its outstanding bills the central bank has been required to adapt to the market and offer price, liquidity and other possible benefits attractive enough for banks and other investors.

If we stay with the BoS balance sheet, the importance of the exchange rate for the central bank may be deduced from the importance of the second part of its balance sheet (II): its increase in time and the level achieved. As we can divide its balance sheet into two parts, in the same manner we can divide its policy into monetary policy and exchange rate policy. All instruments directed at the first part of its balance sheet are to be attributed to the instruments of monetary control. And all central bank transactions with banks and others that change the second part of its balance sheet are instruments of exchange rate policy.

If we keep in mind this division, the central bank has been required to achieve its monetary targets (base money and M1) without any trade-off as concerns the exchange rate. It has had no explicit goal as concerns the exchange rate. The central bank has not been able to have at the same time an independent goal as concerns the exchange rate. It has been able only to try to keep increasing the second part of its balance sheet, precisely only the part II A, as much as possible, taking into account at least two constraints: available funds for covering those sterilisation costs (the major part of its seigniorage) and the feasibility of the sterilisation policy, not only at the present but over a longer period of time. What started at the beginning of 1992 as something transitory has turned out to be still alive almost six years later.

If we look at the central bank with its all activities and instruments, then it differs quite substantially from the central banks of nontransitional economies. If we are not interested in costs, the difference may disappear overnight with a shock. What the central bank or the Government must do is simply opt for either a purely floating exchange rate regime or for a fixed exchange rate regime. All the special problems the central bank has been facing will disappear, but other much greater problems will appear. The experience of transitional economies with a fixed exchange rate regime are well known. On the other hand, no country - transitional or nontransitional - or its central bank has so far dared to completely neglect its exchange rate. The slowly changing reality and/or peculiarities of transitional economy should not be neglected if transition is to be quick enough and within tolerable costs for the most exposed part of the present generation.

The peculiar situation the central banks are facing as concerns monetary and exchange rate policy, for instance BoS, is in general a mirror image of the problems experienced by business enterprises, banks and other financial institutions. And if the central banks and/or monetary systems are still not prepared for a fixed exchange rate regime, this means that the economy is still not ready for such a change. What is important is whether the economy is approaching the possibilities for such change. Before some tentative answers are given in the last part of our paper we must briefly look at banks and the liberalisation of international capital flows.

We have already seen that, besides the central bank, the banks have been required to absorb an important part of foreign exchanges on the basis of so-called minimum foreign currency balances, in the first place for foreign currency deposits by residents, and they have not been allowed to increase their net foreign indebtedness. Nonbanks have been subject to noninterest bearing deposits for foreign indebtedness for the period up to seven years. Portfolio investments have been allowed only through special clients' accounts with banks, and banks have been required to balance those accounts with foreign currency assets so that no net inflow of capital could have occurred. There has been no obstacle for foreigners to purchase newly issued shares and for purchases that have meant direct investments. There are, however, quite important obstacles for the net inflow of capital with, maybe paradoxically, the final goal of preparing the economy in due time for financial liberalisation. They have been directed at preventing a disastrous appreciation of the domestic currency.

Since October 1991 interest rates have been falling, but at the same time the required risk premium for domestic assets or for financial assets in domestic currency has also been declining. However, because the difference between interest rate in Slovenia and interest rate abroad - taking into account nominal depreciation of the domestic currency - has exceeded the required risk premium for investments in domestic (currency) assets, there has been permanent and nondecreasing pressure for the inflow of capital. And this difference in interest rates and pressure on the import of capital emanating from it has had to be attributed to transitional anomalies (the perverse behaviour of business enterprises as exporters and borrowers because they have been striving not to increase but to decrease their value, the decrease of macroeconomic saving provoked by the voucher type of abolishment of the social ownership of business enterprises, etc.). Within this framework the endeavours of the central bank to make everything possible - or everything we have mentioned for the exchange rate to be higher or the domestic currency to be less overvalued - have had their meaning, legitimacy, and accountability.

All restrictions, with the exception of the sterilisation policy of the central bank and limited possibilities for banks to have an open foreign currency position (up to maximum 20 percent of their capital - the same as in other countries), will wither away in a rather short period of time. So all other existing restrictions on international capital flows are only of limited duration. And if the existing restrictions are to enable the country to financially open up with smaller costs, and/or without disruptive consequences for the economy, they would turn out to be useful, necessary, and beneficial. Although it was not known in advance what there would be at the end (would, for instance, the behaviour of business enterprises change and become closer to normal, would macroeconomic saving recover?) the prudent and cautious behaviour of the central bank was the only right approach. Even if finally, by the time when most restrictions on inflow of capital must be lifted, which will be in the next few years, the underlying causes for the sterilisation policy of the central bank and for various restrictions on capital inflow will still remain.

10. CONCLUSIONS

In contrast to the conditions for adhesion to the EU, where existing members must be so kind as to allow new countries to enter, a non-member country - for instance a transitional economy like that of Slovenia - may *de facto* join the European single currency area by its will alone. It must "only" decide to do so, and irrevocably fix its currency to the euro. The Austrians and the Dutch have pegged their currencies to the German Mark, and so *de facto* they entered into monetary union with Germany (Frölich, 1990). It is not at the mercy of member countries at all. There are, of course, some subtle differences between *de facto* and *de iure* membership of the European single currency area, but the crucial question for the country will be whether it will be able to stay in the long run with an unchanged exchange rate. Formally becoming a member is much less important.

But if it depends on the country alone, this does not mean that it is easier for the country, at first, to *de facto* join the European single currency area. It should do so when it can afford to. If we say when it can afford to, we exclude the possibility that it should be done by shock therapy. The country, or its irresponsible politicians, advised by some foreign economists, may, indeed, just irrevocably fix its exchange rate and force everything - prices, wages, interest rates, international capital flows - to adapt to "the reality" of an irrevocably fixed exchange rate.

For a transitional economy it is probably appropriate to talk about two kinds of necessary adaptations to the single European currency or irrevocably fixed exchange rate regime. The second adaptation, if we start with it - which will not be important in the near future or perhaps even never - is the same as that which member countries of the EU have been facing. These are, of course, not just adaptations to the Maastricht criteria. Although it is almost obvious that for a small economy like that of Slovenia, once the first kind of adaptations (we will talk about them immediately) have been made, the benefits of joining the European single currency must outweigh the costs; nevertheless, the problems of labour market flexibility, price and wage rigidity, etc. should be considered as well (De Grauwe, 1994).

The first kind of necessary adaptations are those due to an economy in transition. We have explained the problems Slovenia has been facing and/or the necessary restrictions imposed in the desire or commitment to achieve two goals: stable currency on the one hand, and non-overvalued currency on the other hand. Until both goals can be achieved and sustained without restrictions on international capital flows and without exuberant sterilisation on the part of the central bank, the country should not think about pegging its currency. Still further away should be considerations of irrevocably pegging its currency to the euro, if it is around at that time, or to the basket of European (and some other) currencies, if the euro is not to be around.

So the country must put its house in order if it wants to think about joining the European single currency, either only de facto or also de iure. Putting one's house in order means: solving the problems of the ownership of business enterprises and their proper governance, increasing the saving ratio, and the restructuring of banks, if we stay with economics. So if the country is focusing on joining the European single currency it is focusing in the right direction, although at the end it may find it better not to join the club, or if it turns out that the club is not there, not to irrevocably fix its currency at all and so stay with the one weapon, devaluation and/or revaluation, which would otherwise have been surrendered. Monetary integration again, is neither necessary nor out of question.

NOTES

1 It is not only G. Soros (Soros, 1995) who has been very critical about emerging "real" capitalism in transitional economies, but also many other who have, of course, not been engaged as advisers. G. Soros said (Ribnikar, 1984) for instance to the Russians, you created "un capitalisme pervers qui ne peut que vous mener à la ruine." G.M. von Furstenberg (Furstenburg, 1991) analyses what could have been done for better acceptance of capitalism.

2 As it will be seen, dominant internal ownership may be something like that.

3 Social capital should not be the same as "capital social" in French because it means equity capital and we have emphasised that it is something different. Capital is always relation between the two and, since society is all embracing, the one is always missing. It is just a misnomer invented by politicians, who maybe wanted to emphasise it as something between socialism and capitalism.

4 They analysed theoretically and empirically how efficient self-managed business enterprises were, whether workers would put pressure on wages to be high and increasing, how investment decisions were made, etc. But into nobody's mind came the idea of how such a business enterprise would be born and/or would increase its capital.

5 A critical appraisal of the market-planned economic system and its functioning is to be found in the book: "An Introduction to Financial Economy" (in Slovenian), Pegaz, Ljubljana, 1989, 357 p. (Ribnikar, 1989c).

6 The thesis that it is contrary to the essence of the system for interest rates to be positive in real terms, stated in a paper in 1984 (Ribnikar, 1984) could not be accepted by economists belonging to the establishment at the time.

7 These two simple questions were put and answers were given in the 1984 paper (Ribnikar, 1984). Later a paper in English was published in 1989 about money and finance in Yugoslavia (Ribnikar, 1989a).

8 This is in accordance with the second best theorem according to which "in economies in which there are some distortions, removing one distortion may not be welfare enhancing", as can be found in J.E. Stiglitz (Stiglitz, p. 61).

9 In Slovenia there has been in use almost from the beginning an unsuitable and ugly word "lastninjenje", invented probably by politicians, i.e. something like "ownershipisation" or "propriatisation", that has simply replaced "denationalisation" or "privatisation" among followers.

10 What should have been done and what has been done finally is explained in the book: I. Ribnikar, "Transition in a Slovenian Way" (in Slovenian), CISEF. Ljubljana, 1994, 318 p. (Ribnikar, 1994b).

11 In the majority of cases business enterprises were selling the same goods on the Yugoslav market (to earn income) and on the Western markets (to earn foreign currencies). These business enterprises did not have great problems when the Yugoslav or domestic market shrinked to become the Slovenian market. But business enterprises specialised for ex-Yugoslav market were not able to adapt themselves and they had been increasing their indebtedness or eating into their capital until they vanished or will vanish.

12 If we take into account that neither at the beginning nor later had there been any (proper) equity, then we must say that all nondebt capital had been created in an inflationary way through redistribution of wealth to the burden of lenders.

13 This unscrupulous behaviour had at least two not very pleasant consequences. People will be disappointed or confirmed in their attitudes towards authorities. And then there is a lot of empty space to look for those who have stolen, appropriated for themselves, or

destroyed the amount of wealth that is missing. But politicians and/or their advisers are those whose behaviour had been fraudulent by passing such bad laws.

14 The same people who at first advocated free distribution of shares to all citizens, and preached how important it was that all should be shareholders, now talk about others as genuine, proper, serious owners, and that genuine "privatisation" is ahead of us.

REFERENCES

Calvo, G. A., 1991, "The Perils of Sterilisation", IMF, *Staff Papers*, Vol. 38, No. 4, December 1991.

De Grauwe, P., 1994, "The Economics of Monetary Integration", 2nd ed., Oxford Univ. Press.

Diaz-Alejandro, C., 1985, "Good-bye Financial Repression, Hello Financial Crash", *Journal of Development Economics*, No. 19.

Fischer, S., 1982"Seigniorage and the Case for a National Money", *Journal of Political Economy*, No. 2.

Frölich, H.- P., 1990, "'L'union monétaire' informelle entre la RFA, l'Autriche et les Pays-Bas: un modèle pour le CEE?", Problèmes économiques, No. 2179, 13. 6. 1990.

Furstenburg, G. M. von, 1991, "Pareto-Optimal Privatisation for Gaining Political Support", *Kredit und Kapital,* No 2.

Karol, K. S., 1996, "Les communistes au secours d'Eltsine", *Le Nouvel Observateur*, No 1671, 14. - 20. 11. 1996.

Krugman, P. R., Obstfeld, M., 1996, "International Economics. Theory and Policy", 4th ed., Addison Wesley.

Obstfeld, M., 1982, "Can We Sterilize? Theory and Evidence", *AEA Papers and Proceedings*, May 1982.

Ribnikar, I., 1973, Base Money Creation (in Serbo-Croatian), Narodna banka Slovenije & Institut za spoljnu trgovinu, Ljubljana & Beograd.

Ribnikar, I., 1984, "Financing of Business Enterprises and Inflation" (in Serbo-Croatian), *Socijalizam*, Beograd, No 9.

Ribnikar, I., 1988, "Financing the Economy and the State and Territorial Isolation of the Economy and Banks" (in Serbo-Croatian), *Ekonomist*, No. 2, Zagreb.

Ribnikar, I., 1989a, "Money and Finance in Yugoslavia", in: Lokar, A., Mazek, W. F., Priestley, T. M. S. (editors), In Honor of the Memory of Tuossaint Hočevar (1927-1987), *Slovene Studies*, Vol. 11, No 1-2.

Ribnikar, I., 1989b, "Introduction of the Parallel Currency - the German Mark - would gradually disinflate the inflationary balloon" (in Slovenian), *Delo*, 23. 11. 1989, Ljubljana.

Ribnikar, I., 1989c, An Introduction to Financial Economy (in Slovenian), Pegaz, Ljubljana.

Ribnikar, I., 1991, "Monetary Arrangements, Monetary Soveregnity, Monetary Policy and Seigniorage in a (Con)Federative State" (in Slovenian), *Bančni vestnik*, No. 1-2, Ljubljana.

Ribnikar, I., 1994a, "The Financial System of a Small Emerging Market Economy", *International Review of Financial Analysis*, Vol. 3, No. 2.

Ribnikar, I.,1994b, Transition in a Slovenian Way, (in Slovenian), CISEF, Ljubljana.

Soros, G., 1995, Le défi de l'argent, Plon, Paris.

Stiglitz, J. E., "Financial markets and development", Oxford Review of Economic Policy, Vol. 5, No 4.

Index